Animal Land

Animal Land

THE CREATURES OF CHILDREN'S FICTION

MARGARET BLOUNT

Hutchinson of London

Hutchinson & Co (Publishers) Ltd
3 Fitzroy Square, London W1

London Melbourne Sydney Auckland
Wellington Johannesburg Cape Town
and agencies throughout the world

First published 1974
© Margaret Ingle-Finch 1974

Set in Monotype Garamond
Printed in Great Britain by
Ebenezer Baylis & Son Ltd, The Trinity Press
Worcester and London
and bound by Wm Brendon & Son Ltd
Tiptree, Essex

ISBN 0 09 118410 X

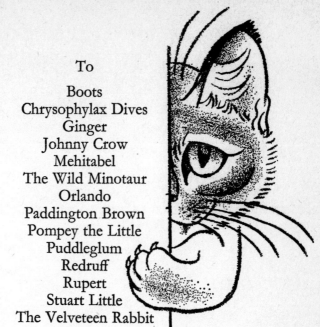

To

Boots
Chrysophylax Dives
Ginger
Johnny Crow
Mehitabel
The Wild Minotaur
Orlando
Paddington Brown
Pompey the Little
Puddleglum
Redruff
Rupert
Stuart Little
The Velveteen Rabbit

Wherever they are

'Brer Rabbit saunter into the house he did, and shake hands with the gals and sat there smokin' his seegyar same ez a town man.'

Uncle Remus, *Joel Chandler Harris*, 1880

Contents

Illustrations

Page 224. Mary Tourtel's illustration to *Rupert and Dapple*.

Page 227. 'The Tables Turned at the Zoo' – an engraving by George du Maurier.

Pages 228 and 231. From *The Jungle Book* by Rudyard Kipling, illustrated by J. L. Kipling (228) and W. H. Drake. (231)

Pages 241 and 243. From *Stuart Little* by E. B. White, illustrated by Garth Williams.

Page 247. From *Thy Servant a Dog* by Rudyard Kipling, illustrated by G. L. Stampa.

Page 249. 'I do not understand' – as above.

Page 252. From *Black Beauty* by Anna Sewell, illustrated by Blampied.

Page 265. From *The Hey Diddle Diddle Picture Book*, written and illustrated by Randolph Caldecott.

Page 279. Moominpapa, from *Finn Family Moomintroll*, written and illustrated by Tove Jansson.

Page 294. 'Reepicheep' – from *The Last Battle* by C. S. Lewis, illustrated by Pauline Baynes.

Pages 303 and 306. From *The Last Battle*, as above.

Page 318. Paddington Bear, from *Paddington Goes To Town* by Michael Bond, illustrated by Peggy Fortnum.

The Author and Publisher acknowledge with thanks permission to reproduce the drawings on the pages indicated from the following copyright holders:

127, George Allen & Unwin Ltd. 177, Associated Book Publishers Ltd. 114, Associated Newspapers Ltd. 211, 212, 219, 224, Beaverbrook Newspapers Ltd. 279, Ernest Benn Ltd. 118, 129, 294, 303, 306, The Bodley Head Ltd. 93, 144, 149, 179, Curtis Brown Ltd. 60, 198, 199 Jonathan Cape Ltd. 98, 106, J. M. Dent & Sons Ltd. 144, (Canada) Doubleday & Co. Inc. 45, Gerald Duckworth & Co. Ltd. 1, 62, Barbara Edwards, 181, Victor Gollancz Ltd. 241, 243, Hamish Hamilton Ltd. 129, 241, 243, (Canada) Harper & Row Publishers 79, William Heinemann Ltd. 198, 199, (Canada) Christopher Lofting. 177, 179, (Canada) McClelland & Stewart. 150, Methuen & Co. Ltd. 129, Penguin Books Ltd. 202, Routledge & Kegan Paul Ltd. 93, 149, (Canada) Charles Scribners Sons. 136, 137, Frederick Warne & Co. Ltd.

Introduction

My grandmother had two stories, instalments of which were repeated on every occasion that we met, by popular request. One was about a colony of rooks and the other about a mouse family. The rooks spent much time and argument building nests and arranging their affairs, all conducted noisily by referendum and voting. The young married rooks who dared to leave the colony or build their nests differently from the prescribed pattern were rigorously put down. The mice had an exciting, fugitive life, menaced constantly by humans, cats and traps. They had, as criminals have, great rewards, and sometimes suffered arbitrary penalties. They had little power over their environment, being transported here and there (whenever Grandma needed a change of scene) hidden in luggage, or accidental stowaways on buses and trains.

Much as I enjoyed these delightful endless serials, I really preferred my father's well-plotted stories about a house with legs, comic fantasy in the Lewis Carroll manner. Not all children are bewitched by animal stories, but again and again these are the kind that everyone when young is given, firstly I think because this kind of story is the type that adults seem to enjoy writing; an animal fantasy is a kind of imaginative launching ground that gives a built in power of insight to narrative – one is half-way there before one has noticed. Secondly, animal stories are the kind that adults enjoy *giving*. They are supposed to be 'improving' in some way, pointing oblique and therefore palatable morals, or helping one's nature study along. Apart from the rare, objective nature stories that do the latter, the animals are not really themselves, but disguised people. Though I did not recognise that Grandma's stories were telling something about democracy and conformity, or the pains and perils of existence on the fringes of a world that is very large, strong and hostile, I realised, as all children do, that animals and birds were not really like those rooks and mice – their lives had been humanised, or 'improved', even though what my grandmother was describing was a countrywoman's accurate comment on animal and bird behaviour.

Why, then, *have* animals at all when people would do as well? The answer lies perhaps in the way people create, and the kind of life they would secretly wish to lead. If one is inclined to fantasy, one sometimes tries to present the kind of world one wishes were true, if only things had not turned out otherwise, and if the aspect of Eden that entrances the writer most is the spectacle of the lion and the lamb living harmoniously together with each other and with men, then intelligent and probably speaking animals will appear. There seems to me to be three distinct kinds of writer who have this wish, and their reasons for choosing animals are almost the same that many people give for being vegetarian – they like the food, they dislike meat or find it disagrees with them, or they are concerned with ethical problems about killing or exploitation. Substitute 'animal' for 'vegetable' and you get, first, the sort of writer who cannot help writing about animals – they are his first love and find their way into his work whether he will or no; besides Jack London, C. S. Lewis or Alison Uttley, there are the great naturalists Ernest Thompson Seton, H. Mortimer Batten, J. W. Fortescue or Denys Watkins Pitchford. The second kind of temperament tends to dislike, or be critical of, the human race and finds animals a more innocent, congenial alternative with which to populate the earth, and includes Swift, T. H. White or Beatrix Potter. The third category, far the largest and also containing writers from category one, is concerned, consciously or unconsciously, with teaching us something. The moral urge is very strong – not in the folklore animal stories, but in the early animal tales of the eighteenth and nineteenth centuries; however, more twentieth-century writers belong to the group than one might think. There are Hugh Lofting, Paul Gallico, Beverley Nichols, and C. S. Lewis once more, and all these numerous creators who start by dressing animals and giving them human voices end by saying more than they intended – anthropomorphism has unexpected results. Animals are beautiful, innocent, funny and strange, and their built-in appeal can be used as a half-way stage towards comment on the human race. One can do this, as perhaps Kenneth Grahame did, almost without realising it.

The great gulf between human and animal can never, in this world, be crossed. All writers who used animals as dramatic material are attempting to cross it and their methods vary; they may leap, build bridges, or even pretend the gulf isn't there at all. Different eras make the approach in different ways – the human attitude to animals is always changing, from the earliest days when it was prob-ably a mixture of greed and awe, through all the stages of amuse-ment, guilt, objective interest, to concern and nostalgia. Awe recognises that animals are enemies and rivals and perhaps magic, and greed uses them. The mixture produces folklore and fairy tales in which animals have magic powers or take over human identities, all set in some far-off time apparently before the gulf was made. Amusement comes next, where the animals pass from objects into characters such as Reynard the Fox – though they are being used to show up human foibles. Guilt follows, and animals are used to represent people in a new way – to teach us how to behave to each other (Mrs Gatty, Charles Kingsley) and how to treat the animals themselves (Anna Sewell, Sarah Trimmer); they are pawns in satire (Orwell) and are even, in a recurrent fantasy, allowed to retaliate on humans who have used them cruelly (C. S. Lewis, Daphne du Maurier). Objective interest in how animals really live takes things a stage further by trying to leap the gulf and identify with what one is writing about, in the way that Henry Williamson or Ernest Thompson Seton achieve (though it is not my intention to treat naturalists' stories in much detail in this book). The great animal fantasies, rising with the decline of religious teaching, build bridges by imagining the results of wish fulfilment in a series of 'If Only's'.

If only the animals could talk; if only toy animals or pets could talk – the idea gives rise to bear stories and Dr Dolittle. Imagining that animals have their own societies on the human pattern, gives many mouse stories. 'If only mythical beasts were true' gives dragon stories, from Beowulf to E. Nesbit. 'If only we could reverse the roles and *become* animals' gives *The Jungle Books*. Fantasy eventually enters a kind of Utopian stage in which animals are used to populate rural Edens or share the world with humans on equal terms. It is as if the human race is wondering, nostalgically, how long the animals will remain and wants to make a truce with them – and also longs to be as uncorrupted as they. Such fantasies often abolish humans altogether, substituting Hobbits or Moomins (like humans but much nicer) or create worlds where humans and animals are really the same, such as Narnia or Paddington Brown's Notting Hill.

Various landmark books show this process happening. *Reynard the Fox* (1481 in the English version) is the first animal satire, *The Life and Perambulations of a Mouse* (1783) the first story concerned with kindness as well as morals, *The Butterfly's Ball* (1807) the first non-moral fantasy, *The History of Pompey the Little* (1751) the first dog book. *Black Beauty* (1877) is the first real animal novel, *The Story of Dr Dolittle* (1922) the first book to consider animals' rights, *The Jungle Books* (1893) the first attempt to enter an animal world, and *Mary Plain* (1930) the first animal to share the human one.

Humanised animal stories were never my own favourites. Perhaps because I was not quite under the spell, I was always filled with curiosity. *How* did the thing work? Maybe one had more critical detachment through not being enslaved. Did Miss Meadows an' de Gals mind being sassed by a rabbit? Why was the bus conductor in Rupert sometimes a man, sometimes a chimpanzee? What did Mr MacGregor *think* when he found the blue jacket with the brass buttons? The whole structure still seems to me curious, odd, sometimes naive, as if the authors had worked some kind of magic or hypnotised themselves into accepting a world that wasn't, and imagined all readers would be hypnotised too, as in the story of the Emperor's New Clothes. One can argue that all fantasy is like this and the hypnotism is very enjoyable; but in one sense animal fantasies are the most down-to-earth stories in which nothing happens that is outside nature, and to me, as a child – and still – this realism is almost a barrier. I could 'take' the tallest sort of magic, Peter Pan at a gulp, Alice *in toto*, being in the usual state of reader's trance, but

Peter Rabbit made me think, and want to ask for details; did the people in the story think the situation odd, or interesting, or funny? Why have the animals there?

The careful balance of credibility can be upset. If one wonders how it works or investigates too hard, the whole thing may fail. The books I have chosen to discuss have, I hope, an integrity that will stand close scrutiny, but one always remembers the sad fate of the Bounceable Ball that died with a sigh when cut open with a pen-knife to see what made it bounce. If one wonders too hard about why the Mole had statues of Garibaldi and the Infant Samuel outside his burrow – or house – one might start wondering too hard about whether he is a man enough to appear in court as a witness at the Toad's trial. Is the Toad such a man, anyway? Thinking about its oddity does not alter the fact that *The Wind in the Willows* is a masterpiece that gives great pleasure on a number of levels; and so do all the great animal stories. For a while one can forget that the gulf is there, a state of mind that brings a unique felicity.

The animals have been very good to us, after all, lending themselves for our entertainment and edification with never a murmur. This book is dedicated to some of their fictional and real selves in gratitude.

PART ONE

Animal Fable

Demades, a famous Greek orator, was once address-ing an assembly at Athens on a subject of great importance and in vain tried to fix the attention of his hearers. They laughed among themselves, watched the sports of the children and in twenty other ways showed their want of concern in the subject of the discourse. Demades, after a short pause, spoke as follows: 'Ceres one day journeyed in company with a swallow and an eel.' At this there was marked attention and every ear strained now to catch the words of the orator.

Aesop on the Power of the Fable

1 Folklore and Fable

For thilke tyme, as I have understoude,
Beestes and birddes koude speke and synge.

'The Nun's Priests Tale', *Chaucer*

'Long ago, when the animals could speak.' The golden age is somewhere in the past – perhaps in Eden or before the Flood, perhaps
nearer, just beyond the memory of the oldest story teller; and in
that time the gulf between animals and men had not been opened,
the distinctions were not so sharp, magic was all about. As youthful
things and creatures are always more alike than adult ones, as seeds
are always more similar than plants and animals that grow more like
themselves and so more different from each other every day, so in
tales that belong to this youthful time animals and people were
more alike, could communicate, have equal stature and often a
similar moral life.

Folklore and myth bring animals nearer to men while fables and
satire, while apparently doing the same thing, do the opposite; they
are divisive and put animals in their place – further off.

The folklore story abounds in talking animals, clever animals that
have an ambiguous or helpful role, or even appear to have private
lives and families on the human model while co-existing with human
masters, owners, or acquaintances. No one knows the origins of
such stories, apart from the obvious racial strains which make a
Japanese story different from an African, Danish, Scottish or English
one. Talking animals seem to be as old as Man; and folklore tales
read like Man's remote dreams, related by someone with dramatic
and narrative flair but little imagination. Things are seldom described, they just *are* so, in a bright shadowless world just beyond
the present where anything can happen and it may be any time at all.
As large as life and quite as natural the animals come and go, changing their shapes and offering help – or vengeance – setting up home
together like the Mouse, The Bird and The Sausage, working in the
kitchen like Tittymouse and Tattymouse, usually on friendly terms
with humans. Function and character can become delightfully,

mysteriously, blurred. In such a story as 'All Gone' (*English Fairy Tales*, Joseph Jacobs collection, 1890) which concerns a friendship between a cat and a mouse, the cat uses as an excuse for its absence, 'I have a favourite cousin who has brought a small handsome son into the world, and I have been asked to be his godmother'; yet what the pair actually *do* is steal butter, which is animal and natural.

On the edge of life the animals are there. Reading these tales you feel that if you could go back far enough, you might have met a witch hare or a talking horse or cow; or joined the animals by being turned into one, or earned their help in impossible tasks imposed by kings or magicians such as picking up grains of sand, or choosing the right princess. Such animals are much nearer to the present climate than one imagines, from the pantomime *Puss in Boots* (who has changed his shape for the occasion) to Brer Rabbit, who is life-like in the same way as Paddington the bear, almost true, somewhere, as long as you don't look too closely. There is not always an obvious moral either, but usually a certain rough justice, plenty of cruelty, deaths, mutilations and revenge. The animals talk quite naturally, answering humans back and being accepted as semi-equals. The cunning ones, cats and foxes, often outwit humans and the more favoured ones, dogs and horses, are not usually as intelligent – perhaps because humans, who made the stories, feared them less. Sometimes the animal kingdom is allowed – as a sort of holiday – power over the human one and a turn at having the upper hand – a recurrent theme of animal vengeance, from 'The Travelling Musicians' to Hitchcock's *The Birds* (based on the Daphne du Maurier story), perhaps prompted by something ever present in the human psyche; guilt at what Man has done to animals made deeper by the knowledge that animals can never 'win'. But such serious themes, leading in the end to the favourite satiric device that animals are morally superior to Man, as in Swift, or Erich Kästner's *The Animals' Conference* are not as common as simple comedy and magic transpositions. Until the Brothers Grimm made them respectable, folk tales were regarded, perhaps, as being rather on the level of comics – regretted by the Wife of Bath who blamed the clergy for suppressing them, compared unfavourably with Aesop and his obvious morals.

The classic 'fairy' tales are adult embellishment of folklore written in the late seventeenth century when the urbanity of the times allowed a greater toleration of fanciful tales with no particular moral uplift – though right is always rewarded and wrong punished. The *Contes de Perrault* are courtly romances, modified and embellished from their folklore origins, sometimes beautiful, like Madame de Villeneuve's *Beauty and the Beast*, or Madame d'Aulnoy's *The White Cat*; but often spoiled by complication. Animal help and the disguised human are favourite themes. The behaviour of the cat in *Puss in Boots* is that of a human in a cat's skin. He advances his master's fortune so that he wins the princess and the kingdom. He is the Clever Servant, and has all the initiative and all the ideas; he can order the peasants about, outwits the ogre and ends by enjoying his share of his master's good luck. The Beast, or the Frog Prince, are more obviously human – but, in his way, so is the Wolf in *Red Riding Hood*. Perrault makes this even more clear by his rhymed moral (A. E. Johnson's translation):

> *All wolves are not of the same sort;*
> *There is one kind with an amenable disposition*
> *Neither noisy, nor hateful, nor angry,*
> *But tame, obliging and gentle,*
> *Following the young maids*
> *In the streets, even into their homes.*
> *Alas! Who does not know that these gentle wolves*
> *Are of all creatures the most dangerous.*

The fairy tales of Hans Andersen are an even further development, with animal servants (*The Tinder Box*) and enchanted humans (*The Ugly Duckling*) given greater depth because their moral, and meaning, is not explicit.

A very old and rather different type of story based on animal folklore is the Beast Fable – the Animal Society theme where animals have taken the place of humans and act out human dramas. *Reynard the Fox* is the most famous, existing in many versions and printed by Caxton three years after *The Canterbury Tales* and before Aesop. Grimm's 'The Tomtit and the Bear' is a good example, dealing with an animal war in which a Fox is a valuable general. In *Reynard the Fox*, many strains and ideas have been developed into an animal epic in which animals are characters in a romance cycle, with plots, sub-plots, heroism, deception, trickery, humour, triumphs, victories, battles and death. In its time, the vogue for Reynard was enormous, but as entertainment for adults the style is quite dead however 'Dogland', 'Babar' and *Finn Family Moomintroll* are very-much-removed relations.

Aesop's Beast Fables, tongue-in-cheek human substitutions, have always been in favour. Perhaps from Caxton's time onwards, they have been regarded as the right books to give to children, recommended by educationists from Locke onwards. They are part of most people's early experience and are the very roots of that kind of humanisation which turns animals into facets of human character, and many writers have changed and revived them. Animals are here 'used' rather than presented and they point the way directly to those moral and satirical tales which were intended, from Swift to Orwell, to show the human race how it ought to behave.

The history of animal stories through these three strains – folklore, fable and romance – is one of growing seriousness; folklore animals are on the whole, a much gayer lot than those in later versions of Aesop. Perhaps the best folklore animal, and certainly the most famous, is Brer Rabbit. Though later in time than the *Reynard* cycle or Aesop, in treatment and essence he is earlier and more primitive and has the genuine amoral wily innocence that fairy-tale animals lack. Hans Andersen sometimes leaves one full of an odd, cold sadness, however delicate the allegory and beautiful the image; compared with this, Grimm's folklore tales are like tomato sauce out of a bottle, and Brer Rabbit comes out of the same jar, full of humour and rather undeserved retribution, of which Uncle Remus offers no explanation except that it *was* so, in the old days when the animals could talk. These African stories (*Uncle Remus*, Joel Chandler Harris, 1880) modified and translated into an American setting, have one or two Aesop themes such as 'The Tortoise and the Hare', 'The Wolf and the Lamb', 'The Dog and the Meat', transformed and improved on, brought to life – the folklore version being a jollier one than the fable; in 'The Tortoise and the Hare' Brer Terrapin defeats Brer Rabbit, not because the rabbit does not try, but by posting various identical members of his own family along the route and at the winning post; and in the 'Bullfrog and the Bear' (Aesop's Wolf and Lamb) the Bullfrog finally escapes, using a 'briar patch' ruse – the Lamb in Aesop is devoured.

On the whole the Uncle Remus stories are kindly in that the weak

animals always win. The whole saga concerns a weak animal winning, and celebrates the victory of a creature that has no natural
weapons, only speed, concealment and cunning, and the reversal of
nature and the likely gives great delight. Everyone wants the weak
and innocent to win and the tyrant to be defeated, and enjoyment is
increased by Brer Rabbit's sly confidence, his deceits and trickeries
that are full of outrageous resource and happy zest. Until the very
end, most of the animals survive to hunt again and they all seem to
belong to some wonderful American past when the Beasts 'had
sense, same like folks', and the humans were not too obtrusive –
indeed, did not even have proper names, but were addressed
ambiguously as Miss Meadows or Mr Man. Their function was to
provide farms and roads and a vaguely law-abiding background
against which the animals eat-or-be-eaten existence could function
more effectively.

"Brer Rabbit 'sembled his fambly, en he swaje ole Miss Cow's bag."

Part of the charm of the *Brer Rabbit* stories is the vernacular way in which the animals talk. Their natural, funny, adult conversations are turned to childlike motives of hide and seek, being one up and outwitting your neighbour by being sharper than he is; a game spiced with danger because they are animals after all, the Fox is *really* out to eat the Rabbit, the evasions concern life or death; but the talk is all casual understatement as neat and careful as a game of tennis played by opponents who are so used to each other's styles that they have a sort of wary relaxation, an alert yet unstrained pleasure in countering and turning the other's attack.

> *'I wanter have some confab wid you, Brer Rabbit,' sez Brer Fox sezee.*
> *'All right, Brer Fox, but you better holler from where you stan'.*
> *I'm monstrous fuller fleas dis mawnin'.'*
> *'I seed Brer B'ar yesterday,' sez Brer Fox sezee, 'en he sorter rake me over de coals kaze you en me ain't made frens and live naberly.'*
> *Brer Rabbit scratch one year wid his off hine-foot sorter jub'usly en den he ups and sez, sezee, 'Supposin' you drap roun termorrer en take dinner wid me. . .'*

And everyone knows that dinner is what Brer Fox had in mind. The game is on, the rabbits raid a convenient human garden for appropriate food, and Brer Fox tries one of his favourite 'dying' ruses, while Brer Rabbit pretends to have to go in search of calamus root. One had the feeling that if one had been lucky enough to live in America in this golden age, these witty talking animals would have been in one's backyard or farm or briar patch; whereas Beatrix Potter's animals with their human clothes and lakeland landscapes belonged to a naturalists' fairy tale 'now' that wasn't and could never be. They might exist, but one could never meet them. As soon as they were clearly observed their clothes would vanish, they would drop on to all fours and run away, like Mrs Tiggy Winkle.

Brer Rabbit was as near a man as a rabbit could ever be; he 'sorter pull his mustarsh and say . . .' The game of chase was exciting and constant; like Tom and Jerry, the prey was always elusive and cunning, the hunter indefatigably animal and incredibly naive, with no one really getting hurt until the strange, rather brutal deaths which come with the stories 'the sad end of —' and the saga is over.

The Tar Baby story is the classic of the collection, with its refrain 'Tar Baby ain't sayin' nothing' and Brer Fox, he lay low'; and the wonderful riposte of 'born an' bred in a briar patch', when the Fox, thinking he has given the Rabbit a fate worse than death, is persuaded to throw his prey among the brambles. The Fox is always the real victim, the Rabbit only the apparent one; the battle is conducted with conversation, those careful, stylised, once-removed remarks in which neither animal says what it means; an elaborate, cumulative game of double dealing in which the Rabbit always *knows*.

The other lucky animal that outwits the rest and is never hurt is the terrapin, even more passive and defensive than the rabbit and at times one up on both Rabbit and Fox. There is the curious episode of the shelf at Miss Meadows's house. Miss Meadows and her sisters are humans who have a privileged place in the story – Rabbit and Fox are rival suitors who visit them. Even the little boy listener to Uncle Remus thinks the situation odd: 'Who was Miss Meadows, Uncle Remus?'

'Don't ax me, honey. She wuz in de tale, Miss Meadows an' de gals wuz, en de tale I give you like h'it wer' gun ter me.' Both Fox and Rabbit show off in front of the ladies, who treat them with polite indulgence. The terrapin is also an accepted caller, and is placed high on a shelf to make up for his lack of stature – and falls off it, knocking the Fox on the head and saving the Rabbit's life (apparently a folk-tale theme from among the Amazonian Indians, where the Tortoise falls from a tree). A. T. Elwes's illustration transforms the shelf into a chimney piece, and the ladies – dressed in the 'aesthetic' fashions of the early eighties – sit round among the fans and bamboo furniture – to me, a child of the thirties, this looked like a golden age indeed.

The way the animals end – as if Tom and Jerry had suddenly become serious and the consequences of each violent act became real instead of imaginary – is death, always in a cruel form. The Bear is stung to death by Bees, the Wolf scalded in a chest, the Fox's head served up in a stew to his unsuspecting wife and children; and the game is finally over. The wise-cracking gaiety is marred, but perhaps one can here, as in Grimm, accept the 'fates' of the bad characters because they have a certain amount of non-animal guilt and wickedness; but the end still seems out of place. It is happier to think of Brer Rabbit at last marrying one of the Gals. Uncle Remus is not sure *which*; but, when pressed, admits it was Miss Molly Cottontail, which makes one wonder if Elwes was wrong, and the Gals were just ancestors of Peter and Benjamin, after all.

Beatrix Potter must have been brought up on this book; there is one strong clue. 'Tobacco, Uncle Remus?' asked the little boy incredulously. 'Rabbit terbarker, honey. You know dis yer life ever-lastin' w'at Miss Sally puts 'mong de cloze in de trunk: well, dat's rabbit terbarker,' '(which is what *we* call lavender)' sold by old Mrs Rabbit in *Benjamin Bunny*.

The impression left by Brer Rabbit is of a string of episodes, each distinct and self-supporting, linked by words such as 'One time' and 'By and by'; and of course by the personality of the narrator. The stories are indeed a series of joined folk tales. Earlier in time, more serious in content and more sophisticated in conception is *Reynard the Fox*, composed of many folk tales but fused, by a coherent plot, into animal epic romance. It is a Beast Saga, in the way that the Rhinegold is a Ring Saga, and concerns the adventures of the fox who, by his superior cunning, manages to get the better of all the animals in the lion's kingdom. There are traces of Oriental (lion and jackal) and European (bear, wolf and fox) tales in its making. So human is the action that there is a strong feeling that the authors (many, preceding the Dutch poet Willems from whom Caxton's version was taken in 1481) found in animals useful actors

REYNARD ATTACKETH LAPRELL THE RABBIT.

who could take the parts allotted to them, rather than creatures with their own habits and characteristics – the animals behave unnaturally and are imagined – for satirical purposes – as inhabiting a mirror world and performing the actions of kings, queens, knights, soldiers and statesmen.

Starewicz (

This tradition was popular enough for many versions, the earliest being a Latin poem written in about 782 in the court of Charlemagne, elaborated and enlarged through the Middle Ages, improved on by court poets until it grew into a kind of parody of the romance of chivalry, and the animals grew names that we remember today: Ysengrim the wolf, Reinardus the fox, Rufanus the lion, Tybalt the cat, Bruno the bear. The same story is used by Goethe in 1794. The plot concerns the Lion king who summons the Fox to court to answer complaints brought against him by the other animals – the Fox refuses to come and evades the Lion by playing tricks on every messenger sent to find him; at last he is brought to court by the Badger. He is condemned to death, but deceives the Lion with a story about hidden treasure and a conspiracy between the Bear and the Wolf. He is allowed to go and look for the treasure, and also on a pilgrimage to Rome; but after further murders, he is outlawed, captured and tried, fights a duel with the Wolf, wins, is forgiven and reinstated.

Turn this story into Robin Hood, without any pretence of the hero being a 'good' character, and the feel is much the same. The animals have a king and a court, own castles and armies, wage wars; there are sieges and rescues, crude humour and vengeance. If there is a moral at all, it is that cunning is better than brute strength, but that is as far as it goes, because the wicked triumph over the weak; however, one is meant to take it all seriously. Caxton tells us that by reading this work 'Men may come to the subtle knowledge of such things as daily are used and had in the counsels of Lords and Prelates, also among Merchants and other common people: to understand the subtle deceits that daily are used in the world.' And perhaps this is nearer the mark. There is considerable satiric intention; corruption of the clergy, mock ordination and confession, plenty of lies and trickery with much recapitulation and reported speech.*
It is clear that this saga had a long, strong life while it ran, but the whole epic, to a twentieth-century person, seems archaic in a way that fairy and folklore tales, with their greater fluctuation in popularity, do not. In Reynard there is humour – of a kind – but no gaiety, and the genre has disappeared.

Kaulbach's 1846 illustrations to Goethe's *Reineke Fuchs* are inte-

*But these ponderous delights are part of the charm of early narrative; see *Beowulf*.

resting in the way they dress the animals. There are affinities with
Elwes and Tenniel in the naturalness of the human postures and
movements shown with great regard for animal anatomy. Faces are
effectively humanised in that weakness, cruelty, pride, etc, are
always there. Even the great Kaulbach, however, could not dress a
bird or a horse, and Chanticleer appears *au naturel* while Reynard
is traveller, knight or tonsured monk in robe and cowl. The trees,
rocks and landscapes often have human faces, which give the pictures a romantic strangeness alien to the beast fable, usually simple
and direct. One illustration shows the Lioness queen suckling two
cubs simultaneously at her two human breasts while reclining on a
day bed, a surrealistic oddity worthy of Ernst; but perhaps it takes
a nineteenth-century illustrator to work the Circean spell and show
the 'real' people hidden in animal skins. One wonders if it would
not be a better story if the spell were taken off and the hero turned
out to be Ulysses – or Robin Hood – all the time.

Chaucer's 'Nun's Priests' Tale' comes somewhere between Reynard and Aesop. The Cock is the hero of the story and the Fox a
mere wicked marauder. The lighthearted parody of a knight and his
lady living in a barnyard belonging to a poor widow is given an
affectionate depth because the Cock and Hen have an heroic beauty
all their own; the absurd, lengthy gravity with which each makes his
point to the other with learned examples from history and literature
parodies the self-important struttings of barnyard birds. The actual
story – the Fox's flattery of the Cock, persuading it to crow with its
eyes shut, seizing it and running off, and the Cock's escape when it
persuades its captor to shout defiance at the pursuit – is very short;
and the action, the bang and clatter comedy of hue and cry, is
shorter still. The greater part of the poem is in the conversations
and justifications of Chanticleer's warning dream, and his lady's
insistence that one of his 'humours' is at fault and he needs a purge.
Few animal poems are more full of unforced delight than this tale of
the Cock with his heraldic beauty and monumental learning, and
the practical Hen, wise in her herb lore; it outclasses fable and folk-
tale and makes them seem pale and insignificant. The sudden detail
that reminds one that the actions are not human, adds to the
pleasure:

2

> '*And with a cluck he gave the troupe a call,*
> *For he had found a seed upon the floor.*'*

The Fox, when he appears, is as courteous and learned, and can cite Boethius and Burnel the Ass; and when the Cock is seized, Chaucer cites Destiny and the Trojan Women. Although there is a moral here and the Nun's Priest tells his audience to take the grain and leave the chaff alone, one should do as Pertelote advises with her remedies for the black or red humour: 'peck them right up, my dear, and swallow whole.' This human Cock and Hen are unsurpassed and it is their bird-nature that gives point to their humanity.

The moral: that is the sombre kernel for which the animals are a covering device. Aesop, the oldest and most influential animal story teller of all, used the attractive power of animals and narrative to get at his audience in a peculiar way, and the method has been seized on, enlarged, used and copied until, in the last century, the animal moral tale becomes almost wearisome. The genius of Aesop was to use the animal as a fixative, in an unforgettable way.

Prudence pays better than greed; or, it is better to keep what one possesses than to lose it while trying to gain the unattainable. This is easy to say but horribly cumbersome to *imagine*. 'A man's reach should not be greater than his grasp' is easier. Easier still is 'a bird in hand is worth two in the bush', which brings with it a Bewick picture of a man with a gun and two dogs and a pheasant; most brains supply pictures which fix abstractions. What Aesop did was to reverse the process so that the image comes first, and so no one forgets the dog dropping the bone to try to grasp the one that is only a reflection. Aesop well knew the power of a story and the graphic, simplified short cut that animals made towards human attention; if the same story began with a man crossing a bridge with a piece of meat in his hand all sorts of other considerations would enter, the least of which being why the man should be silly enough to mistake his reflection for reality. In pointing this sort of moral, human psychology is irrelevant. It is only later that one begins to be dubious and to consider that greed does not pay – not because generosity is better, but because, in a harsh world, prudence is best. The whole thing can be taken two stages further by an artist like

*Neville Coghill's translation.

THE FOX AND THE CROCODILE.

Charles Bennet (*Aesop's Fables rendered into Human Nature*, 1866)
who draws not only the animal agent but the moral too; a valet with
a dog's head is shown rejecting a simple parlourmaid in order to
yearn after 'The Quality' who are having a soirée in the next room.

Aesop's fables have none of the humour of folklore, none of the warm satisfaction of fairy tale – the sudden turn of fortune before the happy ending. They have surface justice or an amused shrug. They have a resemblance to folk tale in their short, plain, factual lack of light and shade, but there the likeness ends. Aesop's animals, behaving not like animals at all but as propositions in Euclid, or, as G. K. Chesterton suggests, pieces in games of chess, are interesting because they are the very beginning of that typecasting which animals have found so difficult to shake off since; but there is a flatness about the stories, a cynical assessment of human nature at its lowest, an acknowledgement that often the good and innocent are duped and that good works often pay, not because they are good, but because nature is sometimes arranged that way.

The people in Aesop are non-figures, the farmer, a man, a boy, an old widow; their interaction with the animals does not seem to belong to any golden age when the animals could speak and people understand, and even Mr McGregor, shadowy as he is, has more character. The people, like the animals, have to be ciphers. If they had any real, complex human attributes, all kinds of chemical reactions might set in and spoil the experiment. The tendency, on reading Aesop, has been to applaud, to remember, and lastly to add one's own moral, to decide perhaps that the Fox that lost the grapes was the most sensible beast ever. 'Some men, when they are too weak to achieve their purpose, blame the times,' says the Greek; but the story also tells one not to bother about what one cannot have. Roger l'Estrange's *Aesop*, 1692, pictures the Fox 'turning off his disappointment with a jest', a kindly interpretation, equally valid, and Samuel Croxall in 1722 was uneasy about the grapes for a different reason – grapes did not grow wild in England and foxes did not like them anyway.

L'Estrange was doubtful about Aesop's moral values, and thought that they might be 'more dangerous than profitable'; but Locke, in his essay on education, 1690, had no doubts at all. Aesop was the best book to offer to children to encourage them to read; because it 'may afford useful reflections to a grown man; and if his memory retain them all his life after, he will not repent to find them there, among his manly thoughts and serious business. If his Aesop has pictures in it, it will entertain him much the better.'

Although Robert Henryson in 1570 and La Fontaine in 1651 are

Aesop's most notable interpreters, his illustrators have given the fables a certain depth and ambiguity. Croxall's *Aesop* has Bewick's beautiful woodcuts which are full of animation, the animals as natural as life, and perhaps the Fox, jumping to reach the grapes is unnatural. If you give the Fox a top hat and a cane the story becomes different, and that is what later illustrators have done, helping too to fix the animal prototypes by showing the Lion to be proud, the Fox devious and crafty. Robert Dodsley's Aesop, 1771, is interesting for its preface, which suggests this very thing – that the animals in the stories should act and speak according to their 'true' natures, perhaps thus applying the 'finishing polish, with the appearance of nature, the effect of art' which was his design in making the lion proud, the owl to speak with 'pomp of phrase', the monkey a buffoon. Literary animals have been doing this ever since, and finding it impossible to take character parts except by wrenching themselves somewhat unhappily and being a Reluctant Dragon, a Cowardly Lion (Frank L. Baum) or a Stupid Fox that is always failing to catch Clever Polly.

Walter Crane's Aesop – 1887 – with 'Portable Morals Pictorially Pointed' has a rather violent streak – foxes and wolves have ferocious snarls, lolling tongues, and there are realistic gin traps. The fables are neatly versified in limerick form with an appended and not always obvious moral, i.e. the Cock and the Pearl, which is about irony (as is much of Aesop), is interpreted as 'If he ask for bread, will ye give him a stone', which is an ironic statement about something quite different.

Ernest Griset's Aesop – 1869 – again shows that violent streak in Victorian illustration to an unpleasant degree. These pictures are, to a present-day eye, unhappy; they appear to belong to that black, sinister, ragged, rather dirty-looking world that one imagines the industrial revolution at its worst to have been happening in, a sort of de-urbanised Doré place, coal-tip countryside. The animals are beautifully drawn apart from the period convention that always makes elephants look pneumatic and lions like angry colonels. One oddity is that Griset dresses the evil animals – wolves and foxes, and seldom the others, and, as always, never birds; it is as if we see ourselves always to be guilty, never innocent or virtuous. Scenes of slaughter and death abound; in 'The Eagle and the Fox', the Eagle is hideous, but equally so are its embryonic young fledglings. And

Griset turns every *character* into an animal, i.e. in 'The Nurse and the Wolf', Nurse and baby look and behave like monkeys and are gratuitously ugly *because* they are wearing clothes. Oddest of all, but pointing to an interesting sympathy of this period, is Griset's treatment of insects. 'The Ant and the Grasshopper' have great charm. The Grasshopper has a mandoline slung at its back and it, and the Ants walk upright. The haymaking ants are as human as insects can be, leaning against the stack with their rakes, mopping their brows. Insects have not had much attention in more recent years. Perhaps Max Fleisher's *Mr Bug goes to Town* film cartoon, 1941* or Don Marquis' *Archy and Mehitabel* are the two most notable.

Far the most interesting illustrator of Aesop is Charles Bennet, whose *Fables of Aesop translated into Human Nature*, 1867, both dresses the animals completely and gives them a contemporary setting which is quite thought provoking, even now; though, in a sense, what he has done is to abolish the animal stereotype. The characters in Bennet are Victorian Londoners with animal heads on, i.e. in 'The Wolf and the Lamb', the Wolf is a Bill Sykes with neckerchief and knobkerry, the Lamb is frock-coated and top-hatted and is garotted with his own gold-studded collar. There never was anything comic about this story, but perhaps there is in Bennet's Ass in the Lion's skin – the Ass is shown smoking in the

*This story is, in its way, about ecology, or the unhappy effect on a community of insects of the building of a new city block. It was drawn by the creator of Popeye and Betty Boop. both of whom displayed hard shells and a galvanic activity comparable with Hoppity the Cricket and Miss Honey Bee in the insect film; and many animal cartoon films have the harsh knock for knock automatism of the insect world.

Mess, pretending to be a Guards officer. Social observation is witty and exact and the applications unexpected. 'The Fox and the Crow' story is given a new dimension when the Crow is a rich widow, the Fox a philanderer, the Cheese not shown or mentioned; and in 'The Fox and the Grapes' a vixen relates to her friend, a parrot, over the tea cups, the story of the man she did not marry. 'The Wolf in Sheep's Clothing' is a policeman, taking supper in the basement with the cook – a sheep. They are dining, ominously, off a leg of lamb.

These animals have a sinister, stylish elegance in keeping with Aesop's message and its worldly application; an ox's horns curl upwards forming the brim of his smart top hat, a crocodile's hide is also his fur-collared, crocodile skin coat, ending in a tail; he is dressed and not dressed, the clothes a part of him. This Aesop is indeed sophisticated. The reader needs to know what Aesop wrote, what animals are like, what the London of the sixties was like, and what civilisation has done to human nature and human ethics since then. Yet this art form, seen here at its finest, is a sort of spiritual dead end. If animals have a message for us now, it is a completely different one.

The tendency to add a Christian moral to Aesop has been as irresistible as the view taken, in the Bestiaries, that animals were specially created for man's edification in symbolic form. While Robert Henryson's Aesop, 1570, written in the reign of James III of Scotland has verse only comparable with Chaucer in its delightful gaiety and wry charm, it is the moral that is important:

> *And als the caus that thay first began*
> *Wes to repreif the haill misleving*
> *Of man, be figure of ane uther thing.*

The Uplandis Mous and the Burges Mous (this is always the favourite fable for treatment; perhaps it owes its popularity to the enduring appeal of mice) converse formally, yet with natural human voices, in seven-line stanzas. The country Mouse has the sort of reality of any finicky adult justifying the delicacy of his appetite by blaming a weak stomach. After expressing disappointment and disgust in no uncertain terms

This burges Mous had lytill will to sing,
Bot hevilie scho kest hir browis doun,

looking, as well as feeling, glum. In the town, the Spencer inter-rupts their feasting; the country mouse is chased by the cat and swoons. One should be content 'with small possession', says Henryson. The moral is so obvious that this fable, were it new today, might be interpreted as a warning about changing one's environment too abruptly. But with 'The Rat and the Frog' ('The Paddock and the Mous') though the charm of the expression is made greater by dialect, age, and gentle, mock-heroic humour, the moral is Henryson's and not Aesop's.

Ane lytill Mous came till ane river syde:
Scho micht not waid, hir schankis wer sa schort;
Scho culd not swym, scho had na hors to ryde.

The Mous agrees to cross the river tied by the leg to the Paddock although greatly worried (and who would not be?) by the Frog's runkillit cheeks, hingand brows, loggerand legs and harsky hyde; after the Mous has quoted some Latin and the Frog sworn to Jupi-ter, they set off, the Frog plunges down, the Mous begins to drown 'till at the last scho cryit for ane preist'. In the end, a hawk eats them both. Aesop's moral is the one about justice and the biter being bit, Henryson's are twofold: don't trust fair words, and another more complicated 'Whereby the beistis may be figurate.' The Frog is man's body, the Mouse his soul, the water is the world, and the hawk, death. The charm, and the parable, co-exist, and point directly to the animal didactic stories of the nineteenth century.

Lastly, as a contrast, one can set beside Henryson *The Just So Stories* of Rudyard Kipling, 1902. Equal in charm, precise in diction, and each apparently with its moral, these tales are part of an in-vented folklore. They appear, like Brer Rabbit, to belong to that time after prehistory but before civilisation when the animals could speak to man and to each other: 'Before the High and Far-off Times'. The incantatory repetitions and oddly comic solemnities enhance the feeling that these animals were the first ever, straight off the ark before any multiplication had taken place: all-the-Elephant-there-was, all-the-Crab-there-was, and so on. The physical attributes which each animal finally gains are of the type of which one is told; don't pull that face, one day it will stick. So the hump, the spots, the skin, the trunk, have 'stuck', and there is no real moral at all; but one thinks again about animal diversity and strangeness, and human myth making.

Some of the stories – 'The Butterfly that Stamped', 'The Cat that Walked by Himself', 'The Beginning of the Armadilloes' – prompt equal thoughts about human oddity. But in 'These High and Far Off Times', humans and animals, as in all folklore tales, were much the same. The Parsee and the Rhinoceros do exactly the same things, taking off their clothes in a heatwave, playing equal tricks on each other; the Whale and the Hibernian Mariner, too, converse and outwit each other in the same manner – their differences are of size and shape rather than quality; nothing has, as yet, been defined. All legends belong to this time, from 'How the Robin got his Red Breast' to 'The War of the Birds and Beasts' and the Batrachomyomachia. The order of things has since been settled, the gulf fixed, and only conscious reversals or magic can cross it; or myth making, of a different sort, such as the invention of Edens where animal and human meet.

2 The Moral Tale

Boy: Frogs cannot speak, can they, Aunt?
Lady: No, my dear, but this man says for the frog what we think
the poor thing would say if it could speak.
Boy: Why, Aunt?
Lady: To teach you, my dear.

Fables in Monosyllables, *Lady Eleanor Fenn*, 1784

'The cat likes it,' says she; 'we cats, you know are said to have
nine lives!'
'Ah! That such a notion had never been taken up,' interrupted
the other.

'Tabby and Tib,' The Adventures of Poor Puss,
Elizabeth Sandham, 1809

While Aesop used animals as human symbols and folk tales use them as characters in semi-human dramas, the true didactic story uses their natural behaviour to point a human moral, and this tradition often bends animal behaviour further towards the human than it should go; you can draw a moral from a butterfly's emerging from a chrysalis, or an ugly duckling becoming a swan, but if you make the chrysalis feel envy or the duckling a wandering outcast you have the beginnings of human fiction.

The didactic story flourished in times that suspected the fairy tale and were concerned with heaven and hell; from the seventeenth to the nineteenth centuries. With notable exceptions such as *The History of Pompey the Little*, most animal stories were of this kind, and the genre is long lasting; even Rupert Bear is didactic if looked at closely. Bunyan used animals and insects as moral symbols in his *Divine Emblems, or Temporal Things Spiritualized*, 1686; the emblems are animal, the morals human.

The Egg's no Chick by falling from the Hen;
Nor Man a Christian till he's born agen,

and

> *The Bee goes out, and Honey home doth bring.*
> *And some who seek that Honey, find a Sting.*
> *Now woulds't thou have the Honey and be free*
> *Fron stinging, in the first place kill the Bee.*
> *This Bee an Emblem truly is of sin . . .*

Which is the opposite of Isaac Watt's bee in *Divine and Moral Songs for Children*, 1715, quoted by Alice, where the bee is the emblem – as it usually is – of industry.* Obliging animals, they could illustrate any virtue or vice the poet wished and even some bad behaviour not their own: 'Let bears and lions growl and fight, for 'tis their nature, too', implies that they are quarrelling, which children should not.

John Newberry's *Tommy Trip's History of Birds and Beasts*, a 'familiar description of each in verse and prose', 1760, does the same thing. No one knows what animals feel, they can only guess. It did not matter anyway when animals could serve as an allurement for children's interest and as examples to be followed or shunned, regardless of their physical nature:

> *Few beasts can with the leopard vie*
> *His beauteous skin allures the eye*
> *His form, like Vice, serves to decoy*
> *Those whom his Nature would destroy.*

or

> *The Bison though neither engaging nor young*
> *Like a flatt'rer can lick*
> *You to death with his Tongue.*

or

> *The crocodile with false perfidious tears*
> *Draws the unwary trav'ler nigh*
> *Who by compassion warm'd no danger fears*
> *But ah! Th'unhappy wretch must die.*

---

*As late as the 1870s bees are still being used to point a moral: in the Rev. F. A. S. Reid's *Comic Insects*, a patriotic one, as the bees are loyal to the Queen.

> *Lessons here of self-reliance,*
> *And 'defence but not defiance'*
> *As Volunteers are taught by the Bee.*
> *As it works on active wing*
> *Self protected with its sting,*
> *'Tis a grand working Model, good to see.*

Whatever the moral, this is unhappily false to the animal. In a sense the Bestiaries, however fabulous, were more honest.* But Tommy Trip's attitude to the Duck is unequivocal:

> *This waddling, hissing, quacking pair*
> *Have but few charms for eye or ear,*
> *But let the cook but spit and baste 'em*
> *And every fool is glad to taste 'em.*

which almost sounds like a verse from *The Bad Child's Book of Beasts*, Hilaire Belloc, 1898. It is a short step from this to attributing human feelings to an animal in order to make the moral more interesting and the point more forcible – to turn the animals from examples to actors, capable of a degree of human vice and virtue. *Jack Dandy's Delight*, 1786, goes in this direction, as animals are credited with moral motives. 'Goats are remarkable in the care of their young, which care, when the dam grows old, is returned with becoming gratitude by the young one who brings her food and water' – attributed to Goldsmith, the book certainly has a feeling of Dr Primrose's gentle preaching.

Indefatigable female moralists and educators are responsible for many of the classic didactic tales, from Sarah Trimmer's *History of the Robins* to Margaret Gatty's *Parables from Nature*, including people with pen names like Arabella Argus or Aunt Affable. Unfortunately, at times, the authoresses cared more for the moral than the story. Mrs Anna Barbauld's *Easy Lessons for Children* and *Evenings at Home*, series published between 1792 and 1796, have various instructive stories, among them 'The Young Mouse, a Fable', which has a moral about filial obedience, but it is rather dull and prosaic. Even Charles Lamb complained about 'Mrs Barbauld's stuff' and that there was nothing for children to read but 'little narratives of puss and a crow and a squirrel'; the ladies were obviously opposed to the fairy-tale tradition and liked beast fables – if they were of the right kind. But the ladies are responsible for a more interesting development, the second kind of moral story which really endeavours to

---

*However far-fetched the notion of the Ichneumon covering himself with mud to attack the Dragon (Physiologus), the moral drawn 'So Christ took on flesh to attack the Devil' does not infer any crusading holiness in the Ichneumon.

Oh! My!

From *Selected Cautionary Verses* by Hilaire Belloc

find out what the animal might be feeling and to convey, through human emotions and speech, its joys and sufferings (rather more of the latter than the former).

Sarah Trimmer's Robins and Dorothy Kilner's Mice are the first stories to unite both types; the parable of human behaviour and the sermon on how animals should be treated, pointing the way to literary landmarks like *Black Beauty*.

Fabulous Histories Designed for the Instruction of Children, Respecting their treatment of Animals. This long title was merely hopeful – the only completed story was Sarah Trimmer's 'History of the Robins', 1786. Mrs Trimmer – an adherent of Robert Raikes, with much charm, kindness and common sense as well as Sunday School tract didactic purpose – used a bird family to teach young readers both how to behave to animals and how they should themselves behave, in a kind of double fable. She did not intend the Robins, Mother,

Father and four children ('to whom for the sake of distinction,' she writes, 'I will give the names Robin, Dicky, Pecksy and Flapsy') to be altogether like real birds and warns adult readers in the 'Advertisement': 'Through an erroneous education many children contract habits of tormenting inferior creatures before they are conscious of giving them pain: or fall into the contrary fault of immoderate tenderness to them'; and also warns child readers that in the story 'the sentiments and affection of a good Father and Mother and a Family of Children are supposed to be possessed by a nest of Redbreasts.'

The robins nest in a garden with other birds, animals and insects; the garden is the world, the creatures its population, but observing all this in godlike fashion are a human family, the Bensons, a mother and a master and miss. They have some unpleasant friends, a cruel Edward Jenkins (a recurrent character in this type of story) and his sister, who are used by Mrs Benson (and Mrs Trimmer) as examples of what not to do. Father Robin must be the only bird ever to talk like Dr Johnson, but Mrs Benson speaks in the same manner.

The young Robins are natural – as human children are – they quarrel, peck each other, are greedy, envy Pecksy for being the parental favourite. They learn to fly, to show curiosity, wonder and fear. Pompous Father Robin teaches by admonition and example, like Mr Fairchild; he is full of such remarks as 'Nothing can be acquired without patience' or 'Never be ashamed but when you commit a fault'. Being a widower before he married their mother, he tells the children of his former nest and mate, describing her death scene: 'She lifted up her languid eyelids and then with feeble accents said . . .'

Mother Robin is rather a snob, as is her friend Mrs Linnet. 'My own nestlings are just ready to fly,' said the Linnet, 'and I hope will make acquaintance with your own: for birds as well instructed as your offspring are, must be very desirable companions.' The chaffinch and sparrow children, who fight and are noisy, are 'rough' and to be avoided; but still all the birds mob the cuckoo (an undesirable and wicked social outcast) and the mocking bird ('properly a native of America but introduced here for the sake of the moral').

Cruel Master Edward Jenkins tells some quite horrid tales of badly treated animals and pets, but Mrs Benson teaches her children to feed the Robin family (by this time they seem human enough to be the poor, to whom the Bensons are kind at Christmas time: only the Robins are very bourgeois, with their own morals and manners and their own poor, and it seems odd that they should accept charity).

Though the human children are taught the unexceptionable lesson – 'As every living creature can feel, we should have a constant regard to these feelings and strive to give happiness rather than inflict misery' – Mrs Robin is heard to say 'No, Dicky, the Linnet has as great a right to the caterpillar as you or I', and Pecksy gives her mother 'a fine fat spider', saying 'Accept, my dear parent, the first tribute of gratitude which I have ever been able to offer you.'

Perhaps the real moral is that animal nature is there for our use, after all, whether as an example to the young, or as something to eat; and the homily ends with the remark that 'we should prefer the happiness of mankind to that of any animal whatever'.

One interesting feature is Mrs Trimmer's dislike of trained animals, or animals acting unnaturally; a 'learned pig' is something to be wondered at but avoided, and at one point a monkey* (probably belonging to cruel Master Jenkins) wrecks a tea table in the Bensons' house. Clearly there is no room in this fable for pets, or perhaps monkeys are too human for comfort.

Dorothy Kilner's *Life and Perambulations of a Mouse*, 1783, breaks new ground – it is quite exciting, full of incident and is told by the Mouse itself (the charming preface describes the Mouse dictating to the authoress) and is the first of those animal autobiographies that were to be so popular in the early years of the nineteenth century. In a way it is the prototype of all mouse stories, which are nearly always about pursuit, courage and cunning, or an integrated underground society perpetually hidden and retreating from Man, yet scoring small victories and surviving in competition with a powerful, hostile world.

The Life and Perambulations of a Mouse is a parable about filial obedience, but there is a real feeling of what it might be like to be a mouse and record one's feelings. Dorothy Kilner's mouse is named

---

*This incident is rather like that in *Evelina* and shows a similar aversion. 'He' (the Captain) 'hauled into the room a monkey; fully dressed, and extravagantly *à la mode*.' The monkey is felt to be unpleasant through no fault of its own.

Nimble, and there is an odd foretaste of Peter Rabbit. Nimble's brother and sisters are Longtail, Softdown and Brighteyes, and their mother, instead of sending them out to gather blackberries – or cheese – sends them out into the wide world with the advice: never be seen, never return to the same place twice. The prohibitions worked in much the same way as: don't go into Mr Mac-Gregor's garden, don't eat anything off the tree of knowledge. 'She was no sooner gone than the thought of being our own directors so charmed out little hearts that we presently forgot our grief at parting from our kind parent: and impatient to use our liberty we all set forward in search of some food, or rather, of some *adventure*.'

The sins of disobedience bring swift retribution, and all the mice, excepting Nimble, come to bad, sad ends, caught by cruel humans, traps, or cat. Their fates were not worth the bird seed and plum cake by which they were lured, but their real faults were in doing what their mother had told them not to do. There is, however, excitement and suspense in their adventurers – in evading traps, escaping from human view, episodes in gamekeeper's cottage and garden, as well as the floor-and-closet life in the house of Mrs Artless and her daughter Ann. (The human family are observed, critically, by the mice.) The story is a great advance in making the animal, as well as the moral, interesting; one feels that this mouse of the eighteenth century is speaking across the gap in time in appropriate words: ' "When," said I, addressing myself to my brother, "shall we grow wise and learn to know that certain evil always attends every deviation from what is right?" '

If a human soul could enter a mouse body, this is what it might have felt like.* Dorothy Kilner's moralising is more kindly than Sarah Trimmer's; and at last Mouse and Dorothy come together when she says 'The author cannot help in *human* form (as well as in that of a *mouse*) . . . warning my little readers to shun all those vices and follies . . .' The affection between mouse and authoress is quite strongly felt, and there is great concern and regret at the helplessness of the mice and their sad treatment by the humans in the story. The reader is moved never to set a mouse trap – as Anna Sewell moved her contemporaries against the bearing rein.

*Real human souls in animal bodies – as distinct from humans whose appearance has been changed by magic – would not have been an acceptable idea at this time: one has to wait for E. Nesbit's *The Cathood of Maurice*, T. H. White's *The Sword in the Stone* or Paul Gallico's *Jennie*.

Animal autobiographies proliferate during this period, the emphasis moving from the animals or birds being used as examples, to animal observation of how cruel, or moral, or amiable the humans are. *The Escapes of a Hare*, *The History of a Field Mouse*, *The Comical Adventures of a Baboon*, *The History of a Goldfinch*, and many others were all written between 1805 and 1822 and nearly all read like tracts written for spoiled children. Mrs Pilkington who had had experience as a governess, appears to speak with feeling in *Marvellous Adventures, or the Vicissitudes of a Cat*, 1802. It is the cat, Grimalkin, who really speaks, and the grim and gloomy narrative proceeds from infanticide – 'orders were given that the whole of (my mother's) progeny should have their existence terminated as soon as they drew breath' (they are drowned in sight of their mother) – to the heroine's death on her mistress's tomb. One wonders how the story was ever written. However, with certain delightful exceptions (*The Curious Adventures of a Field Cricket, Jemmy Donkey*) the convention is that the animals' thoughts appear to speak directly to the reader, with no worries about pens, ink and paper, and how they came to be printed; even a favourite such as Black Beauty communicates in this telepathic manner.

Descriptions of quite refined animal torture, mostly carried out by cruel children may have had some moral effect; one feels that kind children would have been made unhappy by them while cruel or amoral children would have been merely given ideas. Grimalkin's sufferings – physical and mental – make unhappy reading indeed, but her picaresque adventures involve kindness and amusement too. Perhaps the odd charm of the narrative derives from the nature of the humanisation – Grimalkin speaks as a well-brought-up young lady – who happens, accidentally, to have a cat's form – would speak. When she catches her first rat, she is rather loath (as is Peter, the boy in a cat's skin in Paul Gallico's *Jennie*) but she does her duty: 'though I at first felt a little alarmed at the thoughts of an encounter, my courage soon revived.' When put out to board at a farmer's where the cats will not drink skim milk, 'in vain,' she says, 'I attempted to convince them of the folly of their conduct.'

By the end of the story Grimalkin becomes rather more omniscient than a cat should be; she witnesses human drama, creeps under a sofa to see her mistress dance at a party and catch pneumonia, is able to 'know' the contents of letters and is familiar with 'Mr Gray's Ode' (as is Pompey the Little, but the latter is a very well-read dog).

In the days before the RSPCA perhaps certain things needed saying. Successions of cruel and kind-hearted owners are castigated, from those who teach tricks by cruelty or attack animals in fits of bad temper, or leave their care to lazy servants, to those who overfeed them or indulge them to the point of neglecting human suffering. It is to be hoped that children were edified without being too much upset.

Elizabeth Sandham's *The Adventures of Poor Puss*, 1809, has similar episodic treatment, cruelties and human wickedness. Early stories of domestic animals (and there are few stories of any other kind, apart from mice) nearly always see them as victims, often bewailing their lot with human voices; and *The Adventures of Poor Puss* is no exception. The cats shake their heads over human wickedness and act like persecuted saints, never putting out a claw to defend themselves.

Both cats 'move' continually. Constant escapes and changes of owner bring drama into their rather contrived lives. Tib, the younger of the two, does not appear to benefit from her friend's good advice, but her life gives a series of minuscule views of London life during the time of the Peninsular War, as Tib goes from shop to alehouse, boys' school and a Dame school conducted in a garret over another shop. Her sufferings are ingenious and unbearable, and Tabby's prolonged death scene equally so. Among the less cruel tortures is the tying of walnut shells to cats' feet, which, impossible though it sounds, must have been fairly common, as it is mentioned in cautionary and moral tales so often. Perhaps the most interesting episode is Tabby's meeting with an ailurophobe, with the comment that the cat was as frightened as the man: 'His behaviour,' says Tabby, 'was so contrary to what I had expected.'

The Adventures of a Donkey, 1815, is a direct ancestor of *Black Beauty* in many respects. The animals are not held up as moral examples, but there are 'good' and 'bad' ones as there are good and bad humans, lack of speech being the only animal disadvantage. (It took Polynesia the parrot to put this matter right.) Arabella Argus's (as Harvey Darton suggests, the name is impossible) donkey is one of these animal writers that takes up its pen as enthusiastically as a romantic novelist; and composition brings its own reward: 'How authorship affects other Animals, I know not; with me, it was beginning to be an imperious feeling,' writes Jemmy the Donkey.

His narrative does not push the moral too far by the use of melodrama or pathos; Arabella Argus makes an objective attempt to imagine herself inside a four-footed beast and describe what it is like. Similarities to Anna Sewell's masterpiece abound. The donkeys talk to each other and understand human speech; Jemmy's mother advises him to be docile and obedient, as does Black Beauty's. Jemmy is also advised by an older donkey, Balaam, the Merrylegs of the story, and he relates with some feeling what it feels like to be shod, with its strange noises, heaviness and height. His narrative gives considerable information on riding, driving, saddling and being hired on donkey races and the use of blinkers, on the traffic of the day in Fleet Street, Chancery Lane, Holborn and Russell Square, where at the side of the road donkeys drawing carts could be almost knee deep in mud. Jemmy, in a similar manner to Black Beauty, ends up broken-kneed and is bought at last by a kindly lady. His descriptions of London are not intended necessarily to refer to the London of Waterloo, as he writes in retrospect in charming, but – like Eeyore – rather pompous style, 'obtruding his history on the public'. His plea for kind treatment criticises human nature quite gently. 'I, a beast of burden, declare that our fatigue is increased or ameliorated by the temper of those we carry,' he writes; but why humans behave as they do, he cannot tell.

'I feel all the presumption and danger of attempting further analysis of the *human* character,' he says. This is as it should be; the omniscience of the horses in *Black Beauty* is rather unnerving, and the human viewpoints of Tib, Tabby and Grimalkin constantly remind one of their authors, not themselves.

Like Boots, Kipling's dog, Jemmy 'does not understand'.

During the nineteenth century, however lively and objective the story, the moral was always *there*, not a shrugging observation of the less likeable traits of human nature, as in Aesop, but a blueprint on how to behave.

Struwelpeter (Heinrich Hoffmann, 1848) uses animals as typical victims ('Good Dog Tray') or chorus (the cats, in 'Harriet and the Matches') but does allow Tray to change places with Cruel Frederick. And there is that hare, in 'The Man That Went Out Shooting'; it walks off on its hind legs with the Man's gun and spectacles and eventually begins to stalk him (but perhaps this is because it is a *wild* animal – no cat, dog, or horse is allowed even a comic riposte). A book like *The Kitten Pilgrims* took a family of cats towards the Celestial City in the eighties, through encounters with various other animals, each symbolising a sin to be overcome; Worm Sloth, Hippopotamus Unconcern, Monkey Fun (early in the story made a

The green man wakes, and sees her place
The spectacles upon her face;
And now she's trying, all she can,
To shoot the sleepy green-coat man.
He cries and screams and runs away;
The hare runs after him all day,
And hears him call out every where,
"Help! Fire! Help! The Hare! The Hare!"

friend of, and a great help in dealing with later trials) and lastly
Giant Self, a vast cat. This is animal fable based on human allegory,
as delightfully twice-removed as Bennet's Aesop. The Rev. F. A. S.
Reid's *Comic Insects* takes a rather more naturalistic and anatomical
view of such fabulous material as caterpillars growing into butterflies and the slothful snail wearily scanning the future through a
telescope and the Drill-Serjeant Bee. (As in many Victorian illustrations, the insects are lovingly drawn but rather too large for comfort – a death's head hawk moth caterpillar is shown as big as a
child.)

Even Southey's version of *The Three Bears*, 1834, has a moral
ring. In the original version, the little old woman, 'If she had been
a good little old woman, . . . would have waited till the Bears came
home, and then, perhaps, they would have asked her to breakfast:
for they were good Bears – a little rough or so, as the manner of
Bears is, but for all that very good natured and hospitable.' As it is,
she gets what she deserves for inquisitive marauding.

Margaret Gatty's *Parables from Nature*, 1855, take a very exact,
naturalist's view of the divine order, and though at first the stories
appear to be mere examples of animals with a moral, they share
some of the wonder that the writers of the Bestiaries must have felt

and point the way towards Kingsley and Ernest Thompson Seton. Mrs Gatty was the author of a two volume book on British Sea-weeds, and her parables are rather like a nature series current in the nineteen-thirties known as 'Beasts – or Birds – Shown to the Children', in which the animals discuss their attributes and habitat with one another. This quite entertaining series had no morals. Mrs Gatty's *have*, but her animals and insects – plenty of these, for metamorphosis is a fruitful moral symbol – discuss their affairs similarly: ' "Let me hire you as a nurse for my poor children," said a Butterfly to a quiet Caterpillar who was strolling along a cabbage leaf in her odd, lumbering way.' The Butterfly dies and the Cater-pillar is left anxiously guarding the eggs, comforted by a passing Lark (who does not eat eggs or caterpillar). The eggs turn into caterpillars and caterpillar into a butterfly; the story is called 'A Lesson of Faith'.

Mrs Gatty's most interesting parable is that comic delight 'Inferior Animals', which foreshadows not *Animal Farm*, but Kipling; yet the satire is almost as sophisticated as that of Swift. The rooks are holding a counsel. The subject is Man. The meeting is addressed in turn by those learned authorities Mr Ravenwing, Mr Yellowhead, Mr Greylegs. 'Why Man?' says Mr Ravenwing, sounding like a religious programme on television. 'One of the most puzzling *whys* in connection with Man is, *why he wears clothes?*' The birds decide that clothes are probably vestigial feathers, or that Man, having either lost or not yet evolved feathers, is trying to reproduce them artificially, to become, in fact, a Rook. Further proof is supplied (in this coal-using and mining era) by his efforts to attain his original colour – black. Another proof of his need to resume his original life in trees is his continued effort to soar in the air – by balloon. The rooks debate Man as a fallen Rook, arguing delightfully from data, drawing all the wrong conclusions with invincible superiority.

Mrs Gatty edited *Aunt Judy's Magazine*, 1866–73, which first pub-lished 'Bruno's Revenge', and was a great admirer of *The Water Babies*, which is, in part, so much like some *Parables from Nature* enlarged and given a continuous plot. It is perhaps unfortunate that Charles Kingsley felt that he had to be a didactic writer. *The Water Babies*, 1863, has a moral, the un-Voltairean one that your soul makes your body, just as a snail makes its shell; but the constant sermons included in the narrative hold it up, both from a child's and from an adult's point of view.

Kingsley was a devoted naturalist, but managed to combine this love with the sports of shooting and fishing, perhaps an easier matter in the last century than it is now. *The Water Babies* divides into three well-defined parts – Tom as a chimney sweep, Tom in the river, and Tom in the sea searching for Mother Carey. Having started with the wonderful, touching first chapter (written we are told, quite incredibly, in half an hour), the story continues quite differently: in 'The Natural Parables', in come the newts and trout and caddis worms and dragonfly, the salmon and the others, all talking to Tom in underwater language, as if life were full of those pills the author speaks of: 'I have tried in all sorts of queer ways to make children and grown up folk understand that there is a miraculous and divine element underlying all physical nature. And if I have wrapped up my parable in seeming Tom-fooleries, it is because so only could I get the pill swallowed.'

The river creatures converse, gossip and sing (and teach Tom not to maul or hurt them) both as themselves, and as human types – the caddis worms are victims of fashion, the mayfly conceited and empty headed, the otter proud and sentimental, the salmon a fine gentleman with perfect manners. They do nothing out of their natural history, but their talk fixes it in one's mind with pointed images; the mayfly's empty, demented singing as it floats away downstream, the lobster in the pot, a bigoted old Blimp refusing to bend his opinions to escape by the only possible retreat. There is an uncomfortable lesson too in the Last of the Gairfowl who drove the Second to Last Gairfowl off her rock because he was her deceased sister's husband, the hooded crow republicans who cannot allow anyone to be different from themselves, the poor Tom-toddies, wretched children growing into vegetables, a vision so unhappy that it has haunted me all my life.

In *The Water Babies* there is murder, tragedy, shipwreck and sudden death, but the effect is softened by the justice of the two great Fairies who arrange the fates of all the creatures in this natural and supernatural history – and as Tom is half supernatural himself, justice is seen to be done.

Finally, two moral fairy tales that use animals as a means towards making their point, obliquely: *Pinocchio* and *The Ugly Duckling*.

Collodi's *Pinocchio*, 1883, is a gay but slightly macabre quest-fairy tale. Pinocchio is the puppet pilgrim and his goal is to be turned into a real boy. Like *The Water Babies* and *The Three Pearls*, it is an allegory of life, but far nearer to folktale in feeling with its shadeless black and white issues, the quick rewards of virtue and sharp punishment of wrongdoing. Animals – notably those two villains the Cat and the Fox – play their traditional parts as the hero's semi-equals who in this story ensnare him by greed. But when he does wrong he is tried by animals and his worst fate is to be turned into one, and throughout his adventures his companion is a kind of externalised conscience, a Cricket with a voice, and his good angel is the Blue Fairy with her snail servant.

Pinocchio falls from grace with the monotonous regularity of most humans, doll though he is. Again and again he is put on the right road, again and again he behaves foolishly, tells lies to save himself, resents advice, dashes here and there in pursuit of pleasure, steals, is taken in by the simplest ruses, is filled with remorse and repentance and immediately goes wrong again – one wonders why the Blue Fairy and the Cricket don't give up. The moral message is quite clear – one may sin many times and still be forgiven – but the implicit allegory is that it takes a long time to grow up. The delightful gaiety is mixed with much that is harsh and rather violent (as in many folk tales). Pinocchio kills the Cricket by throwing a block of wood at it in chapter four; its subsequent appearances are as a ghost. When the Blue Fairy first appears at a window after admonishing invisibly like Hamlet's father, she tells Pinocchio that she is dead, waiting for the hearse to take her away; there is the feeling that Pinocchio's sins have caused her death, or illness, or sorrow. He sins constantly, and she 'dies' more than once. He is always trying to find her, to beg forgiveness, and is always being swept away in another direction.

His main persecutors, the Fox and the Cat, are archetypal deceivers, like characters out of Reynard. They part him from his money. Pretending to be lame and blind, they trick him again and again. He is surrounded by deceitful, threatening or predatory animals, fanciful symbols of life's hazards. When ill, he is cured by an owl and a crow; when sent to prison he is judged by a gorilla with mastiff policemen. He is pursued by a dog and sharks and eventually swallowed by one of the latter. The misery and humiliation he suffers from being turned into a donkey (beguiled, with his friend Lampwick into going to live in the Fun City of Toyland) is being made to perform in a circus. When he is lamed during a trick, he is sold for drumskin. The most eerie part of the story is the gradualness of the transformation. Just as Pinocchio's nose grows larger with every lie he tells, so his ears grow longer with each foolishness; he runs on hands and feet, his back becomes covered with hair, and at last muzzle and tail appear. The Disney film of 1939 – still the most attractive and stylish of the full-length cartoons – handles the death and funeral themes cautiously, but the donkey transformation is horrifying. Each boy is frightened by what he sees happening in the other, without realising what he himself is becoming.

Pinocchio is a young *Pilgrim's Progress*, with animal tempters, avengers and judges. Pinocchio is always saying 'Oh! how I wish I could have been a good *child*.' It *is* the same old thing – obedience brings you to heaven, the reverse gets you nowhere.

In *The Ugly Duckling*, Hans Andersen uses animal symbolism to tell a disguised human story. It unites animal transformation and animal moral tale in a unique way; it is about an unrecognised metamorphosis that really isn't one at all. The Duckling only appears to be a strange outcast because no one knows what he really is, even his mother, who took trouble in hatching and defending him, gives up at last, wishing he had never been born. The pathos of this strange and beautiful fable is quite new to the form. The Aesop elements are there: the proud turkey cock, the old duck with the red rag of honour, and the incident when the animals quarrel over an eel head which is seized by the cat; and there is a house too, where the cat is master and the hen mistress. But there is far more than barnyard comedy in the rejection of the Duckling and his efforts to do what his nature demands, always thwarted by animals who, when he wants to swim, tell him to lay eggs or purr. Thrown out, hunted, half-starved, frozen, when he eventually meets the swans, his life has become so wretched and hopeless that he is only conscious of ugliness so great that he expects death.

Perhaps Hans Andersen was writing about himself. Everyone interprets the fable in his own way, for the story has an echo in

everyone. As a fairy tale it is, like many of Andersen's, very odd.
The happy climax is so long delayed that it almost does not happen,
unlike Cinderella (with the same plot) where we *know* the heroine is
favoured and only unrecognised by an odd quirk that magic will
soon put right. The long sufferings of the lonely duck are alien to
the setting which (Orwell always excepted) from Chaucer to Hepzibah Hen is usually gay and superficial. The moral is the one about
appearance and reality, expressed by birds so memorably and
wonderfully that there is no need to call the story a Parable from
Nature; these simple symbols have expressed universal truth as only
a story teller of genius can do.

The moral tale is by no means dead; morals may change, but
crusading purpose goes on, and animals are an acceptable disguise
– as they have always been – for plain speaking, leaving the reader
the choice of appreciating what is said at its face value or letting it
affect him more deeply. If animals are concerned the moral may be
twofold, involving the truth for which the animals are symbols, and
the no less important truth that they share the living world with
humans and should be treated accordingly. One cannot write an
animal story without bringing in one or both of these principles:
wonder, and guilt.

Good modern examples with both elements strongly present
are *The Tree That Sat Down* and its sequel *The Stream That Stood Still*
by Beverley Nichols. *The Tree That Sat Down*, 1945, introduces The
Woodland in the same sense that it appears in *Winnie the Pooh* or, as
a garden in *The History of the Robins* – some semi-enclosed place
where animals live their lives and go about their business in a world
smaller, more parochial than the real one, and more or less cut off
from it apart from, in this case, a few human characters. *The Tree
That Sat Down* is a carefully worked out moral tale (it is too kindly
for satire) on commercialism; its message is strongly and amusingly
presented. If Mr Nichols does not, as has been suggested, carry on
the tradition of Kenneth Grahame, he works more along the
didactic lines of *The Water Babies* or *The Three Pearls* (the Hon.
J. W. Fortescue, 1916).

The animals in wood and stream are not exactly humans in disguise – they are deputising for them, and show us, rather uncomfortably, what happens when wicked characters – the evil Sam and
his accomplice the witch – are determined to exploit and corrupt an

essentially innocent world. Good kind Judy and her Grandmother
have a shop in which they sell everything the animals need. Their
rival, wicked Sam, sells in *his* shop a substance called Wake-o which
galvanises anyone who takes it into stupid action so that they either
need more, or some other expensive product to cure them. Sam also
advertises and introduces other evil things called Progress and
Competition, and plays on the animals' vanity, credulity and
covetousness, even selling them empty boxes labelled *Nichts* and
Rien – carefully sealed. The simple animals (necessary here, as
humans would not be so innocent) queue to buy them.

> *It looked such a good parcel that Mrs Rabbit felt it must be worth
> five shillings. As Sam handed it to her, he said 'I suppose you understand
> how to undo this parcel?'*
>
> *'How to undo it?' Mrs Rabbit blinked at him in bewilderment. She
> did not know what he meant.*
>
> *'You must not undo it in daylight,' Sam said, 'otherwise all the goodness
> goes out of the* Nichts. *They must never be exposed to the sun.'*
>
> *'No,' muttered Mrs Rabbit. 'I quite understand.'*

Such wickedness does not go unpunished. Judy herself is incorruptible – she will not buy an evilly enchanted Hoover – but is
nearly killed by a bear with a past who has escaped from a circus
and is being blackmailed by the witch and Sam. Sam is at last tried
and condemned by an animal court whose role is twofold: to defend
innocence against profiteering and to maintain the gulf or gap that
has always existed between human and animal, making sure that it
is never crossed. Judy is fairylike, Sam a very human human. The
story may not be to everyone's taste, but the pill is interesting.

The theme of the similarly highly moral *The Stream That Stood
Still* is as modern, told in a manner more like the moral tales of the
past. Jill, the daughter of the now grown-up Judy, has to undergo
trials with great unselfish endeavour to save her brother Jack from
the jaws of a pike, an evil city millionaire changed into a fish for
eating the substance of widows and orphans. To do this, Jill has to
adopt an underwater life, make friends with the fish and persuade
them to act with her.

The real message is that concerted action and goodwill of many
weak creatures will sometimes overthrow a single, strong, well-
armed tyrant. The underwater world is more obtrusively humanised

than Tom's river – the sticklebacks belong to a regiment, the minnows are a ladies' finishing school, the fish have police and magistrates – but the moral is impeccable and the substitute drama enables it to be absorbed painlessly and permanently. Perhaps today there is less need to be coy about stories with a message.

The pike's captive: human who fish

3 Four Satires

I return . . . to apply those excellent lessons of virtue which I learned among the Houyhnhnms; to instruct the Yahoos of my own family, as far as I shall find them docile animals; to behold my figure often in a glass and thus, if possible, habituate myself, by time, to tolerate the sight of a human creature.

Gulliver's Travels, *Swift*

The animal satire is rather more rare than one might think. Animal moral fable is the more usual form, often having a certain amount of interest and attention given to the animals' real lives, which satire does not do. Animal fables, other than Aesop, are softened with kindness, where satire has only bite, attacking humans by using animal substitutes or people wearing animal masks.

An Arthur Rackham illustration to *Gulliver's Travels*

True satire, like *Gulliver's Travels* or *Animal Farm*, uses animal disguises only to show the human race to itself in caricature. At first sight, Gulliver's voyage to the Houyhnhnms is a tables-turned story in which the functions of animal and man are neatly reversed, as in *The Jungle Book*; the horses are disguised people, the people disguised animals. But the difference is that here there is no real disguise – the horses *are* people, of a specialised sort. They are reasoning beasts, and the Yahoos are people too. The black streak of bitterness that makes this last book of *Gulliver's Travels* so bleak an experience that even Gulliver is irreversibly changed by it, colours all human nature, the best and the worst. The best is too good to be portrayed in human terms, and horses, the noblest of beasts, embody it. The worst parts of human nature, the meanest and most degraded, are given human form. For an even sharper lesson the two species could have been two different kinds of ape, but Swift's dislike and disgust for the human body perhaps led him to choose, as the rational and speech-using leaders, the one animal that cannot be humanised. The equine form and face are as far from the human kind as one can get; even a reptile does not look too odd on its hind legs, but to imagine a horse like this is impossible.

One can't help comparing Gulliver's first meeting with the horses to Ransome's encounter with the Hross in *Out of the Silent Planet*. Both men are expecting an animal and find a human intelligence – yet while C. S. Lewis (not writing satire) manages to make his account of that meeting one of the most moving passages in the book, Swift's hero, seeing a familiar animal, is at first less wary and at the end less filled with wonder and awe; satire has no numinosity. 'I did not much like my present situation,' notes Gulliver, 'and I at last concluded they must needs be magicians,' and he produces the gifts he had in readiness for savages. These are naïve reactions, and the idea that (being conjurors) the animals are conversing does not surprise him. Perhaps the difference is that Ransome's mind is full of the idea of an unattainable Eden in which humans and animals are equal – which is, in a way, what he finds in Malacandra – while Gulliver, a seasoned traveller, is an objective observer and has to be unemotional. The transition from concluding that the rational horses are 'all necromancy and magic' to the realisation that they are the masters and the humans are dumb and bestial, is hardly noticed.

The horses are a singularly innocent society, as inhuman as the Yahoos are sub-human, yet each *is* human in intention. The horses do not steal or fight and cannot understand a lie; it is 'the thing which is not', a phrase also used among the Hrossa who are similarly innocent. The horses are almost too perfect, they have no weaknesses, they live in clean spacious stables among fields full of oats, share their children in Platonic amity, do not fear or mourn for death, do not blame the Yahoos for being miserable, dirty and incorrigible.

As fantasy, the fourth voyage falls short of Gulliver's other three travels. Who built the stables, and why do the horses live in this odd, semi-human way? And who planted the oats, made the pottery and did the cooking? The explanation of the hoof and pastern used as a kind of finger and thumb does not overcome horse resistance to human likeness. The horses' manner of sitting back on their haunches recalls a fallen cabhorse or Tom Cobley's old mare writing her will; but as a satiric device for undermining European confidence, the horse, the least human, or the ape, the most human, are admirable.

Gulliver (as soon as he has learned horse language) makes the great mistake common to many science-fiction heroes who visit alien cultures: he starts to tell the truth about his own society and unleashes the contempt and incomprehension of the inhabitants. Professor Cavor made this mistake with the Selenites; explaining human institutions never goes well. The scene is set for the simple, Spartan virtues of the horses and the hopeless vices of the Yahoos: the drawbacks of the human frame, the soft, useless feet, awkward placing of the eyes, inability of the mouth to eat without having food put in it by the hands, and the whole body's need for artificial covering; the defects of the reason which make for wars, the misapplied intelligence, which gives rise to the profession of lawyer; the miseries which cause criminality, disease and drink. Self-disgust can go no further. The horses' suspicions are confirmed; the Yahoos, when wild, are not even good monkeys – when allowed power, they get out of hand. The reader's shame at being a Yahoo almost makes him regard horses with superstitious dislike for ever.

Karel Capek's *Insect Play*, 1923, too, shows Man up in a poor light, as do most 'generic' satires; Birds, Frogs and the Bandar-Log. Its three acts take three unhappier human characteristics: man's pleasure-seeking superficiality, his small-minded, money-loving selfishness, and his futile ideas of war and conquest. Butter-

An Authur Rackham illustration to *Gulliver's Travels*

flies, beetles and ants act out these themes in a miniature world, while a human tramp who falls asleep in a wood is the baffled, unhappy chorus. That these creatures are acting according to their natures makes the human parallel even more effective – it always does. The wily fox and boastful cock were not chosen arbitrarily by Aesop. The insects are human, and of course human actors as well, disguised as butterflies or ants, acting out human dramas in an insect-behaviour convention.

The amorous pursuit of the butterflies, their shallow disregard for involvement or thought of any kind, and their equally casual deaths are rather alien to the present climate, but not to that of 1923. The creepers and crawlers are unhappily constant. So are the dung beetles with their savings, the piratical ichneumon, the innocent, duped crickets (no one has, I believe, written about an *evil* cricket – cheerful, happy good nature is the rule), the idealistic and poetic chrysalis killed as soon as it is born. The warlike ants with their rival dictators and incantatory cries of Peace, Science, Progress and the Good of the Whole, fighting territorial battles were, when written about, prophetic. The anthill has symbolised the city or the state ever since cities got large enough to frighten, and states powerful enough to make prisoners of the ignorant. It is difficult to use ants, as a population, in any other way. T. H. White's ant colony in *The Once and Future King* teaches the same lesson of tyranny and mindless obedience.

In the second two satires, Orwell's *Animal Farm* and Erich

Kästner's *The Animals' Conference*, there is something more than human problems being acted out in an animal mirror world – the animals also take over and show Man how to do better; failing, in Orwell, and succeeding, in Kästner's equally valid, but light-hearted fantasy.

Animal Farm starts with the familiar animal vengeance theme – a guilt-ridden preoccupation with some authors from Arthur Machen to C. S. Lewis. In this recurrent drama, as in the *Animal Farm* Battle of the Cowshed, the animals always win – at first; even with their limited weapons. The fable is about a suppressed and and mistreated class, and so about revolution, but it is not always a finally successful one. Part of the story always puts Man at an initial disadvantage – he loses his own weapons and meets armed animals when he is disarmed, or as in *Animal Farm*, only appears to have shotguns.

Animal Farm has been called a satire on dictatorship, but it is a chronicle of the sad sameness of human nature and the ultimate absorption of every revolutionary movement – the endlessly turning wheel of conquest, power, corruption and decline. If you removed the moral, it would be no more memorable than the kind of sermon that tells one what ought to be done by giving a gloomy and prophetic chain of consequences that will be brought about if one persists in the way one is going. The actual story of *Animal Farm* is likewise very simple – initial success, then slowly accelerating disaster until the inevitable climax when it is seen that the animals have only moved into worse slavery than they endured under Farmer Jones.

What makes the fable memorable is the simple but cogent characterisation that the animal actors are able to give to their parts, and the beautiful logic of each downward step whereby the pig Napoleon – who starts off with his ally the visionary Snowball and mouthpiece, Squeaker, by directing the revolution, drinking the surplus milk and doing no work – ends by sleeping in a bed, drinking with men and selling the animals into human slavery for his personal profit. The animals are, like most animals, well meaning but naïve, and they are bullied and duped apparently with their own connivance; innocent farm animals are as uncomfortably exploited in reality, unable to defend themselves; the fable is twofold. Capek makes his insects poignant; the Orwell animals in this ingeniously simple, deceptively short novella linger so unhappily in the mind that one tends, after one has noted that all revolutions spawn tyrants, to think of the short, foolish lives of all sheep, the exploitation of all poultry, the toil and deaths of all horses. When one has read of the herd that bleats nothing but slogans, the hens that die in futile revolt when their eggs are taken, the sad death of Boxer the shire horse when he is too old for work, farm animals spring to mind when one should be drawing the human parallel. The nearer satire material is to truth, the less effective it becomes. Orwell's masterpiece succeeds by showing us that the pig Napoleon *is* human; he finally becomes a member of the human race, while the animals remain ambiguous.

The humanity of the other animals is simple and two dimensional, as is the way of fables. Squeaker, the propaganda mouthpiece, 'had a way of skipping from side to side and whisking his tail which was somehow very persuasive'; even this description is double edged. Benjamin the donkey is another Eeyore character who always looks on the black side. Stubborn, canny endurance has always enabled donkeys to live and work. Muriel the goat is more intelligent than she looks. Millie the mare is empty headed and vain and soon leaves the animal revolution for happy human bondage. The cat manages to stay on both sides and disappears when there is trouble. None of this is very foreign to natural animal behaviour – apart from Napoleon who, in becoming dictator with the help of Snowball, shows power lust, wit and cunning, and no animal nature at all. He was a man all the time, leading the trustful animals along the dismal downward path of exploitation, forced confessions, execution, secret police, bureaucracy, extravagance and bending and reversal of the rules and promises of the glorious revolutionary dawn.

When the pigs are fully humanised, the animals are back where they began with the exploitation of all beasts, ready for animal vengeance to begin again. The fable works, but not entirely on the level the author intended. One reads it and ends by feeling shame – like Gulliver – at being human, as well as shame that men can exploit the ideals of their fellow men. It is almost as if not Orwell but a committee of wise animals had written the story, arranging their characters to interest us in human revolutionary parallels in order to draw our attention to an animal plight: animal fable in reverse. One wishes to change the famous slogan to ALL ANIMALS ARE AS EQUAL AS POSSIBLE.*

The Animals' Conference, Erich Kästner, 1955, is a lighter hearted satire, but its propaganda is just as acid. The dreadful human race, the animals decide, is responsible for spoiling the entire planet and making life impossible for animals and the innocent – in this case, every nation's children.

How often, and how uncomfortably, one has thought just the same thing. But this is animal vengeance with no violence. Erich Kästner tells the story of how the animals – mostly living peacefully in the depths of Africa – suddenly wake up to the state of the world and decide to do something about it. They do not intend to usurp the human position, but copy the human design for getting things done – the conference, committee or parliament. The basic joke is, of course, not that they succeed (they have to) but that in order to succeed, they beat Man at his own game. The moral is serious, the means amusing, helped by the illustrations of Walter Trier who turns the animals into cheerful Bruin-Boys characters, full of colour and delight. Their names and remarks are rather comic-paper, too: Oscar the elephant, Paul the polar bear, and Louie the lion who says things like 'If I wasn't so blond I'd turn purple with rage this very minute'. They all seem to have, in some unspecified way, houses, furniture and newspapers. Their animal natures are merely suggested, as when Oscar has done some concentrated telephoning he was 'worn out with the effort and had to mop his brow. His handkerchief was four yards long and four yards wide.'

But when the conference is called, fantasy takes off with the satire, delightfully. All the animals – even animals out of books and history – join the conference, have themselves made beautiful and set off for the Animal Skyscraper with the slogan: 'We'll bring order into the world all right. We're not people.' In scenes of wonderful release and jollity they frighten all the frontier guards and laugh at them, abolishing such silly human institutions. The Animal Hotel (wonderfully drawn by Trier) has rooms adapted for every kind of bird, beast and fish; and they are all interviewed and photo-

---

*The Halas and Bachelor cartoon of 1954 is too sad for children or the unwary and reinforces this feeling; animal actors are dramatising themselves, not showing us ourselves in altered form.

graphed and representative children of all colours – red, white, brown, black and yellow – join them. They pass a resolution that war, revolution and hardship be outlawed, and relay it by television and radio to all human schools and the rival conference that the humans have arranged, led by a nasty belligerent human called General Rage Miller, who threatens force.

The animals' victory is achieved, of course, not by force but by united effort and cunning: the tactical destruction by the rats and the moths of what they consider to be the *real* enemy – the things that make the humans pompous – paper and clothes, especially documents and uniforms. They are abolishing, in clothes and written communications, two of the chief differences between men and animals; but as a sanction it is very effective. 'Our Patience is Exhausted,' announces Oscar the elephant, and the statesmen sign. All frontiers are abolished. There are to be no more soldiers, or ammunition; science, officials and documents are to be kept to a minimum; teaching is to be the highest paid profession. The people, amid scenes of rejoicing, name the animals honorary citizens of the earth.

The liberating gaiety of this fable is an antidote to the pessimism of *Animal Farm* and the book deserves a wider public. Walter Trier's* pictures are at their best in crowd and animation scenes, full of beauty and comic invention; the long line of flamingoes at the conference telephone switchboard is a delight to the eye; so are the groups of animals racing to the conference by air, land and sea, on wings, magic carpets, trains and icebergs, and entertaining the children on a holiday island. Beside them, the people look rather thin, ordinary and silly, and above all, *all the same*, which is a salutary lesson in itself. If you give animals human roles to play, no Utopia should be populated by only one race, even if it is the human one.

*Some may remember his pleasing and witty covers for *Lilliput* Magazine, from its first issue onwards.

4 People with Heads

The didactic animal story of the Divine Emblems kind seems now as archaic as the language in which it was written, and it was super-seded by the animal story from which moral lessons were drawn from natural history. An odd hybrid, half in fable and half out of it, is the device of taking a human body – literally or figuratively – and putting an animal head on it and seeing what happens. You can't help being a little didactic, often amusing, interesting and some-times satiric, and the genre gives rise to some of the oddest, pleasantest – and silliest – of the children's book animals, those in cartoons and comics as well as the inspired hybrids in Lear and Carroll. One can draw any conclusions one wishes, or none at all. As in the *Rupert* stories, a supreme example of this kind of art, you may get quite an interesting fairy tale, but the method also gives rise to a tale like 'Rupert and the Circus Clown', a didactic story in an equally interesting disguise.

Most stories in this genre are lighthearted, some merely strange, and there is often a feeling that the medium has run away with the writer and the device was more interesting and important than the message. Pictures are, for the first time, of primary interest – the transformation is something that has to be seen, as in *The Headlong Career and Woful Ending of Precocious Piggy* by Thomas Hood, in which the pig leaves the farm and seeks his fortune in the world. ('What, leaving your mother, you foolish pig?' Pigling Bland had no choice, and a rather happier end.) Piggy tries everything, wear-ing the most fashionable and appropriate clothes, including cigar and top hat. He tries landscape gardening, driving a horse, dancing, including a *bal masqué*, but eventually goes to a fair and takes to drink. In the end, the butcher arrives. Anyone who finds Beatrix

Potter harsh should take note of this 'Rake's Progress', and other picture books and annuals intended for the Victorian child (though Piggy is of slightly earlier date). Perhaps the butcher would have come anyway, whether Piggy had left home or not; the moral is rather ambiguous.

Nursery rhymes like 'Cock Robin' or 'Old Mother Hubbard' are very much of this kind. 'The Ballad of Cock Robin and Jenny Wren', which has appeared at different times and in many versions, some not intended for children at all, has a kind of arbitrary truth. No one can imagine it differently; the Bull who can Pull, the Sparrow with the Arrow are comedy characters acting out a tragic drama that, were they human would sound very different, more like a tragedy of jealousy. As it is, the animals' rhyming actions are direct forerunners of Leslie Brooke's delightful *Johnny Crow* in that there is no reason – other than rhyme – *for* their actions. Old Mother

Hubbard is similar. After the poor Dog's disappointment he performs a variety of semi-human acts just for the fun of it, in the
manner of the Learned Pig that so worried the 'Lady' in Mrs
Trimmer's *History of the Robins*, who had always considered animals
as 'Mere machines, actuated by the unerring hand of Providence'.
Such an animal is Deborah Dent's Donkey, in *The Child's Toy Book*
(or *Pleasing Tales in words of one or two syllables*, James Bishop, 1838).
The donkey performs, like Old Mother Hubbard's Dog or Precocious Piggy; it becomes a lawyer, an artist, a schoolteacher (changing sex) and a doctor.

> *You'll get high in practice and pocket a fee*
> *Since many a jackass (all parties agree)*
> *For physic is famous, though silly as thee –*

In slides the moral. The Donkey's clothes are appropriate for each
role, the fun is emphasised, the satire minimal.

Dame Trot's Cat (*Aunt Louisa's Toy Books*, 1878) has even more
fun without being cumbered by a moral at all. She takes over the
house in her mistress's absence, teaches the Dog to dance, and wears
fashionable clothes.

> *'You're quite a grand lady, Miss Pussy,' said she*
> *And Pussy affectedly answered 'oui oui',*
> *She thought it beneath her to utter a mew*
> *While wearing a dress of a fashion so new.*

This child with a cat's head dressing up in mother's clothes is really
enjoying itself – when amusement is the prime motive, animals
oblige the artist. Somewhere between Deborah Dent's cynical
Donkey, and Dame Trot's frivolous Cat comes the apotheosis of
the style in a story in the *Poll Parrot Picture Book* of the late sixties in
which cats are placed in social situations of the most boring kind.
When one has taken in the odd transformation which has happened
to the people who have cats' heads on them (and cats' names like
Minnie and Muff) – heads that, on the necks of ladies with deep
décolletage, fade gradually into human flesh – the tale is not very
interesting. The cats have tea, play croquet and blind man's buff.
'Taking advantage of the game, Minnie slipped out of the room to
help Muff to prepare the supper. Muff told her mistress she thought
the mice were not so fresh as they ought to be. Minnie determined

to give the butcher a good scolding the next morning . . .' Meanwhile, the gentlemen smoke cigars in the garden.

Perhaps the style reflects a marked delight in stuffing animals and putting them into lifelike scenes, or even worse, dressing their bodies and putting them into lifelike human scenes as in the Bramber Museum collection which must have used the bodies of fifty or sixty kittens.* This odd fashion still lingers in the realistic picture-book styles in which dogs and cats act out fairy tales and nursery rhymes for no apparent reason:

> *This fine Pussy Prince is knocked all of a heap*
> *By the sight of this plump Pussy Princess, asleep†*

Illustrators' clever humanisations may transcend banal verses. Walter Crane's 'Mother Hubbard' is, of course, stylish and beautiful. Perhaps the dog which assumes various disguises is made more attractive by being a poodle. One almost expects this favourite circus breed to behave in this way, and it looks at home in a wig and tricorne. The same artist's *The Three Bears* are rather fierce and incongruous in their Kate Greenaway clothes; and in his *Animal Alphabets* he manages an attractive spider and an unpleasant unicorn which prove perhaps that character will out, in spite of conventions of beauty and ugliness, strokeability or the reverse.

Even Aesop is transformed in this manner and rendered as harmless – apart from the abrupt ending – as a Victorian At Home, in the delightful *Miss Browne, Superior Mouse*, a picture book of the nineties written and illustrated by Madeline Hall. The transformation – from the era when such devices were worn – describes the gay and pretty world in which Miss Browne, an urban and fashionable young lady with a tiny waist and gigot sleeves goes to stay with her cousins the Greys, rustics (in a cottage) with sunbonnets. Miss Browne retains her beautiful hat for luncheon. Everyone in the street is a mouse; take away the heads and everyone is a person.

The style survives – a fairly recent example is Maurice Sendak's *Higgledy Piggledy Pop*, a rather frightening fairy tale acted chiefly by animals, about a spoiled girl whose greed is stronger than her fears

---

*By Walter Potter of Bramber, Sussex, 1835–1918, master of humorous taxidermy. Other small animals had scenes of their own, all now collectors' items.

†*Frolicsome Friends*, Warne picture book of the 1920s.

and which eventually leads to self-sacrificing courage. But the heroine's part is played by a Sealyham with stage ambitions and the other actors are a cat, a pig, a lion, and two humans. The pictures, in Tenniel-style naturalistic black and white, underline the story's sinister charm.

The animal autobiography that started with *Life and Perambula-*

The cats' musical evening from *The Poll Parrot Picture Book*

tions of a Mouse seems at times an extraordinary genre, the ultimate in the Bramber Museum all-change-heads technique being perhaps Alfred Elwes's *Adventures of a Dog* and *Adventures of a Bear*. The work of Dorothy Kilner, Mrs Pilkington, Elizabeth Sandham and Mary

Elliott (*The Adventures of a Parrot, a Greyhound, a Cat and a Monkey* and *Rambles of a Butterfly*) have some slight reference to natural history, and Arabella Argus's work had considerable lifelike qualities; but in Alfred Elwes's *Adventures of a Dog*, 1857, animal life plays no part at all.

It is a purely human life story – the Dog moves from rags to riches, or rather, respectability and a competence. There is a strange, embarrassing archness about the text – the realism of the illustrations (Elwes was the illustrator of *Brer Rabbit*) is serious, beyond all doubt. But as with human autobiography, there is a valedictory preface written by a certain Minette Cattina, Upper Mews, Caneville; and the Dog – who starts by being a destitute puppy – is concerned with his struggles in the world, which he recounts with coy gravity. The mixture is very strange. The dogs in the story are dogs in name only; an old dog 'had lately invented a novel match for lighting pipes and cigars . . . he wanted some active young dogs to dispose of his wares. I became his agent.'

The hero's first adventure as a salesman is disastrous; a 'Lady Doggess' firmly repulses him (the word bitch is never mentioned). Later, when kissed by 'A Lady Puppy' he 'gambols like a mad thing'. He eventually becomes a manservant to Sir John Bull, protecting his estate when 'curs' make a raid. His adventures include selling meat in a butcher's shop and escaping from a flood from which he returns on crutches; he ends by becoming chief of police, marrying the beautiful Fida, his first love, and is philanthropic towards puppies ever after.

This anomalous work was by no means isolated. It was a sequel to the popular bear story, and one finds others such as *The Frogs' Parish Clerk and his Adventures in Strange Lands* by Thomas Archer, 1866, a reptilian romance taking place in Batrachia or Frogland, though here other animals, birds and insects take part. Similarities are great, except that the frog story is told in a historical convention, and there is more reference to animal appearance and anatomy and to other species. The human world may, in theory, be going on up above all the time – it is not mentioned. These frog-headed people do not need it. The hero, Rana, rises from humble parish clerk to wandering troubadour, to statesman, general and eventually king, always true to his love, Sauriana. Some earlier and more traditional strains appear – the 'King Log' story out of *Aesop*, and

'The Frog's Wooing'. But the other events are pure romantic adventure; battles, court scenes, a duel, the Mouselanders Wedding, the war of the Mandibles and the Locusts, and a frog rebellion. 'How can I be true to Sauriana if I am false to my country?' asks the hero.

The imagination that shaped this tale is of the same kind that delighted in *Reynard the Fox* and prompted C. S. Lewis to compose his 'Animal-Land' fantasies as a boy; there is a pleasure in animal actors and the remote, once-removed curiosities of their lives; the ordinary doings of people seem direct and dull. *The Curious Adventures of a Field Cricket*, 1881, translated from the French of Dr Ernest Candeze, is part of the vogue. Partiality for insects can go no further. The bizarre fashion even embraced the 'True Confession' type of narrative, as in the *Public and Private Life of Animals*, another translation wherein the animal characters explain, among other things, how they took to drink or crime.

The Curious Adventures of a Field Cricket reads rather like Henty, or the non-scientific parts of Jules Verne. This autobiography is perhaps the most psychological but least humanised of the group. After the traumatic sight (in 'My Childhood and Youth') of his his entire family eaten by a nightingale, the Cricket has various adventures among other insects, about whose ways he seems ignorant.

There is the old problem of giving a mouse, a horse, or an insect, a human head or psyche. The horse's sufferings may be many, an insect's life is violent and horrific, but the screw is turned quite unbearably by the observing human consciousness. The horrors of the Cricket's life read like science fiction, or the strange wars fought in drops of water under the microscope. His adventures have some unconscious humour – when offered food by a mole cricket, he relates 'she pushed it towards me. It was neither more nor less than a spider. "Thank you," I said, "I don't want anything more." ' But his eyewitness account of ichneumon grubs eating larvae is like one of those detailed accounts of cannibalism towards the end of Ballantyne's *Coral Island* before the natives are converted, with the added refinement that the hero cricket believes that he himself is carrying an ichneumon parasite, and feels pain: 'But my sufferings were all mental.'

After daring escapes from a mole and frogs and 'Monsters of the Deep' (horrific underwater life) he befriends a small ant who behaves rather like Little Nell and becomes the most human and endearing character in the saga. The tale is interesting and vivid and physically almost possible (the only 'war' is an ant war which happens in reality), but the feeling these adventures leave behind them is that the method has engulfed the matter, and that there is profuse, almost surrealistic indiscipline of details – something like the contents of the Great Exhibition of 1851. The careful narrative of *Black Beauty*, though earlier than *The Curious Adventures of a Field Cricket*,* is, in comparison, adult and mature.

It seems to be accepted that the 'Nonsense' animals and creatures in Edward Lear and Lewis Carroll have semi-human faces that disguise various aspects of human eccentricity, gaiety, sadness, tragedy and childish quirks. Lear's creatures amuse by their incongruity, but their human strains are nearly always sad ones. Happy endings are reserved for the characters who retain an obviously animal appearance – they have love affairs and sail away to some far

---

*Watership Down, Richard Adams, 1972, is oddly near, in technique and feeling, to this book. Mr Adams' work is completely original, but he has, perhaps unknowingly, used a method of animal writing that has not been repeated since 1881.

country where miscegenation or odd friendships will not matter. The Duck and Kangaroo, Daddy Long Legs and Fly, Owl and Pussy Cat all end in a pleasing idyll. It is the anomalies, the half and halfers, the Pobbles, Jumblies, Dong and Yonghy Bonghy Bo who have that built-in melancholy that mules are said to have and who experience loss or hopelessness. It is interesting to see, too, Lear's illustrations to his limericks which are full of human animal adventures. How like the partners are; the Old Man in the Tree, the Old Man who said Hush, the Old Man with the Owl, the Old Man in a Marsh. All seem to have family resemblances to the Bees, Birds, Owls and Frogs who are amusing or plaguing them – sometimes there is little to choose between each pair. Even Lear and his cat Foss are alike, but it seems to bring little pleasure.

Though the odd, solitary outcasts have no happiness, the more domesticated birds – the Pelican King and Queen (anxious about their daughter's marriage to an outsider with no webs to his feet)

and the delightfully suburban Sparrows – have a kind of human bliss because they are trying to be as like humans as possible. The Sparrows, who assume clothes which they buy in a shop, are happy because they have kept up with the Joneses:

> Said they, 'We trust that cold or pain
> We shall never feel again
> While perched on tree or house or steeple
> We now shall look like other people—'

which was probably what the Pobble, Yonghy Bonghy Bo and Dong were trying, and failing, to do all the time.

This note of anxiety is not present in the *Alice* books. Characters like the Mock Turtle or the Dormouse may be conscious of their own shortcomings but they are never trying to become something different; they are so human that they seem to be actors in carnival masks. The convention that these characters are humans with altered heads suits actors and illustrators – Jonathan Miller in his *Alice* film abandoned the masks and the human characters beneath appeared without any loss of meaning or humour. Heads and bodies are reversible. Tenniel or Rackham can give the Caterpillar or the March Hare or even the White Knight's Horse an animal body and a human face, or the Red and White Queens' faces reminiscent of Pug and Mastiff. Though animals, or people, often *appear* to be turning into something else – Queen into kitten, baby into pig, Queen into sheep; Cheshire Cat growing and fading like a

film dissolve or phantasmagoria, gnat as big as a chicken, it is because they exist in a child's dream in which reality is blurred and logic displaced, full of confusing adventures peopled with grotesques; only animal diversity can provide enough of them. There is no real reason for a caterpillar to smoke a hookah on a mushroom or a hare and a dormouse to be having tea or for a Mock Turtle to be sad and tell its life story. But there is one feature which nearly all the creatures have in common – an adult, slightly patronising attitude towards Alice. Perhaps this is the way in which human adults used to treat small girls to whom they were always polite, but whom they found immature, absurd and perhaps just a little boring. Alice returns this attitude with interest and is equally polite and on the whole, not overawed.

Children find the Wonderland creatures strange, interesting and unfunny, while adults are amused by comic likenesses. Jonathan Miller's vision of Gryphon and Mock Turtle as two rather literary and philosophic dons on a Sussex beach illuminates the whole feeling. The unreal population of Wonderland is just the Grown Ups, after all – those odd, immense, inexplicable touchy characters full of quirks and prejudices, sometimes difficult to know, often hard to please. Adults don't come in this size any more unfortunately, though there may be a few rare ones about still. But at least in Wonderland there is no *instruction*. A sheep may teach one not to catch a crab, but there is no moral lesson to be drawn in the Mrs

Gatty manner:

'I *can't explain* myself, *I'm afraid, sir,' said Alice, 'because I'm not myself, you see.'*
'*I don't see,' said the Caterpillar.*
'*I'm afraid I can't put it more clearly,' Alice replied very politely, 'for I can't understand it myself to begin with; and being so many different sizes in a day is very confusing.'*
'*It isn't,' said the Caterpillar.*
'*Well, perhaps you haven't found it so yet,' said Alice, 'but when you have to turn into a chrysalis – you will some day, you know – and then after that into a butterfly, I should think you'll feel it a little queer won't you?'*
'*Not a bit,' said the Caterpillar.*

But of course this donnish old character who will presently tell Alice to Clear her Mind of Cant will always stay in a changeless old age; metamorphosis, whatever Mrs Gatty may have said, isn't a human experience.

Mrs Gatty was, in a way, the sponsor of *Sylvie and Bruno*, Lewis Carroll's uneven, extraordinary and little read successor to *Wonderland* and *Through the Looking Glass*. Two chapters of it appeared first

in short story form in *Aunt Judy's Magazine* in 1867. The two volume
final version, the result of years of thought, note-taking, reminis-
cence, reported and overheard conversations of children, and containing nonsense verse that included *The Hunting of the Snark*
probably fulfils its author's wish to write a book as different as
possible from *Alice*.

At times Sylvie is very *like* Alice. She is a sedate, kind, very moral
little girl, the delightful elder sister to the baby Bruno; but both
children have an odd, dual character. Sometimes they are in a real
world populated by humans including Carroll himself as narrator –
this he calls 'Outland' – and sometimes they are fairy people in the
Michael Drayton or *Butterfly's Ball* manner, minute creatures three
inches high – and into this fairy land the narrator follows them
through his own dreams. In fairy land the children's dealings with
animals are closer to nature than anything in Alice. Sylvie and
Bruno, though their footsteps are dogged by this rather eccentric,
professorial observer, are not children talking to adults made bearable because they are wearing animal and carnival masks. The
animals are not 'characters'; they are talking birds, beetles, mice and
frogs to whom the children, as fairies, do 'good'; at one point Bruno
entertains and amuses a frog audience with scenes from Shakespeare.

The isolated exception to this kindness to tiny animals theme is
the visit that children and observer pay to Dogland. As in *Miss
Browne, Superior Mouse*, everyone in sight has been changed. There is
a mastiff sentry, dressed in a scarlet collar and carrying a musket,
who talks a language known as Doggee, who addresses the children
in a series of barks: 'Oobooh, hooh, boohooyah.' This is easily
understood: 'Sylvie spoke Doggee very prettily.' The noise is as
far as print will go, a fairly accurate rendering of the sound a dog
makes, as 'Houyhnhnm' is like a whinny. 'A couple of stray humans,'
the dog remarks in a rather scathing manner, and asks them what
dog they belong to. One is ready for a reversal of roles incident with
the Dog King keeping human pets – but nothing like this happens.
The anecdote has the same picture book oddity as *Deborah Dent's
Donkey* or *Dame Trot's Cat* – one is never allowed to forget that,
though the Dog King's palace is staffed with bloodhounds and bull-
dogs for bodyguards and greyhounds for ladies in waiting, they are
all Man's Best Friend when off duty. There is some pleasant pedantic
fun in the details about scratching on the door of the Royal Kennel

and pricking up your ears when the King speaks, but when Sylvie absentmindedly pats His Majesty on the head, the king smiles and wags his tail; a stick-throwing incident follows which greatly gratifies His Majesty and the court. Dogland is as interesting an idea as Horseland or Flatland, but nothing actually happens there. One is reminded of William Tenn's story *Null-P* in which an intelligent race of retrievers breed men selectively to encourage proficiency in stick throwing until the development of a machine that does the job better and makes men obsolete – which says something interesting about intelligence and domestication. *Dogland* says nothing except that, given a voice, Man's Best Friend has nothing to say.

> '*He said "Bosh!"* ' *said Sylvie.*
> '*What is Bosh! in Doggee?*' *I enquired.*
> '*It's the same as in English,*' *said Sylvie.* '*Only when a dog says it, it's a sort of whisper that's half a cough and half a bark. Nero, say "Bosh!"* '
> *And Nero (the Dog King) who had been gambolling round us again said 'Bosh!' several times and I found that Sylvie's description of the sound was perfectly accurate.*

It is all fun, of course, but most of the real amusement in *Sylvie and Bruno* lies with the human characters (the Professor, the Other Professor), the delightful Gardener's Songs ('He thought he saw – He looked again, and found it was'), and the various devices and inventions that rival the White Knight (the umbrella boots for horizontal rain when the barometer goes sideways, the discourse on gravity and weightlessness with tea rising out of cups, and the magic watch for making time go backwards). To modern taste, Bruno's baby talk is an unsurmountable barrier. Baby talk was popular in the eighteen eighties* but sentences like 'It isn't bed time. The owls hasn't gone to bed and I s'a'nt go to seep wizout oo sings to me' need purging or translation. Bruno does, however, have the last word on mouse stories.

> '*Once there were a Mouse – a little tiny Mouse –*'
> '*Did nothing ever happen to it, Bruno?*' *I asked . . .*
> '*Nothing ever happened to it . . . it were too tiny,*' *Bruno explained.*

This method of giving humans transformed heads or animals

---

*'So popular as to become almost a disease' – Roger Lancelyn Green

transformed bodies can lead to ingenious absurdities like *The Adventures of a Dog* or almost frighteningly obsessional preoccupation with method, like the work of Louis Wain. In Don Marquis's lively verbal cartoon *Archy and Mehitabel*, 1931, the human/animal exchange is not exactly of bodies but of souls. Archy, the insect with a human soul is a man with an insect's view of life, and the result is satire, fantasy and sharp moral stings in about equal proportion. As Madame Blavatsky's ego went into a white horse, so the soul of a *vers libre* poet has passed into a cockroach. It lives in a nest of old poems on the floor of the editorial office of the New York *Sun* and communicates by bouncing, head downwards, on typewriter keys; cannot manage capitals, does not bother with punctuation and can only just change to a new line. Once again, the method is part of the charm. Archy's poems are a mixture of philosophy, history, requests for food and suggestions to the typewriter's owner as to how things can be improved.

Archy, the cockroach – transformed from one of the world's most sensitive creatures to one of the lowliest, toughest and most indestructible, yet with an abiding urge for self-expression – comments on life from the underside. He is very funny, in spite of his small, lugubrious ego; in telling his 'boss' what it is like to be an insect he is doing the same as Capek and showing that the insect world – the one we seem to be looking at in so many animated cartoons – is, with its eternal ambitions, predators, victims, heroes and villains, very like the human one – terribly, wonderfully and morbidly like it. In doing so he shows up the human world as small and insignificant, and man's life as short and senseless as that of a beetle accidentally stepped on or blown out to sea. Yet the philosophy, humour and courage with which Archy greets this situation makes it bearable; and the riotous enjoyment that his disreputable companion Mehitabel the cat gets out of life makes it something heroic – a dance of death charade in circumstances of impossibly comic gloom.

Archy's world is not an entirely insect one. It is a floor-level place inhabited by various scavengers and drop-outs: a rat, Mehitabel the cat, a parrot and other animal and insect characters mostly living off each other and their human hosts; a world that suggests cartoon treatment but is too verbally vivid and amusing to need it. The short *vers libre* lines that describe these goings on have the throw away, punch-drunk ingenuity of Tom and Jerry at their best, while being far more subtle than anything so visual.

Most of the animals have transmigrated human souls in them and the parallels are devastatingly exact:

> *he (the rat) is jealous of my poetry . . .*
> *he was a punk poet himself*
> *and after he has read it he sneers*
> *and then eats it*

Archy deals with the world in a Peanuts mock-profundity which is, nevertheless, very moral underneath. The ruthless competition of life is stressed again and again, and so is the inevitability of death, in a kind of miniature nihilism. The worm and the beetle meditating on the Cosmic All in the intestines of a robin are all nevertheless devoured by Mehitabel. 'Believe,' says Archy, 'that everything is for you until you discover that you are for it.' The Aesopian Mouse and Frog have been given a new setting and a new twist, as have the Spider and the Fly who argue until the fly is eaten: 'the end would have been just the same if neither of us had spoken at all.' The smallness of human life is Archy's constant theme – how everyone, and every insect thinks it is the centre of the universe until it is eaten or trodden underfoot. Insect conversation is as pompous, and also as subtle and sadly logical, as that of humans. Archy and a flea talking:

> *parted each feeling*
> *superior to the other and is not that*
> *feeling after all one of the great*
> *desiderata of social intercourse*

And his philosophy puts man in a very low place:

> *the bees got their*
> *governmental system settled*
> *millions of years ago*

As much a mentor as the Talking Cricket, he is still full of his own shortcomings: ready to talk about the evils of drink in a hornet's gangland life story, to transpose Aesop, to declare war against Man by rousing the insects to revolution, to indulge in self-pity because he is not a butterfly and that 'with the soul of a hamlet, he is doomed always to wallow in farce'. But transformations are seldom comfortable.

Mehitabel, the indestructible Nellie Wallace alley cat with the soul of Cleopatra, is happier with her lot. Always a lady, avoiding matrimony and motherhood with desperate adroitness, *toujours gai* and always dancing, she has endless, haggard romantic escapades, undying stringy vitality and an indescribable past, having gone through more lives than she can count and known so many swell gents in her time that she has forgotten them all. She is Archy's companion, the main subject of his verses, and inhabits the oddest dark dimension, a kind of shadow of the human world above. She, Archy and the lively, irrepressible outcasts and vermin among whom they move are outside time, older than men, remembering Shakespeare at first hand, talking to Pharaohs in their tombs, full of transmigrations, ghosts, remains and old memories, that 'gaiety with a necrological turn' that the cat with the soul of François Villon uses to Mehitabel in his lyric epitaphs. The whole sad, witty, rueful but ever hopeful chorus of talking, singing, dancing creatures are like human life seen under a transforming microscope by the Martian with whom Archy is in contact by radio – by which medium cockroach and biped sound much the same.

'Comic' or cartoon animals have been much maligned. They are similar to various members of the human race – some are likeable and some the reverse – but I have never found them violent or corrupting. If you take a comic situation and transform all the actors into animals, or even half of the actors so that there is animal/ human interplay, no one is ever bewitched into thinking that these are real animals. For most children they are useful scapegoats who are able to do and say things that a child is not able to do or say, and the comic release is increased.

The Bruin Boys, Mrs Hippo's Boarding School, Dr Jumbo's Academy, Dame Foxe's School of the twenties and thirties were all devices to gather together a group or gang of well-defined characters who had unlikely, unpunished (or barely punished; just the food-and-treats-withheld variety) and invariably successful adventures in which, as disguised children, they triumphed over adults – who often had grinning, victorious faces and so did not mind being worsted. All was good humoured and above all reliable. It was the life one longed to lead and led only in dreams – cheerful anarchy and a kind of indiarubber immunity to hurt and pain. For rewards

there were gorgeous, four coloured banquets and 'hampers' (I was
a child who had little interest in *real* food) and lots of simple, inevitable happy artifices in which the most unlikely ruses came off well.
Nothing overbalanced, no missiles failed to reach their targets and
all kinds of merry wheezes succeeded where, in real life, intense
effort would have produced equally inevitable failure, mess, blame
and cleaning-up afterwards.

There was no magic at all attached to these characters. They were
the clever but slightly tamed boys who had all the bouncy adventures one always wanted but could never manage to get. Stories –
doubtless apocryphal – about what went on in boys' schools were,
to me, full of comedy and thrills, the epitome of what seemed to
happen to the Bruin Boys and in the Jungle Academy all the time.
Perhaps for that reason I rejected the Bruin Girls as strange and
unamusing, which seems a little unfair.

'Angel and her Merry Playmates' in *Puck* was similarly enjoyable,
partly because it had a heroine with no less than three clowns as
friends/brothers, and partly because she had a variety of pets, zoo
animals, who invariably triumphed. The combination never seemed
odd; the 'pets' wore suits with Eton collars and bow ties, the clowns
had circus clothes, Angel was normal (i.e. oneself) and they all lived
with a responsible adult father/manager/ringmaster called Jolly Joe
Jinks. Their adventures were usually about simple rewards such as
the gaining or losing of food or prizes or treats; buns, cake, or jam
were the most popular. Most of the remarks both animals and chil-

dren made had cunning and apparently endless variants on the
phrase 'he said'. He lisped, simpered, smiled, chuckled, growled,
stammered, gurgled, laughed, gasped, cooed, grumbled or panted.
The pets were always artful, the children always surprised. That the
pets are not of the orthodox kind but Jungle Animals never seemed
to worry anyone; perhaps they were all trained members of some
circus that never appeared. Really the pets are another set of
younger, licensed children, who have the wit to do things that
Angel and the clowns never think of.

Different animal permutations abounded between the wars. Dame
Fox and her boys – very similar to the Bruin Boys and Tiger Tim –
were farm animals only, and Dr Jumbo's school and Jungle Town,
also in *Puck*, had every kind of animal with much fun to be obtained
from the smallness of creatures like ants and flies and the vastness of
hippos and elephants. Variety was the spice of these whole-page
pictures showing in marvellous detail, places such as the Jungle-
town Theatre, hat-shop or Christmas party.

The even more popular Bruin Boys of *Rainbow* and *Tiger Tim's
Weekly* had no illusions about being trained or tricky animals. They
were boys in Mrs Bruin's school/boarding establishment. They had
pop-eyed, grinning, animal-approximated faces, Eton collars
(obligatory wear for comic strip animals; Bill Badger had one and
so did Teddy Tail) and striped trousers. Tiger Tim alone had a
striped suit and frilled collar. They continued never to grow up.
Diversity of animal contours and sizes made them easily individual,

even though their faces were so alike. Tiger Tim, Jacko, Jumbo, Bobby *et al* with Porkyboy, the Bunter of the stories, showed what boarding-school life might be, but never could be. They were schoolboys made neuter and funnier than real. Their life excluded adults at the same time as being essentially on good terms with them. Mrs Bruin went through all the stages of amazement, incredulity, scolding and punishment but she always forgave and everything ended with a hamper or a feast; it was school with the sting out. Cartoons about real boys might have had the same effect but the credibility gap would have been oddly greater. In the cosy, tamed world of characters who were toys, pets, friends, circus animals on the spree, one could believe in anything.

Comic animals in school seem to have disappeared in favour of creatures who live in little houses of their own and have a moderately idealised, suburban existence – not often a jungle one. The animals too have changed – they are rabbits, hamsters and guinea pigs, dogs and cats with the occasional bear or seal. They still do things that children would like to do and cannot – but equally often they get into impossible scrapes which make a child spectator feel superior, all through an inordinate passion for jam or buns or because they are simple minded, like Harold Hare, or conceited (most frog stories, a legacy from Kenneth Grahame). Perhaps H. M. Talintyres' *Jerrywangle* is still in the Bruin Boys tradition with cat and humanised elephants and others (Uncle Oojah permanently in pyjamas) and one lonely boy.

The Bruin Boys sometimes had a few humans around to give the illusion that the whole thing was really happening somewhere. But those lively animals Korky the cat and Biffo the bear are anarchic members of a very human world: you can almost see the actor inside the animal skin. Simple greed and slapstick, disconcerting one's enemies or inflicting some hurt on them – always unreal – is circus humour, whether one has a cat's head or a white face and red nose.

Walt Disney's Mickey, Donald, Pluto and Goofy are human self-parody – no one can say that Mickey is mouselike – and dogs and cats in Disney cartoons are usually human bullies. Pluto is not always a dog except in his relationship to humans and cats. In one memorable episode he is captured, tried and almost executed by a cats' Ku Klux Klan; but the cats, too, are ambiguous. Mickey's irrepressibility has some resemblance to a mouse's faculty of survival and multiplication under odds. Otherwise he is the Little Man, who, Sir Osbert Sitwell insisted, has in this century inherited the world. He is one of the few humanised animals with any sort of sex life; he and Minnie behave like a suburban couple with a stylised, jerky immutability. They are the Little Man and Little Woman pursued by forces bigger than both of them, always triumphing over their adversities as little men and younger sons should – the audience anaesthetised to violence because it is happening to a mouse who is not only their representative but an unlikely, mechanised robot figure whose human attributes are thus given armour-plating.

Mickey was always topical. *Plane Crazy*, 1928, was linked to the Lindbergh flight, *Gallopin' Gaucho* to Fairbanks epics, and the musical hits from the *Silly Symphonies* and cartoons such as *Snow White* came to symbolise defiance to the enemy in the Second World War, or the right sort of *Music While You Work*. The secondary characters – Pete the bully, Pluto the pup, Goofy and Donald – are typecast humans acting out single themes as faithfully as characters out of Ben Jonson. Ingenuity of action and animation re-dressed the basic jokes freshly each time. Donald Duck's furious, garrulous innocence goes through various stylised distortions as his emotions mount. His sailor hat and coat take part as vividly as his face. Even his tools, fishing rod, golf clubs and garden shears become extensions of his vivid *persona* which is a human one, birdlike only in name.

Other Disney animals tend to be less fully dressed but no less human. Jiminy Cricket, the walking (but fallible) conscience, upstages Pinocchio in a way that Collodi did not intend; he is full of chirpy gaiety with nothing ghostlike in his appearances. The Fox and Cat in the same story are bland, evil human rogues. Dumbo the elephant, although he has a circus background and elephant mother, has human ambitions and humanly psychological dreams and fears (of mice) and a desire for the apparently impossible – flying; in one episode of the film, he even consults a bird psychiatrist about them. Bambi too has human reactions and a prettified, non-animal face.

Disney's very faults – whimsy, vulgarity and gratuitous terror – are ones that writers about animals cannot share if what they create is to have valid life. Humanised animals are in a different class from 'real' ones and are sometimes even enhanced and illuminated by crude, vulgar or horrific treatment; it is ourselves we see in such work – often suspect, never innocent.

PART TWO
Animal Fantasy

*Free! The word and the thought alone were worth fifty
blankets. He was warm from end to end as he thought
of the jolly world outside, waiting eagerly for him to
make his triumphal entrance, ready to serve him and
play up to him, anxious to help him and to keep him
company, as it had always been in days of old before
misfortune fell on him. He shook himself and combed
the dry leaves out of his hair with his fingers; and,
his toilet complete, marched forth into the comfortable
morning sun, cold but confident, hungry but hopeful,
all nervous terrors of yesterday dispelled by rest and
sleep and frank and heartening sunshine.*

'The Further Adventures of Toad',
The Wind in The Willows, *Kenneth Grahame*

5 Mythical Beasts and Magic

'*Ah, what* is *it now?*' *the Unicorn cried eagerly. 'You'll never guess! I couldn't.*'

The Lion looked at Alice wearily. 'Are you animal – or vegetable – or mineral?' *he said, yawning at every other word.*

'*It's a fabulous monster!*' *the Unicorn cried out, before Alice could reply.*

Through the Looking Glass, *Lewis Carroll*

Magic animals that talk and grant wishes have appeared in folk tales since the beginning of time, like the little red calf that befriends the Scottish Cinderella or the mice and rats that become footmen and coachman in the Perrault version. In these stories the animals are usually recognisable and not outlandish – their strangeness lies in magic or bewitchment happening to an ordinary beast like a cat, a rat, a donkey. The genius for inventing creatures that aren't and never were, does not seem to be a native one; really outstanding beasts like minotaurs, harpies and centaurs belong to stories of gods and heroes that have been translated into English without being changed or *used*, apart from the kind of imaginative transference whereby a poet like Gavin Douglas could make the Aeneid sound as if it were happening in Scotland.

Minotaurs and others of half-human appearance do not seem to have travelled well enough to transplant themselves into stories. But they, and other animals made up from a mixture of parts, seem to have been accepted as facts in the popular Bestiaries; the descriptions proliferated in the telling with all the force of apparent eye-witness accounts, permeated with religious symbolism which lends them awe and wonder.

Bestiaries – with Hellenic, Asiatic and Egyptian sources – are responsible for the perpetuation of several mythical animals and classical hybrids and for the misinterpretations of many more; and

each illustrator, from the eighth century onwards added flourishes and often humanised faces, whether the creature was a Mantichora or Gorgon (positively true, in Topsell's *Historie of Fourefooted Beasts*) or the Dipsa ('so small that when you step on him you do not see him').

Nearly every animal in a Bestiary was symbolic of a human virtue or vice, and as often described – like the animals in *Tommy Trip* – as possessing them. Morals abound until the animals' very existence becomes a moral of some kind – as St Augustine remarked, it did not particularly matter if certain animals existed at all – the important thing was what they *meant*. The extraordinary assurance of the scribes (and limners) in dividing the beasts into 'good' and 'wicked' is equalled by their seriousness in describing winged bulls, sphinxes, dragons and mantichorae in sentences introduced by words like 'moreover', 'verily', 'therefore', 'thus', or 'and so'.

It is in human nature to want mythical animals to be true, or to wish that they were, and make up stories in which they are. Mr Richard Hoggart* has described the manner in which with the world more closely defined, we use 'face savers' such as 'in one sense', 'in a way', 'perhaps', and 'I suppose'. It is face saving that takes the magical and mythical talking animals out of fairy-tale settings and puts them into contemporary ones; they are slightly tamed by being known, but at the same time grow even more interesting by contrast with the kind of story – such as those of E. Nesbit – which is rooted in real life. They have always appeared

*Reith Lectures, 1970.

to have varying degrees of humanity, from the Bestiary lions with their fashionable twelfth-century crimped manes and trefoliated tails to the lesser beasts whose sorrowful, humorous, worried expressions reflect what they are doing: 'wicked' beasts eating people with various degrees of enjoyment, the sad, apprehensive elephant carrying a turreted 'castle' containing four Norman knights, the camel apologetic for its wavy back and the unicorn, to whom is given the motives and equipment of chivalry, 'often fighting with elephants'. There is an extraordinary feeling in the Bestiaries of the wonder and strangeness of the living world, full of freaks, beauty, dangers, mixtures and myths that might be true somewhere. The mermaid and unicorn exist, so do Basilisks and the Mantichora, the man-beast. (Topsell, the sixteenth-century Arthur Mee, shows him with a human face looking quite handsome if he had not too many teeth and 'the head and face of a female like unto a Badger's'.)

Everyone almost expects frogs to leap out of fountains and talk in human speech to princesses; but when the story is about ordinary, everyday humans, the introduced mythical beasts are really strange, ominous, helpful or wonderful. Heraldic animals and fabulous birds seem to fit this role – the birds almost better than the beasts. They have always been a favourite device for prophecy and warning from the bird with bright feathers carrying the millstone in *The Juniper Tree* to Poe's Raven. Birds have less obvious physical presence than animals – they may fly away or disappear, and seem naturally proud and arbitrary. In reality they often look arrogant, gay, heartless or beautiful – they seldom look humble unless there is something wrong with them; and there seems to be an unwritten law that magic animals are ancient, powerful, experienced, educated and erudite. Birds have this look, whether heraldic or real, from the Gryphon to Dudu the raven in Mrs Molesworth's *The Tapestry Room*.

Mrs Molesworth was, indeed, the first writer to take such a bird out of a fairy tale* and place it in what one feels to be the right setting – a contemporary one. *The Cuckoo Clock*, written in 1877, has in it a bird character who besides being very moral is *there* in the

---

*Frances Browne's Christmas Cuckoo from *Granny's Wonderful Chair*, 1856, is given a fairy-tale setting. It seems quite natural that he is a luck bringer with his golden and merry leaves, enabling the brothers Scrub and Spare to try their fortunes at court.

4

clock. The arbiter of time, punctuality, rules and rightness, he is also *there* in a different kind of reality, always heralded by 'the faint coming sound' and able to take the lonely child Griselda on magic adventures. The old moral tales took a long time to fade; the Cuckoo from the clock insists on Griselda's doing as she is told, attending to her lessons and being patient. But he provides the companionship she needs until she is lonely no longer and he can turn once more to wood. He is stern, logical and philosophical.

'The sea is so strange, and so dreadfully big . . .'

'You have a great deal to learn,' he says, 'don't you know that *everything's* alive?' And later, 'Time! What is time? Ah, Griselda you have a *very* great deal to learn.' But from being sometimes irritatingly superior, he passes at the end of the story to a great solemnity as he takes Griselda to the desolate sea on the other side of the moon.

The Carved Lions, in 1895, similarly dominate their story with hardly a word between them – symbols of strength and protection and images of lost joy in this early school tale which has a truth about it that has hardly been equalled since. But Mrs Molesworth's Dudu the Raven in *The Tapestry Room*, 1879, is a real bird, though so old that it has magic, immortal qualities. It has lived on a terrace of an old chateau as long as the family has lived there. It is, in a way, a 'fairy', but like the Cuckoo, has a distinct and humorous character of its own. It is also traditional in being stately and well mannered – as are the children, Jeanne and Hugh, most of the time. It is their guide and mentor in a fairy world that happens, mysteriously and only in moonlight, in a certain room in the chateau – the tapestry chamber – in which the children can enter the tapestry itself by wearing special shoes called Wall Climbers.

Dudu is a stately, well-mannered, but rather forbidding bird. The child Jeanne has a kind of rapport with him. In the beginning of the story he hops on the window sill outside the pane, like Poe's Raven, and she remarks that he seems *about* to speak 'as if he would say "Let me in, Mademoiselle: why do you mock me by calling me if you won't let me in?"' Later, when he does talk, he is rather admonitory; he reads thoughts and acts like a teacher or nursemaid, becoming powerful and almost frightening. Bird companions are not always comfortable. The children in their dream world are always expecting him to appear. He is more than a friend; he is the engineer of their fates.

Frank R. Stockton's fabulous bird of the same era – the late seventies – is similarly forbidding, but treated with greater humour. In 'The Griffin and the Minor Canon', a contribution to Mary Mapes Dodge's *St Nicholas Magazine*, the Griffin is powerful and frightening enough to be almost a winged dragon. Humour is the only way of treating such a creature if it is not to be an enemy. The Griffin is somewhere between the magic, all powerful Dudu and E. Nesbit's Phoenix, and as conceited as every fabulous bird ever conceived. It appears in a little French town populated with humans who are cowardly, gossiping, malingering and selfish, and once again is concerned with putting them right, but even more with its own image (carved on the town cathedral).

The odd love affair that develops between the bird and a modest minor Canon – the only person able to influence or control it – ends sadly, when the townspeople drive the Canon away, hoping that the Griffin will follow him and trouble them no more. The Griffin tries to take over the town, becoming an overbearing schoolmasterly figure, giving lessons to a class of bad boys and girls, acting as doctor to those who are ill, literally frightening them into health again, driving the poor, as well as the ill, willy nilly towards better things. Maurice Sendak's illustrations to the new edition show him at one point staring hungrily at what looks like a dole queue, but it is a deputation to the mayor. The humans, like the citizens of Hamelin or the Five Children who encountered It, do not want to be good.

The Griffin is the perfect example of that strange harshness that seems to be the property of mythical birds. It menaces people for their own good, saying with lofty contempt, 'There were only two good things in this town: the Minor Canon and the stone image of myself.' There is an ambiguity even in its love for the Canon whom it follows about. Is the attraction potential food? Maurice Sendak gives it an heraldic look – that of changeless, watchful hunger. The only occasion on which the Griffin's expression alters is when he has taken over the role of doctor and is putting thermometers into patients' mouths, with tired disgust.

This oddly moral nature of talking birds seems self-perpetuating. Bird omens and oracles are more familiar than bird friends; perhaps we love birds less than we think. Their formality and frequency in heraldic design, as crests or emblems may have something to do with it – their decorative properties give them a didactic coldness. E. Nesbit's Phoenix, of *The Phoenix and the Carpet*, 1904, is hardly a cold bird, but it is, like the others, proud, vain, beautiful, condescending and extraordinarily well educated. It is in full command of every situation, and far more than a device for granting wishes, as was the Psammead who preceded him – indeed, the Carpet does this.

Many of the E. Nesbit books suffer from having been written as serial stories and often the joins show – the events are arranged so that each chapter has a self-contained plot and climax. With *Five Children and It* the granting of wishes divides the book into neat episodes. *The Phoenix and the Carpet* does tend to develop in the same way, with the Carpet transporting the children to distant places or bringing strange things – such as the hundred and ninety-nine cats from Persia – to the house in Camden Town. A magic carpet alone would have provided scope for adventure; the Phoenix helps the magic by being able to explain the properties of the Carpet and suggest ways in which it might be used. Its faults are its vanity, its delicate nerves, its constant demand for homage of various kinds and tendency to view London life of the nineties in terms of temples, priests ritual and classical knowledge.

'Good, old, beautiful Phoenix,' said Robert.
The Phoenix fluttered at once on to his wrist. 'This amiable youth,'
it said, 'has miraculously been able to put the whole meaning of
the seven thousand lines of Greek invocation into one English hexameter.'

It understands all languages 'as easy as kissing your claw', even that of contemporary street urchins.

'I say, slosh 'em in the geseech and get clear off with the swag's wot I
say,' urged Herbert.
'Forbear,' repeated the Phoenix sternly. 'Who pinched the click off
of the old bloke in Aldermanbury?'

It visits the head office of The Phoenix Fire Insurance Company 'expressing in graceful phrases the pleasure it felt in finding itself at last in its own temple'. But the Phoenix is not awkwardly moral – it is far too conceited for that. Its greatest didactic effort is tactful, but ill-received – when the children wish, standing on the Carpet, to do good, the Carpet stays in its place, and the Phoenix hints that there is no need for it to move at all. Robert says with deep disgust, 'It's like the end of a fairy story in a Sunday magazine. How perfectly beastly.'

The Phoenix's greatest fault is its tendency to over excitement, brought on by vanity; and when it sets a theatre on fire, flapping its golden wings and crying 'Well done, my servants! Ye have my favour, and my countenance', getting carried away by the limelight, the children feel it has gone too far. This is a curious episode in which no one gets hurt and the Phoenix is contrite afterwards, managing to tell the absent parents (always absent, in E. Nesbit's magic stories) that their children are safe, and to undo the damage it has caused. This magnificent bird – quite the most engaging, both of magic birds and of E. Nesbit's 'creatures' – at last lays its egg and departs in votive fire; and one is left wondering where, and when, it will be reborn.

E. Nesbit never wrote about, and did not really understand, 'only' children; the nearest she got was the delectable Mabel of *The Enchanted Castle*. In a way, the quirky magic creatures take their place. The Psammead, who in *Five Children and It* and *The Story of the Amulet* grants wishes and directs the adventures, is quite the most memorable, unlike anything except itself – ugly and strange as a monkey-tarantula.

> *It was worth looking at. Its eyes were on long horns like a snail's eyes, and it could move them in and out like telescopes: it had ears like bat's ears and its tubby body was shaped like a spider's and covered with thick soft fur; its arms and legs were furry too and it had hands and feet like a monkey's.*

It was, of course, a sand-fairy, spoke perfect English, and was irascible, water-hating, and had already lived for five thousand years; it had, also, to its own detriment, to grant wishes, puffing itself and swelling with obvious difficulty and danger. The wishes are the ones every child – perhaps every adult – wishes once in their lives; to be beautiful, to be rich, to fly, to go into the past, to see real Red Indians, to be a different age, to be stronger than one's enemies. Throughout the disasters brought on by the logical application of these wishes to everyday circumstances, the Psammead maintains its dignity and character and endears itself to children and readers, who asked for more. In *The Story of the Amulet*, 1906, the Psammead appeared again. Its long life had given it a sarcastic manner with people, 'I quite thought I had dreamed you all. I do have very odd dreams sometimes' and it treats their wishes with black humour:

> *Wings? Take care you are not flying too high at sunset. There was a little Ninevite boy I heard of once – one of King Sennacherib's sons. One day he wished for wings and got them, and at sunset he fell slap on to one of the winged lions at the top of his father's great staircase – well, it's not a pretty story. But I believe the boy enjoyed himself very much until then.*

It gets tired of the children, cross with them, almost pathetic in its inability to escape its wish-granting fate: 'If you know how I hate to blow myself out with other people's wishes – and then to wake up every morning and know you've got to do it' – and begs them never to tell the grown-ups of its presence. 'Scientific people would hit on some way of making things last after sunset. And they'd wish for a graduated income-tax and old-age pensions and manhood suffrage and free secondary education' – with the hint that all these things would go as wrong as the more direct and childish wishes for wealth and beauty.

In *The Story of the Amulet*, the Psammead is there to interpret and guide, from the moment when bedraggled, dusty and thin it calls to the children from a pet-shop cage 'in downright common English' and is sold to them for two pounds ten. This magnificent story of adventures in the past, based on a good deal of research into Babylonian and Egyptian antiquities is, I think, the best ever written in this genre. The 'time' adventures in the *Arden* books have not got the coherence, continuity and excitement of the search for the missing half of the Amulet, involving a chase through time to find a moment at which both halves existed. The Psammead goes everywhere with the children. It gets them out of trouble and is rescued in turn. It is its irascible, proud, reluctant, lovable self, always grumbling, always referring acidly to the good old Megatherium days, picking up contemporary slang with amazing ease yet moralising about the present, saying things like 'You've got your country into such a mess that there's no room for half your children – and no one to want them' – and 'There'll be a National Cage built for me at Westminster and I shall have to work at politics.'

After the adventure with the Phoenix at the Garrick Theatre, one would have thought that the children would have known better than to take the Psammead to the Hippodrome; but this was done, and 'the wishes of the people round them were granted so suddenly and so surprisingly that at last the Psammead had to be taken hurriedly home by Anthea'. As a magic companion, the Psammead is quirky, surprising, crusty as an old misogynist, irrepressible and unforgettably strange. It leaves at last, departing for Baalbec, complaining, 'I shall be found out . . . I *know* they'll make me go into Parliament – hateful place – all mud and no sand.'

As a fabulous animal, it is a triumph. The imagination of monks and limners of the Bestiaries could not produce a creature of such oddity, yet with such unity: even Mallory's Questing Beast is a mixture of parts with the joins showing.

The Mouldiwarp (and its brothers) in the *Arden* books is less of a character, partly because it is not really present in the plot in the way Psammead and Phoenix are. 'Harding's Luck' and 'The House of Arden' – one blending strangely into the other – are again concerned with adventures in the past, and the white mole who appears to the children Edred and Elfrida is their family crest come alive; or rather, an immortal magic animal with powers over past and future, which they are able to see and speak to. It is rather like Dudu the Raven, except that it speaks what is supposed to be broad Sussex, but which reads as nothing in particular. This rather moral – and again, irascible – little animal is there to help the Arden children find the family treasure, and to make them kind and wise: rather a difficult task, as the two are more than usually obtuse and quarrelsome and are, indeed, the most unlikeable children E. Nesbit ever wrote about.

Heraldic creatures or mythical mixtures of parts are supposed to have been created that way, complete and finished. But creatures that have grown warped and monstrous with time and misfortune symbolise too much that is warped in human nature for comfort. It is difficult to be objective about those very moral works, George Macdonald's *Princess and the Goblin* and *The Princess and Curdie*. The first one frightened me so profoundly as a child that I was afraid to go to sleep – yet it was pleasing, enjoyable, wonderful. It had that primal house or castle in it that one knows from Bluebeard to Kafka and Gormenghast, with something strange in the attic and something horrible in the cellar. Both books are rich source material for the work of C. S. Lewis and J. R. R. Tolkien. The evil, stonehearted, soft-footed goblins who can only live in the dark, and their creatures, are described – the goblins as less than human and the creatures more than animal – with a vagueness that enhances their terror. From domestic stock, the creatures had, underground, grown in all directions like potatoes 'the various parts of their bodies assuming, in an apparently arbitrary and self-willed manner, the most abnormal developments' and 'their countenances had grown in grostesque resemblance to the human; while their owners had sunk towards them, they had risen towards their owners.'

Their first appearance is surprisingly like that of the strange creatures in the film *Freaks*, Tod Browning's horror classic, ill-defined
and full of menace.* As the Princess and her nurse flee down from
the hills, trying to get home before it is dark, 'the something in the
middle of the way which had looked like a great lump of earth
brought down by the rain, began to move. One after another it shot
out four long things, like two arms and two legs, but it was too
dark to tell what they were.'

The creatures come out from the mines through an entrance made
by a stream, opened prematurely by the goblins. Like phantoms
from the deep unconscious, they gambol on the palace lawns in the
dark. Even the Fairy Grandmother and Curdie were ineffective

*The plots of *Freaks* and *The Princess and Curdie* have similarities – one's sympathy is enlisted
for the good-hearted monstrosities, one is turned against the apparently normal. 'Animal'
vengeance occurs in both stories and by this means corruption is exposed and given a just
reward.

comfort for this reader; Arthur Hughes's illustrations to the original edition of 1872, all darkness and inclined heads confined by the borders of the pictures, did not help.

The Princess and Curdie, 1883, has little of this fearsome mystery; but in it the creatures are redeemed and the wicked humans in the story turn into creatures. Curdie, who is given a mission to save the kingdom and rescue the Princess once again, is also given a gift – that of seeing the animal in the human by means of its hands, which turn into the paws of the beast it most resembles. His companion is Lina, the ugliest dog in the world, described in detail and so not frightening.

> *She had a very short body and very long legs made like an elephant's, her tail which dragged on the floor behind her, was twice as long and quite as thick as her body. Her head was something between that of a polar bear and a snake. Her eyes were dark green with a yellow light in them. Her under teeth came up like a fringe of icicles, only very white, outside of her upper lip. Her throat looked as if the hair had been plucked off.*

This dog, with the hands of a girl, has a shining soul. Curdie looks at it in pity: 'if he could but pull the child out of the beast!' The lesson of the story is not to judge by appearances. The creatures reappear, tamed by Lina, and accompany Curdie on his quest. Seen in daylight they are pitiful and laughable – 'a strange torrent of deformity', including Legserpent illustrated opposite grasping a priest, Ballbody, a tapir with an iron nose, a huge scorpion and a centipede three feet long. Curdie realises their true worth, and that humans and animals have figuratively changed places. Inside the wicked and fat Doctor Kelman there is something thin and nasty trying to get out: 'The round body he shows', says Curdie, 'is but the case of a serpent. Perhaps the creature lies there, as in its nest, coiled round and round inside.'

The scene in the castle kitchen when the animals rout the humans – who have claws of birds of prey, trotters of pigs or no hands at all but serpentine appendages – directly foreshadows the animal vengeance scene in *That Hideous Strength*. And the final army of creatures that goes to fight for the king against his enemies is like the animals' last stand in the final Narnia book, except that right is here victorious. Lina is purified by magic fire; the creatures vanish, carrying their victims; 'What became of them I have never heard.'

There are such strong theological overtones in *The Princess and Curdie* that one wonders whether 'their own place' to which the creatures and victims go, is purgatory. Perhaps there they will eventually become human, as Lina will, and the victims turn into the animals into which they have allowed themselves to grow.

Making up animals by adding heads, bodies and legs is something anyone can do – all the parts necessary for some kind of life are there in the imagination, waiting to be fitted together. Lacking the genius that made the Dong, the Quangle-Wangle, the Mock Turtle or the Psammead, one leaves them in an ephemeral state; but in some cases they get out. A curious book published in 1897 consists of nothing but made up animals – this was *Animal Land Where there are no People* by Sybil Corbet,* taken seriously enough by Andrew Lang for him to write an introduction. He states that these creatures exist 'in a happy vein of nonsense', and are a child's invisible playmates, named in the 'spontaneous inevitable way' that Adam and Eve named the animals in Eden. But one feels that they must have been rather like '*des personnages tout a fait etrangers à ma*

---

*Sybil Corbet was aged 6 at the time. Unlike Daisy Ashford, her imagination was visual.

The Toop

This Animal is very kind and comes into every Garden. It pulls long grass and eats it

The Stoop

This Animal looks at everything but never touches

The Booba

This is a funny little Animal. It makes
no noise and runs

famille qui se mettaient à défiler autour de moi,' who haunted Anatole France in the dark. Here creatures very like Legserpent and Ballbody, and the Iron Tapir are pictured and their oddly human attributes compensate for the lack of humanity in their world.

'This creature does everything it is told to do and eats pumice stone.' 'This animal has such dainty little ways of pulling up potatoes.' 'This beast is larger than any table and is always there.' 'This animal loves boiling fish.' The creatures romp and cavort fearsomely, though we are assured that most of them are harmless; and Mervyn Peake composed creatures of a very similar nature in that short, strange work, *Captain Slaughterboard Drops Anchor*, 1945. The story is an idyll that tells how a murderous pirate captain was entranced and tamed by a small animal/human called the Yellow Creature, and retired with it to a tropical island to live peacefully and happily, doing nothing but eating fruit and catching fish. But it is told in the visual language of Breughel and Bosch. It all happens in a beautiful, grotesque paradise of 'little green islands with undiscovered edges,' with whales swimming round them. The whales are happily chewing daisies and the only recognisable animal is an elephant – but who is to judge what is beautiful, as the animals are all different from each other and all animal and human nature.

Captain Slaughterboard is recognisable as a small-brained thug and his crew are frightening caricatures of men. But when he sees the island with its fantastic fauna, he remarks 'there are some preposterous creatures over there! I must catch one.' The Yellow Creature 'as bright as butter' is the only one to let itself be caught. It is a long-eared, half-hairy biped with huge eyes and eyebrows sprouting like antennae. The bosun, Billy Bottle, looks equally fantastic. The other creatures are semi-human travesties. The Balleroon, the Dignipomp (fins, webbed feet and Roman nose), the Mousterache (a tufty, human-faced poodle), the Saggerdroop, the Sleeka (a water version of the urban Spiv) and the Plummet, a vast-eyed, underwater but disconcertingly semi-human fish. The Yellow Creature never learns to speak; it just says 'Yo-ho'. It and the Captain get rid of the crew, do pirate dances when the moon is full, and live on the island with the other creatures 'who were really very friendly'. They catch fish of decorated, grotesque, jewelled, enormous beauty. This is gentle nightmare, a bad dream with the evil removed so that what remains is strangeness and goodwill. Every odd anomaly that one has ever seen in the aquarium or tropical house might be saying: look at me long enough and there's nothing to fear. It is a view that has a certain validity. For these rioting imaginations, even the variety of the animal world has not been enough.

One wonders whether animals have human fantasies; whether the Houyhnhnms 'improved' the Yahoos by speculating about them. But this boring race seem to have had few imaginative gifts. In the *Mr Neverlost* books, A. Turnbull, 1932–4, impossible animals do show an interest in the human race as specimens. These are early *Dr Who* stories – science fiction treated as fairy tale but with interesting ideas and considerable wit and invention. An underground society of animals called the Angry Beasts – vast prototypes and amalgams of the above world beasts – tend to collect humans and compile notes about them. An enormous prick-eared pig corners the heroine and questions her: Wild or tame? Pest or useful? Changing the coat in winter? It decides she is Carniherbivorous and makes her a cage. The Angry Beasts do not really care for bipeds, but each, as in Captain Slaughterboard's paradise, seems to be the

only one of its kind and the quarrelling that goes on is inevitable. One feels that this is a kind of tyrannosaurus behaviour that leads, equally inevitably, to the extinction of the species.

Animals cannot help behaving according to their appearance, from the inhuman hauteur of a bird to the friendly charm of furry, strokable creatures whose flatter faces and larger eyes have a recognisably anthropoid look. A Unicorn, straight out of a Bestiary unmodified, is one fabulous beast who can never appear homely, or quite tamed. Even centaurs may be domesticated with some difficulty, but Unicorns resist – they are always unattainable, unique, a distant flash of white among the trees, a vision of a firebird that can never be caught. As such, they appear in various stories – in Elizabeth Goudge's *The Little White Horse*, 1946, the Unicorn appears mysteriously and vanishes like a dream: 'For one flashing moment she saw him perfectly, clear cut as a cameo against the darkness, and the proud curve of the neck, the flowing white mane and tail, the flash of the silver hoofs were utterly strange and yet utterly familiar.'

There is a fearful symmetry about a Unicorn that must provoke awe and perhaps terror. As a symbol of goodness this one is rather passive, but the whole tone of the book is rather bland: ' "We are of Viking ancestry and great fighters" (said Sir Benjamin). "Yes," sighed Miss Heliotrope. "When Maria was little, I has great trouble in getting her to eat rice pudding." ' In the same story is a dog who is a lion in disguise, but one feels that the disguise is really the other way round.

Alan Garner's work has the opposite effect. The terrors are not only psychological, but tangible. In *Elidor*, 1965, which has a strong Arthur Machen flavour, when children (why children? *The Owl Service* has improved things by growing the participants up a bit) find their way into an archaic, Celtic, legendary place, they let loose Findhorn the Unicorn, whose death shakes the stars. The Unicorn's mythical beauty and submission to a virgin's power is described, most movingly in T. H. White's *The Witch in the Wood*, where Gawaine and his brothers trap one with the help of a kitchenmaid. As it lays its head on her knee, 'the eyes, circled by a sad and beautiful darkness, were so sorrowful, lordly, gentle and nobly tragic that they killed all other emotions except love;' and Meg the kitchenmaid becomes royal in her acknowledgement of the homage. The Unicorn's violent death is described in terms of the unruly family of boys' hatred of themselves for what they have done. In *Elidor* the same scene is described with added strangeness, as it happens in a city slum to a beast which, to the uninitiated, is invisible.

It is no accident that the Unicorn Jewel is Tirian the king's dearest friend in C. S. Lewis' *The Last Battle*, 1956. 'They loved each other like brothers and had each saved the other's life in the wars.' It is Jewel who is given the great affirmative Credo at the end when all the redeemed characters have passed into heaven: 'He stamped his right fore-hoof on the ground and neighed, and then cried: "I have come here at last! This is my real country! I belong here. This is the land I have been looking for all my life though I never knew it till now." '

Alice's Unicorn is rather more worldly, but still regal. As in most of the *Looking Glass* creatures there is an air (lent by Tenniel perhaps) of political or social cartoon. The Unicorn has the air of a bored dandy: 'He turned round and stood for some time looking at her with an air of the deepest disgust. "What – is – this?" He said at last . . . "is it alive?" "It can talk," said Haigha solemnly. The Unicorn looked dreamily at Alice and said "Talk, child." ' He and the Lion sit on either side of the White King eyeing the crown like Prime Minister and Leader of the Opposition spoiling for an election.

In *The Birthday Unicorn* (Janice Elliott, 1970) the nearest modern approach to political comedy since *The Animals' Conference*, a Unicorn manages to achieve its ambition and gain the crown – for a while. A Unicorn, it seems, can never be less than beautiful and dignified, even when it is so much involved in contemporary life that it gives television interviews. This likeable fantasy reads like an animated cartoon; characters appear, make a remark, and disappear again. The stars of the story are a Unicorn and a Dodo, the observer is the usual small boy whose eccentric parents are, most of the time, away exploring or being famous personalities. When Dodo and Unicorn appear as birthday presents, they quickly assume positions not only of equality but importance among the humans. There is no mystery, no question of concealing a magic creature from parents and authorities; neither animal has the usual fears of discovery or being put in a zoo, though at one point they are kidnapped by an enterprising circus manager. Their magic presence is more powerful than anything they encounter and their strong personalities dwarf those of the people: they both have star quality. The Unicorn is proud, beautiful, conceited and a wizard; life, as often happens for the handsome, is in some ways easy for it. The Dodo, a more complex character always falling on its beak and crying – an association with the pool of tears? – is jealous of the Unicorn's success.

As the Unicorn remarks, 'There is nothing so marvellous people can't get used to it'; and *people* (though surprised at the mythical and extinct nature of the pair) let them speak and think, though not dress, like humans without comment. 'The Unicorn crossed its hoofs and smiled into the camera: it took no notice of the questions but said it was very, *very* happy to be there.' It also turns politicians into toads, makes speeches, dissolves parliament and, for a while, takes over the monarchy. Its reign is full of splendid processions and parties and the free opening of Buckingham Palace gardens. It is, in short, a 'just, wise, and handsome monarch'; and this is a classic case of the animal dictating its own story. If the tale is to be about dazzling beauty and popularity, then a Unicorn will in some ways play the part more convincingly than a human who brings inevitable psychological overtones of, probably, being a youngest son. A cowardly, cringing Unicorn, like Frank L. Baum's cowardly lion, is there to be cured; and to my mind 'homely' dragons are only valid if they have had a splendid past.

If a mere magic agent is required Flook (Wally Fawkes and George Melly, 1948 onwards) is probably one of the most successful ever devised. His situation is that of a magic pet, or helper, but the

effect is one of sharp but kindly satire. Rufus, the child in the story, who has aged a little in outlook during his twenty years of life but not at all in appearance, was once living with an uncle and aunt of sparse ideas and wooden-headed unamiability who refused to let him keep any pets. He collected some pleasing jam-jars full of newts and frog spawn and put them in the bath, from which Uncle at once pulled out the plug. Rufus's unhappy dreams that followed concerned a little prehistoric animal who was being chased up a volcano by iguanodons and cave men. Rufus rescued the creature by grabbing it and waking up – to find that Flook was real, round, mouse-eared, trunked and furry, able to turn itself into a barometer or the Albert Memorial at will, just by screwing up its face and shaking with effort. This inspired creation launched Rufus into full-scale, contemporary adventures and soon developed the usual magic-animal attributes – conceit, near-perfect knowledge of worldly affairs, long memory, good education and kindly concern both for Rufus, his special friend, and mankind in general.

Flook is never unbearably conceited or notably soft-hearted. He is wily, self-important, quick-witted, fond of drink, a master of disguise, never at a loss, sometimes angry, as bouncing as Mickey Mouse, as resilient as a cat, always ready to engineer a happy ending, censorious but tolerant, never taken in by the constant stream of phonies that surrounds him. One has to accept the convention – used in other satires such as *The Birthday Unicorn* or near-satires such as the *Paddington* books – that the animal can speak, is recognised by others without undue surprise, and can perform occasional magic. Then one can only admire the way in which, having graduated from the temporary defeat of Bodger, the one-time school bully, he takes on contemporary unpleasantness such as vast office blocks, muck-raking journalists, crooked politicians, trend-setting maniacs or any exploitation of the weak or ignorant. From slightly acid fairy tale this series has become the sort of story in which, while laughing at the felicity with which the mat is pulled from under recognisable idiocies, one sees oneself rather uncomfortably. An animal agent, besides giving advice, is the perfect neutral castigator, and Flook is one of the best to date. He is human enough to be likeable, animal enough to be other, beyond reproach or human laws.

6 Dragons

Dragons have always been thought of – and described – with a mixture of fear and attraction. They lurk everywhere in the Bestiaries as the ultimate deterrent, the ultimate comparison: 'Not even a dragon . . .' The Bestiary limner is hypnotised into drawing dragonish animals, thrilled by their deadliness. The 'Cocodryllus' is really described quite accurately: 'It breeds in the river Nile. An animal with four feet, amphibious, generally about thirty feet long, armed with horrible teeth and claws. So great is the hardness of its skin that no blow can hurt it . . . it incubates its eggs in the earth.' But since none of his readers have ever seen one, short of fire-breathing, this could very well *be* a dragon. The drawing shows a pointed-eared, lean, long-legged, fanged beast with a plumed tail and bird claws.

Folklore dragons always talk – their semi-human nature has a wily intelligence. Sometimes they are regal, sometimes cowardly, less often have some sort of home life with a dragoness or even an old mother. Oriental ones are magical, weather bringing, godlike masters of rain, wind and storm, or sometimes turn out to be wizards in disguise. Northern ones are jewel-loving with fiery or poisonous breath; they are often curiously merry or sardonic in the way that creatures who think themselves invincible may be – but they can be beaten, or more often outwitted through some weakness or soft spot. They are long lived, unhappy, and their hoarded

wealth brings no one any good. Beowulf and Sigurd ultimately gain nothing except fame from their dragon conquests.

If dragons are present – and their fascination is such that they always will be – they cannot co-exist. As is made quite clear in the tales where they keep their true nature, dragons are entirely self-regarding: 'Once I had a mate. It was a pity that I ate her.' The dragon will amass all the wealth it can find or steal, keep it for ever and kill all comers or other dragons.

Stories must, therefore, be about heroic conquest by men; or else the dragonish character must be changed so that the dragon is small, young, friendly, funny, or reluctant – de-natured in some way, otherwise it cannot be approachable, cannot exist except as a thing for which death is violent and inevitable.

Kenneth Grahame's *The Reluctant Dragon*, 1899, is the prototype of most modern story-book dragons that are, in theory, possible to live with. Its sting has been removed, it is an Indian without bow and arrow and scalping knife, a Bull who likes flowers rather than fighting. As creatures of mythical evil in old tales, dragons' honeyed tongues add to their terror and power, and like most semi-magic animals they are old, experienced and learned. This one has all the proper attributes, with one more – a *fin de siècle* weariness; he has lived too long and reacted against being intense and taking all those pre-Raphaelite knights in armour seriously. He is an Edwardian dilettante who likes company and composing a little verse and has left fighting to all the other fellows who were so active and *earnest* and all that sort of thing. Unfortunately, he would probably have

been just in time to enlist in the First World War. When St George appears, his reaction is 'I don't want to know the fellow at all. I'm sure he's not nice. Say he can write if he likes, but I can't give him an interview.'

The medieval setting is quite illusory. The boy, who, although he is supposed to be living in the middle of it, is obviously going to grow up with exactly the same social manners as the dragon, complains aggrievedly that the whole affair of the challenge is being treated 'as if it were an invitation to tea and croquet'. The amusement of the narrative is that child, knight and monster *do* behave as if tea and croquet were being discussed, with perhaps a few amateur theatricals added. Nothing is what it seems; the fight is rigged, the dragon is the life and soul of the subsequent party – and when dragon, knight and boy set off for home arm in arm afterwards, the dragon appears to have diminished in size, the boy and knight have grown, and the three revellers seem oddly similar.

This near-perfect story is just long enough. Perhaps the joke should have stopped there, but the idea was inevitably magnetic and a host of other reluctant beasts with soft centres have followed. E. Nesbit's dragons of the same era at least retained most of their fearsomeness but could often be caught, or charmed, with kindness, which is a good compromise. 'Justnowland' from *The Magic World*, 1912, has a formidable dragon and a city of bewitched crows (the capitalists) and pigeons (the workers) and ends, typically, in Fabian Utopia. As in *The Aunt and Amabel*, a child is isolated in a room as punishment for having tried – and failed – to do an adult a good turn. In each case the Aunt is the real dragon, a grim, misunderstanding tyrant, and the child an innocent little saint. Whereas H. H. Munro in a similar story like *The Lumber Room* allows the child to wreak horrid vengeance on the Aunt, E. Nesbit merely gives her child compensatory dreams. (H. H. Munro's views were loaded by unhappy childhood experience perhaps, but were Aunts always so terrible? A childhood blessed with a large number can be greatly enriched.) There is, in this story though, a sinister adult ring; Elsie the child has been much influenced by Foxe's *Book of Martyrs*. 'It was a horrible book – the thick oleographs, their guarding sheets of tissue paper sticking to the prints like bandages to a wound . . . it was a book that made you afraid to go to bed: but it was a book you could not help reading.' When the giant crow takes her to the

enchanted city to tame the dragon who has turned the people to
birds, she goes in the spirit of martyrdom. But the dragon has a
melting heart after all, like Boris Karloff's (but not Mary Shelley's)
monster. 'I've been so lonely,' it sobs. 'No one to love me. You do
love me, don't you?' A kiss removes the spell, kindness is the key to
this rather moral tale, in which the bird populace, turned back to
men, swear that 'in future we shall not be rich and poor, but fellow-
workers, and each will do his best for his brothers'. The Aunt,
unfortunately, remains untamed.

E. Nesbit had a weakness for saurian monsters, which she usually
calls megatheriums – there is even one in 'The Enchanted Castle'.
The Book of Dragons, 1900, has them in great variety. These short
stories are interesting in their embryo themes elaborated on in later
books – and for the brisk, jocular humour which takes the edge
from the horror of the monstrous, without detracting from its
strangeness. E. Nesbit has been criticised for not possessing the
numinous qualities of George Macdonald nor opening, as Roger
Lancelyn Green suggests, more than an 'occasional chink' of the
magic casement. But the chinks are all the more dazzlingly effective
when they do come; Gerald and the stone dinosaur in the dark
garden, Phillip in the hall of silver pillars in the Magic City, the
present and the past on either side of the Amulet and the whole
long, hot, strange afternoon on which the Enchanted Castle is
found (as perfect an opening chapter as that of any novel ever
written). The dragon stories have no such wonderful moments, but
ideas, often full of fascinating logic, proliferate. There are lines that
one longs to produce and make into a theorem. *The Book of Beasts*
has the idea which is the nucleus of *The Magic City* – that of pictures
in a book, a Bestiary, full of the fabulous, jumping off the page:
wonderful if the picture is of a peacock, but 'What if it had been a
worm, a snake, or a revolutionary?' thinks the boy king to whom
the book belongs. A dragon flies out; ten years later, in *The Magic
City*, it was the Hippogriff and a giant Sloth. Lionel, the king, has
to open the book again and let out a Manticora to fight the dragon;
but it is a failure, rubbing its eyes with its hand and mewing pitifully.
It puts its tail between its legs and hides behind the town hall, eating
all the cats in the night.* 'The Island of the Whirlpools' has a

---

*A dismal record for one of this creature's few appearances in fiction. The one in R. Eddison's
The Worm Ouroborus is much more effective.

dragon and a griffin and the complicated calculations necessary for a prince to navigate tides which happen and monsters which sleep, at different times each day on a sort of sliding scale. Here is the beginning of the spell of the god Arithmos, of *The Enchanted Castle*, 1907; and in 'Kind Little Edmund', Cockatrice, Dragon* and Drackling have links with the Phoenix and Psammead with their stories of legend and prehistory, doubtful tempers and fondness for giving good advice.

H. R. Millar's dragons drawn for this book have infinite variety; no two appear to share similar genes. Likewise, the stories are different, not only in subject but in type, and so full of invention that the book deserves to be, and should be, reprinted with the rest.†

But these dragons are exceptional; domesticated monsters are the rule and facetious treatment is the most usual. C. S. Forester's *Poo Poo and the Dragons*, 1942, is one of the best kindly-but-vast stories, of a type which seemed to have lapsed between the wars. Harold Heavyside Brown meets his dragons by the simple but perfect method of 'wandering up' inside one of the fuchsia flowers on a bush in the garden. Inside he finds a dragon on a vacant piece of land. Doglike, it follows him home, wagging its tail, squirming and wriggling. Later, it brings a friend and they both make themselves useful, mowing the lawn, polishing the floor, and laughing at jokes. They sleep in the garden with their heads in Harold's bedroom. C. S. Forester makes the best of mythical and domestic worlds by giving Harold Heavyside and dragon friends magic adventures inside the fuchsia at night and school comedy with the dragons learning to read and spell in the daytime. These highly intelligent beasts, who act throughout like huge talking dogs, have equally huge and simple emotions of joy, disappointment, laughter and tears and are accepted by the neighbours as rather a nuisance, but not surprising. There are delightful scenes such as the dragons running behind the car like carriage dogs (amusingly shown by

---

*The scene in this tale in which the Dragon goes down a hole inside a mountain cave to the central fires is so like that in C. S. Lewis's *Perelandra* that a comparison is interesting: 'When the last joint of her tail had gone, Edmund slammed down the inner door.' Nesbit.
'As he saw the last section of its tripartite body wobble on the edge of the aperture . . . Ransome almost laughed.' Lewis. The monsters are different, but the central fires, the hole, the disconcertingly 'mechanised' aspects of the dragonish, are the same.
†And has been: *The Complete Book of Dragons*, Hamish Hamilton, 1972. Illustrated by Eric Blegvad.

Robert Lawson's illustrations rather in the W. Heath Robinson style of naturalistic comedy), and watching for trains to come out of a tunnel as mice from a mousehole. The facetious treatment and comment – the *Just So Stories* Best Beloved manner – is perhaps less acceptable now than when the book was written.

The ultimate domesticated dragon is perhaps Rosemary Weir's *Albert*, whose only traditional property is that he lives in Cornwall. Albert has been 'spoiled'. He wants to go round doing good; and in the end becomes so humanised that, like a young animal 'fixed' by human company, he almost thinks he is a member of the human race. His child-accompaniments are named Tony and Mary-Ann. He tidies up the kitchen, makes porridge and helps Tony's father build a haystack, furnishing his own cave with a bed and blankets. He is a vegetarian and likes seaweed. One so amiable and meek would appear to have most of the human virtues, but Albert has three human drawbacks – he is lonely, sorry for himself and does not like the dark. A dragon can sink no lower. He is obviously in need of psychiatric help and Mary-Ann suggests gardening or carpentry; but in the end child adoption is the only compensation for his solitary state and Albert takes in a rather ungrateful baby centaur. Bringing up the centaur leads to adventures rather like those in *Helen's Babies*: 'Never mind,' says Tony, 'Centaurs are different from people like us.' This comforts Albert until Tony adds, 'You and the Centaur are fabulous beasts.' One wishes that they were.

A better compromise is reached in *The Dragon of an Ordinary Family*, by Margaret Mahy, 1969. Ordinary families are human-sized, and all dragons start by being small. Traditionally hatched out of eggs like the Cocodryllus, baby dragons are tiny, as Princess Thora, daughter of the Jarl Hraud found in the saga of Ragnar Lothbrog. The problem of growth is as great as that of man-eating fierceness. The Ordinary Family's dragon is bought as a pet, rather cheaply as it turns out, and its breed and pedigree come into question. But as, like most traditional dragons, it is the only one, there is nothing to compare it with. It grows and grows, never speaking until it is of enormous size, large enough to be sold to a handbag factory. The awful problems of the suburban family who have acquired a vast Pyreneean-mountain-mongrel by mistake ring so unhappily true that one is reassured when the tale turns to fantasy and the dragon flies the family to the Isles of Magic, full of princesses and youngest sons. They sail back on a charter-flight magic carpet, leaving the dragon in its true home.

Rosemary Manning in *Green Smoke*, 1957, almost has the best of both worlds, the fabulous and the homely. R. Dragon, of obvious ancestry, also lives in Cornwall – a useful county, as there could always be a deserted beach or forgotten and inaccessible cove where such a creature might live. The charm of this one is that it has a past, remembering the days of King Arthur, and telling Susan, the child who finds it, many stories of Cornish history and myth. This Cornwall is full of saints, giants, mermaids and knights and is a lot more impressive and exciting than that of the present day. But the story solves, or deals, with two other problems inherent in the genre – first, that of making the dragon both romantic and plausible as a companion (it has, it confesses, eaten maidens but now has turned to the buns that picnickers leave: the Roman Empire fell thus and maybe, one feels, that is why dragons are extinct now); and second, the problem of how to keep the grown-ups quiet when one is off on one's own having semi-magic adventures. Rosemary Manning's Mother is the sort who plays along with a child's fantasy, honouring the child's words without considering their meaning: 'Going to find the dragon? Don't let him eat you,' and packing up a parcel of food in the way that mothers have of giving a sweet to Binker as well as Christopher Robin. In a really nasty story such as John Collier's *Thus I refute Beelzy* or H. H. Munro's *Sredni Vashtar*, the dragon would shortly appear and eat this kind of parent. But R. Dragon is, alas, tamed by time, as usual almost too much so. 'I am your kind dragon who loves you,' it says, 'and I will tell you stories, even without buns.'

Perhaps it was softened up by Christianity, the onset of which – with the wrong food – seems to have spelled death to its kind. When some Saints approached one day it decided to roar in the hope that they would go away, but St Petroc merely said, 'Come along. Good boy! Come to master,' and gave it a drink made of water and church floor dust, which must have broken its spirit. Domesticity, sweeping out its cave with a brush and pan and keeping its teeth in a box, is an anticlimax for any dragon; but perhaps anticlimax is the penalty of out-living one's age.

All-out farce with no shades of pathos is simpler to handle.

Monsters are adaptable enough to survive the treatment: it is when you take them too seriously – like 'Godzilla' or 'The Beast from 20,000 Fathoms' – that farce crashes in, unasked. J. B. S. Haldane's *My Friend Mr Leakey* (1937) turns a dragon into a rather dangerous comic dog. It is small but otherwise dragonlike in the full sense, apart from its human tricks like wearing asbestos boots (it is practically red hot and sleeps on burning coals), grilling fish and making toast with its breath. Mr Leakey, a real magician, has animal servants who were once people. 'Turning people into animals is easy,' he remarks. 'It is turning them back again that is difficult.' In each case the human suffered some handicap which the animal has overcome. Oliver, an octopus who was a waiter who lost his legs, now hangs by an arm from the ceiling, using his other arms to serve his master. Leopold, a beetle who runs round the table passing the salt and pepper, was a swindler rescued from prison. Animal-human transformation can go no further than Mr Leakey's fancy-dress party at which the magician changes the guests not into the animal they are most like, but the one they *hope* they are like. Circe missed some amusement here, for there are oddities like Lady-into-Butterfly: 'You've no idea,' Mr Leakey remarks, 'how ugly a butterfly looks when it's as big as an albatross.' Pompey the dragon is picked up by a lady Jinn and fed lumps of sulphur while she murmurs, 'I don't like to see a dragon too fat.' He is as excited by heat as dogs are by game and almost gets lost in a volcano.

Naomi Mitchison's *Graeme and the Dragon*, 1954, has humour of a less schoolboy kind. It is an inventive story of the E. Nesbit type, and the dragon's only handicap is, once more, its small size. All the problems of the genre are neatly solved. The time is the present, but the dragon is not de-natured. It has, of course, human speech and thinks it is delightful to set fire to things (Graeme's devotion to bonfires is what attracts its attention in the first place). It is conceited, unpredictable, and a dangerous pet; but it is small (and magic, later in the story, makes it even smaller), having been bewitched and sent into an enchanted sleep. Its attitude to its own past is that of Rip Van Winkle; it thinks lorries and trains are legless dragons, and thinks, too, that Graeme looks tender and eatable. The boy has to be one jump ahead, and to keep his new friend hidden, but parents and adults on the whole, only see what they want, or expect to see. When a Roc appears in the sky 'people thought it was a flying saucer or an advertisement for something, the kind of thing they were used to.'

But the dragon is a creature that can't be lost or got rid of; many knights have had this experience. Graeme's dragon can only be temporarily cowed by such things as clockwork toys, which it thinks are lorries under a spell. It is a very logical beast, but like the gullible adults tends to interpret phenomena in terms of what it already knows. When taken on a steam train, it decides it has been swallowed; the train is hungry and people get in, after which the train breathes fire and smoke in the usual way. But the Dragon is intelligent enough to wonder if it has a communication cord inside its own body, and if so, why various princesses it devoured in the past never pulled it.

Dragons are never comfortable. If you make them so, you rob them of their worth. The dragon as an all-devouring monster, entirely evil and without conscience, winter bringing and breathing not only fire but poison – as the one that has to be slain in William Croft-Dickinson's *Borrobil* (1944), is the dreadful, speechless worm that holds the land under its power. It is defeated rather easily, by one stroke; but this sort of dragon is a fearful obstacle to surmount and to attack him is like trying to climb an erupting volcano. An even more formidable opponent is the dragon, greedy with its hoard and full of cunning, who not only fights but answers back, and may win by guile as well as strength.

Apollyon was one of these, with his wings, scales, fire, smoke and lion's mouth that taunts Christian, using, oddly enough, a lot of the depressing arguments that Smaug, Chiefest and Greatest, uses. The battle that followed lasted half a day but one has to imagine it – Bunyan does not help. Not so the author of *Beowulf* who describes the fight with the dragon blow by blow as if he had been there. One learns, as if one had not always known without needing to be told (there is a rightness about traditional behaviour like the inevitable shape of a spoon, a boat or a plough), that dragons are greedy, vengeful, cannibalistic, hate the human race and know to the last goblet the worth of the hoards which they can neither use nor appreciate, and have, somewhere, a soft, weak spot. Beowulf is almost burned to death in the combat and is aided at the last minute by Wiglaf. (Wiglaf has to make formal speeches about ancient history during the fatal seconds. Everyone in *Beowulf* does this and so do people in *Le Morte d'Arthur*; and now that battle action is formalised quite differently such hold-ups are comic and delightful. Only in trial, or court scenes now can one get an idea of what such recapitulated description must have *felt* like when heard: 'Now will you please describe again in your own words exactly what happened on the night of October the fifteenth last.')

The only dragon in C. S. Lewis's *Narnia* cycle is an enchanted one – a dragonised boy who is being taught a lesson. It is reluctant in a rather new and dreadful fashion because it has a dragon's body and a human soul, and the body's instincts – eating sheep, and another dragon – operate mechanically and in spite of its human brain. It cannot speak and the brain cannot control a reptilian nervous system. It tries to express itself in writing on wet sand, but fails lamentably. As always in C. S. Lewis, what is said raises, without wasting a word, far more questions than perhaps it should in a children's story; or rather, the levels of meaning multiply. One lesson anyway is very clearly stated – it is dangerous and unlucky to touch anything that is part of a dragon's hoard, as Beowulf, Sigurd, Eustace Scrubb and Bilbo Baggins found to their cost.

J. R. R. Tolkien's Smaug, whose numinous presence is part of the fascination of *The Hobbit* and who is also the reason for Bilbo's great journey, behaves wonderfully, inevitably and in definitive fashion. 'Smaug lay, with wings folded like an immeasurable bat, turned partly on one side so that the hobbit could see his underparts and his long pale belly crusted with gems and fragments of gold from his long lying on his costly bed.' Bilbo is, of course, no dragon slayer (this is wisely left to the few men in the story) but a child substitute; but Smaug is no tame dragon. Bilbo's only defence is his invisibility. The cunning of Smaug is very great, and so is Bilbo's peril. The conversation which he has with the dragon is a model of brinkmanship and a kind of terrifying comedy.

This dragon is never underestimated and never – in a tale which has already had its share of perils, monsters, strangeness and suspense – less than the 'Chiefest and Greatest of all Calamities' as Bilbo, inspired by desperate bravado and fear, names him. The dragon in turn flatters his intended victim, sneers at him, tries to lull him into a sense of false security, tries to hint that he knows more than he does, tries to plant mistrust, depression and despair.

Bilbo, in turn, uses flattery to Smaug, is drawn on to boast, to try riddles, to tell more than he should, and barely escapes with his life, having seen the proverbial weak spot at the last minute.* Smaug is satanic in his use of lies, which leave an after taste of unhappiness and suspicion, and his hoard with its fabulous Arkenstone causes the breaking of the band of dwarfs just as the Ring does in the adventure's continuation, or the Apple of Discord on Olympus. Smaug's eventual death in a storm of fire and water is magnificent, ruinous and final. No speeches interrupt the action which is traditionally and rightly a man and dragon combat with no magic, no stealth, no words.

Shelob in *The Two Towers*, 1954, is not nearly as awesome or frightening to me. Her terror relies on something far more physical – a purely human dislike of spiders, bad smells and the dark. In battle and defeat she bubbles, hisses and gurgles. Revulsion and disgust are no substitute for awe.

Chrysophylax Dives (*Farmer Giles of Ham*, 1949), my favourite dragon – how can one get to *like* one's persecutors? – has far less

---

*This whole episode brought immediate recognition to this child; it was just the way in which one was tempted to handle monsters or evil characters in nightmares. One tried to flatter, to talk or, worse than Bilbo, to act like Scheherazade and try to entertain or make them laugh – anything to put off the awful hour of eating or annihilation. But then, I had not got an invisible ring.

grandeur than Smaug; he is lazy, astute, talkative and wily, knowing when it is more profitable to retire and recoup his losses than to stand and fight. But he is always dangerous and to be reckoned with. Farmer Giles with his mare and his dog is another reluctant hero, ridiculous in his home-made chain mail, but like Bilbo he has a secret weapon, the sword Caudimordax which will not stay in its sheath if a dragon is within five miles. Luck, circumstances and a certain honest persistence favour him. Bilbo and Giles are, of course, just like you or me, which accounts for their success: a bit more persistent perhaps, but given their luck and weapons one feels one might have done as well. The great heroes like Beowulf often leave one rather cold.

Talk between dragon and man is as natural as talk between man and man, or, in this story, man and dog. The dragon is more intelligent, powerful and better educated than the man, but, as is made clear, has a wicked heart, though not a very bold one. He prefers a meal that he does not have to fight for. To distract Giles, he says ' "Excuse me! Haven't you dropped something?" (An ancient trick, but it succeeded.)' There are several similar polite exchanges between dragon and man in their pre-battle encounters:

' "Excuse my asking, but were you looking for me, by any chance?"

' "No indeed," said the farmer, "who'd a' thought of seeing you here? I was just going for a ride," and this is repeated when Giles – in company with several lazy, vain and incompetent knights – traces Chrysophylax to his lair.

' "Were you looking for me, by any chance?" said Giles.

' "No indeed," said Chrysophylax. "I was just flying about." '

They argue about treasure and compensation like insurance assessors, but here the man has the edge: 'few had ever outlasted Farmer Giles at a bargaining.' The mare expresses her reluctance and distrust of the whole episode by looks and gesture. Garm, the dog, behaves – with words – in the manner that dogs always use. When danger comes he barks under his master's window.

'*Help! Help! Help!*' *cried Garm. The window opened suddenly and a well-aimed bottle came flying out.*

'*Ow!*' *said the dog, jumping aside with practised skill.* '*Help! help! help!*'

Out popped the farmer's head. 'Drat you, dog! What be you a-doing?' said he.

'Nothing,' said the dog.

'I'll give you nothing! I'll flay the skin off you in the morning,' said the farmer, slamming the window.

'Help! help! help!' cried the dog.

This story is full of comic scholarship and has some of Pauline Baynes's most witty drawings. In it, truth and reality are never in question; it tells of a time when dragons were rare but by no means extinct.

In Maurice Sendak's *Where the Wild Things Are* (1967) the monsters are not 'day-time life' real, but just as real as the child Max in the country that he goes to after dark. Being sent to bed for naughtiness was once perhaps part of everyone's experience; it certainly was of mine. The creatures who inhabit Max's night country are as familiar in type, if not in form – mine were rather more attenuated; I was a very thin child – as if they had always been there.

These fanged and clawed, hairy, scaled, crested, semi-human beings are first tamed (by the magic trick of staring into their eyes) and then joined in a wild dance by Max who becomes their king. If only Mr Sendak had been writing and drawing when I was a child, I might have been spared several years of nightmare dreams. The Wild Things acknowledge Max to be the wildest thing of all, and when he leaves for home, beg him to return; awe is still there, but terror has left, which is how all dragons should end, unslain and happily alive in a magic limbo.

My own dragons too must have always existed. They waited until I was six and was shown pictures of the stone monsters at the Crystal Palace; that gave them form, and the slight upsets involved in a move from one house and district to another gave them a way in. Once in, they soon ceased even to try. They had found a pleasant home in my dreams and were able to terrify just by their presence without doing any work at all.* After a while they took to wearing clothes and comic hats and later still got decadent and didn't even bother to appear: the numinous horror that they projected was enough. It took me months and years to work out the idea that knights in armour usually beat dragons and to think the armour into the dreams, piece by piece. I had them beaten at last. This solution is offered to anyone who suffers from this particular trouble, but I think Maurice Sendak's is much better.

*'So secure that all he needs to do is to indicate that he is about to threaten without actually bothering to carry it through,' 'Behaviour of Leaders', *The Human Zoo,* Desmond Morris.

7 Dressed Animals and Others

I can see that little town still, with its river and bridge and shipping, the cheeses and barrels piled high on the quays, the high pitched roofs and the bright green shutters. I am vaguer about the inhabitants, but I think they were anthropomorphised Mice — 'dressed mice' as I would have called them then, with woollen comforters and wide trousers like Dutchmen, and pipes in their mouths . . . I may have wished, and wished intensely, that I might find this town in reality and go to it. But that was because I had first imagined the town and judged it to be simply delightful, almost adorable in its own right. My only reason for wishing to go to it was its adorableness.

Psycho-analysis and Literary Criticism, *C. S. Lewis*

Nostalgia is always with us; perhaps it always was, from the days of Saxons looking at Norman towers and thinking how ugly they were and wishing they were not there. Things being much better *then* is the theme of much English poetry, and because our society is an urban one, the better time belongs to the immediate but vanished past when the towns were smaller or the countryside larger. The whole process of human living is to see the rural past vanishing perhaps never to return, as if one were, from an ever faster non-stop train watching a series of stations fly by, all as lovely as Adlestrop, hardly noticed until gone. A countryside populated by small, indigenous animals is many people's wish, hope, and memory; but such a place, if it is to give imaginative satisfaction, has to be happy and romanticised.

Animal life is not happy in the human sense; it is merely neutral. Human life can be, might be, more often is not, but always has, the possibility. Giving these small animals human qualities is to put them out of reach of inevitable fear, pain and death which is their natural lot. But the device also waves a magic wand and makes humans small, giving them animal qualities and cutting them off from human miseries and frustrations, sexual pangs, jealousy, bitterness and revenge, so that these minute societies have the best of both worlds.

If you are going to imagine that animals have human lives in snug, rural, or ground level communities, you can imagine them at any time; in the remote past when the animals could speak and humans understand (folklore) or now (only you can't see it: it is somehow invisible or nocturnal or stealthily existing just out of sight). The animals are tiny human replicas, dressed in human clothes with a doll-like charm, happy with animal innocence allied to human consciences. This deliberately romantic device becomes, at its best (*The Wind in The Willows*, *The Little Grey Men*, *Tales of Sam Pig and Brock the Badger*), a delicate art form not given to extravagant fantasy but descriptive of an idealised rural life full of pleasing, holiday amusement, and that 'adorableness' of miniature beauty that makes a baby hedgehog seem both comic and magic at the same time.

One knows that life is not like this; one cannot help wishing, sometimes that it were. It is not easy to keep the truth out of these little worlds. A great novel like *The Wind in The Willows* does not entirely succeed, and is all the better for the hints of what is left unsaid. But the happy, Utopian truce from hunting, catching, eating, evil and pain with animal doings described in human terms just for the sheer joy of it, was made by William Roscoe when he wrote *The Butterfly's Ball* in 1807. This poem was so disarmingly different from the moral, instructive and didactic animal tales that had gone before, that it could be said to be the first of the new type, in which animals are dressed or humanised for gaiety and charm rather than for amusement or strangeness.

The Butterfly's Ball is, as Harvey Darton says, with its sequels and successors, 'cheerful good fun of a simple kind'. Its enormous popularity – it, and Lady Dorset's *The Peacock at Home* sold 40,000 copies during their first year – was a sign of its refreshing newness and lighthearted fun. The verse jingles easily and the animals, birds and insects are all enjoying themselves in company with children and observing the natural truce towards each other.

And then came the Moth, with his plumage of Down
And the Hornet in jacket of Yellow and Brown,
Who with him the Wasp his Companion did bring
But they promised that Evening, to lay by their Sting.

The numerous imitators carried on the fun with *The Lions'*
Masquerade, The Elephants' Ball, The Wedding Among the Flowers.
Illustrations show the Peacock's At Home rather like the Assembly
rooms at Bath; the young birds are dancing, the older ones sit down,
delightfully, to cards. At the Lions' Masquerade all the animals are
in witty fancy dress, the Horse as a Houyhnhnm, the Wolf in
Sheep's clothing, the Bear as Caliban. It is elegant and pleasing and
as unlike the ballet sequence in *Fantasia* as it is possible to be. The
eighteenth-century convention that all butterflies' wings were round
and all moths' semicircular only adds to the charm.

Illustration is a prerequisite of this kind of entertainment. There
is an enormous gap in time between William Roscoe and Leslie
Brooke – a hundred years between *The Butterfly's Ball* and *Johnny*
Crow's Party – but the feeling and the gaiety are exactly the same.
For no reason at all other than pleasure in a new Eden, Johnny
Crow acts as host to an assortment of animals, all behaving with
cheerful and characteristic idiosyncrasy, enjoying themselves and
pleasing the human eye at the same time. Of all animal illustrators
Leslie Brooke is among the most endearing. He is perhaps less
stylish than Walter Crane but shows a greater feeling for the
animals, which are by no means all dressed. The comic human
actions they perform, the apt, polysyllabic rhymes that describe
them, have a charm and rightness that needs no narrative.

The Three Bears in *The Golden Goose Book*, 1905, are not dressed;
they live in a charming house that seems to have been transported
to the wood from Hampstead Garden Suburb; they are not fearsome except by their sheer size. Their animal faces have deftly
indicated human expressions of surprise and censure at their discoveries and absurd parental pride in the antics of the small Bear
who wails and grouses like a child or jumps and somersaults in
excited fun and naughtiness. Their bear home is full of fancies with
punning human words, pictures, ornaments and books turned into
their bear equivalents. The Three Little Pigs are similar. The Wolf
is cynical and worldly looking, and the last Pig sitting by the fire is

like the satisfied man who has taken out a life-insurance policy –
which, as the story is about prudence, is quite fitting.

The justly popular *Johnny Crow* books (1903–7, and *Johnny Crow's
New Garden*, 1935) are in the direct *Butterfly's Ball* tradition. The
animals who join Johnny Crow in his garden are all enjoying themselves in absurd yet never caricatured parodies of human acts which
rhyme with their names. One has the feeling that after the odd
masquerade they will presently go away and be themselves once
more. The Ape, measuring the Bear for a suit of clothes, is playing
at looking like Uriah Heep, and the Stork giving his philosophic
talk looks like a stage professor, desiccated and slightly dishevelled.
The Whale, boring everyone with his very long tale, indicates the
vastness of the boredom by boring the Hippopotamus. The feli-
citous rhymes increase the fun:

> *The Cockatoo*
> *Said Comment vous portez vous?*
> *And the Gander*
> *Didn't understand her*
> *But the Flamingo*
> *Talked the same lingo . . .*
> *And the Porcupine*
> *Said Wake me if for talk you pine*

All the while the animals play enthusiastic croquet in the background. They are beautifully drawn and coloured and the combination of delicacy, charm and absurdity is quite irresistible; they are
showing us themselves as they might be if, for a moment, one
could invite them to parody humans in the kindest fashion. The
device works in two ways; as the Bear, who sings a Sentimental
Air, looks exactly like a certain kind of operatic baritone, or the
Stork looks donnish, so humans sometimes show animal nature by
reminding one of a bear or a stork. The animals are having fun in the
most unforced and natural manner, and some of them, the Mouse,
the Giraffe and the Duckling, are laughing at us, or themselves.

Maurice Sendak's *Alligators All Around* is a present-day version
of the same animal carnival. In this cheerful alphabet alligators
indulge in eccentric, original acts to different letters as if dancing in
different keys on each page. There is more surrealism than in
Johnny Crow; the alligators are Forever Fooling, Entertaining

Elephants, Keeping Kangaroos, Looking Like Lions, Wearing Wigs or Riding Reindeer. The simple, effective drawings which make the alligators appear to mime for our pleasure give the same feeling of the animals' conscious enjoyment.

In the work of Leslie Brooke, animals' clothes are assumed for amusement only – perhaps the Bear thought that his black coat and striped trousers were correct wear for his Sentimental Air. But Peter Rabbit's blue jacket with the brass buttons is a natural part of him, a serious matter when lost, as a child's would be – all the more serious because it was quite new. One has to love animals to draw them so beautifully and write about them so confidently. Whatever Beatrix Potter's feelings were, they were perfectly in tune with those of children who shared the same liking. This kind of scaled-down human world has, on the whole, a warm feeling, as if the teller of such tales were trying to re-enter a lost Arcadia by persuading his listeners that somewhere life was like this, just the same as it had always been, and in some miniature animal surroundings, better. Necessarily, this kind of fantasy deals with small animals only. The clothes they wear have made them charming, their world pretty, deathless and painless, their human social life cheerful and law abiding without hunting, killing, persecution or meat.* The animals, often suiting their audience, are often young, inexperienced and behaving irresponsibly like children; if old they are eccentric or 'quaint' and their surroundings have the cosy charm of an old-fashioned doll's house.

Story teller and audience must be in tune – if they are not, the failure is worse than in any other category. Someone who tries his best to write what he thinks children, or any reader, will actually *like* probably will not succeed; but someone who amuses a child by pleasing himself, as Beatrix Potter did in her letter to Noel Moore, and Kenneth Grahame in his stories told to Alastair, probably will write a classic. There is often a sense in such work of a return to childhood – not that of the reader, but one's own. It is no coincidence that many of the stories in this category originate in tales told to the author's children so that writer and child share a past in the present, a familiar and charming world in which nothing really goes wrong, set in an idealised countryside that the writer has

*People don't eat people – so what kind of diet do humanised carnivores have? C. S. Lewis found a good way out of the dilemma in Narnia.

"Oh yes, please! my dear Ribby; and may I have a lump upon my nose?"

known – for no other reason than that these places and their animal populations were Adorable.

Mr MacGregor's Garden is the most perfect vegetable and flower garden ever seen – its vague topography makes it one's *idea* of what an old-fashioned country garden should be. The interesting adventures that Peter Rabbit had there have, at first sight, a familiar moral basis of filial obedience, but that is not what one remembers them for; it is the rural magic, the delicate beauty of the pictures, the few words, precise and perfect, that describe them, and the idealised view of the longed-for North Country of Beatrix Potter's childhood holidays to which she eventually returned. It is true that there are constant themes of eating or being eaten – Jeremy Fisher's butterfly sandwich, Ribby's mouse pie, Mr Tod's designs on Jemima Puddle-duck or Tommy Brock's or Mr MacGregor's capture of the rabbit babies or Flopsy Bunnies – but these are treated with matter-of-fact unconcern. Sex and death never appear, and one knows that the rabbit babies will be rescued from Tommy Brock's oven. Children may be more struck by the 'unfairness' of Jemima's not being allowed to lay her eggs where she wanted, and their being eaten afterwards by the dog rescuers; on the other hand Squirrel Nutkin, who had been silly and rude, probably deserved to lose his tail to Old Brown. The point has often been made that all these happenings could occur in real life, and perhaps it is in this reality, miniature but distinct, that the magic lies. That this beautiful, idealised place – Lancashire, Westmorland or Cumberland – could and possibly did have these small dramas in lake, burrow and hedgerow made the fantasy more real and the pleasure more possible, the animals' humanity (apart from doubts about Jemima Puddleduck's ability to fly in a shawl) more natural.

Nothing is strange and there are no stereotypes: the humanisation varies and is often blurred. Squirrel Nutkin does not wear clothes at all, neither does Jemima Puddleduck when she and Mr Tod are at their most natural – when she is sitting on her clutch of eggs, or he is turning them over. Tom Kitten and his sisters, forced into best clothes, take them off; the cat Ribby is dressed in a lilac silk gown but her guest Duchess, the little dog, has no clothes at all. Dr Maggotty the Magpie who attends her is discovered putting nails into a bottle of ink and doing, saying and looking no more than what he is – a bird. There is similar ambiguity in the animals' houses. Some of them are real, if idealised, burrows or holes; others, the domestic ones of cats or dogs, are real houses, and there is a slight suggestion in such stories as 'The Pie and the Patty Pan' or 'Ginger and Pickles', that all the inhabitants of Sawrey apart from two children have been turned into animals, or better still were animals anyway. As animals these villagers are charming, delightful, comic, beautiful, simple and pleasing in spite of occasional and quite natural and blameless predatory behaviour. In this kind of transformed world real people would not do: they bring with them all kinds of rivalries and human tensions that would spoil the atmosphere of slightly transformed, almost dreamlike, reality – not quite in the world, yet as clear as one's best memories.

> *She was running, running, running up the hill – and where was her white frilled cap? and her shawl? and her gown – and her petticoat? And how small she had grown – and how covered with Prickles.*

Was it all true, or not? It could have been. This is one of the essential ingredients of nostalgia; the grain of truth has to be there, round which the pearl may form.

The work of Alison Uttley has many of the same strains. There is the same Northern countryside, populated exclusively by small animals living their lives in holes, burrows and tiny houses. Margaret Tempest's illustrations to the *Little Grey Rabbit* books (1929 onwards) have clear, simple attractiveness without the topographical detail that makes Beatrix Potter's lakeland scenery and interiors so much a part of her stories. The animals – rabbits, moles, mice, squirrels and hedgehogs – are engaging, but look rather as if they have been made up and dressed by a soft toy designer. Each book insists on not only 'animal living', but human country life – the fire from wood, water from the well, candles made of rushes. The animals all live in a village community, though there are a few families – the Rats, and the Hedgehogs – among them. The magic truce is observed all the time: no predators, no marauders, Wise Owl does not catch mice, the Rat only steals a few provisions and makes up for it by giving unexpected presents.

All the characters, whether adult or babies, are children in an idealised world where children are never naughty and nothing goes wrong. They live in their playhouses in a rural past surrounded, as in all Alison Uttley's work, with beauty remembered and described.

> *The fire crackled in the chimney, sweet smells filled the kitchen – the scent of the burning logs and the smell of dried lavender which hung from the ceiling and the fragrance of the green holly . . . The silver moon shone down in the white fields making them glitter with a strange and beautiful light.*

Sometimes the animals – Fuzzypeg the hedgehog or the dormouse children – talk in baby language. The Hare, though apparently adult, is an irresponsible adult-child, afraid of his shadow, saying things like 'I think it's time for my birthday. It's weeks and weeks since I had a birthday –' Squirrel, Hare and Rabbit live together, the two ladies adult enough to cook, bake, keep house and do the shopping, yet able to enjoy games, tricks, picnics, circuses and parties, as children would – and as Alison Uttley *did*. There are numerous parallels in *A Country Child* and *Ambush of Young Days*. At Jonathan Rabbit's school the lessons are about flowers and nursery rhymes and there are moral judgements which have little or nothing to do with animal behaviour. The Rat has a knot tied in his tail as a reminder of past wickedness, which only undoes itself, gradually, with each good deed: 'A pity you don't do more work, Rat,' comments Wise Owl rather sternly. And at Christmas: 'Across the snowy fields padded little dark creatures, all filled with curiosity to see the glowing lights in the tree. Some were thin and some were lame, and many were poor, for it had been a hard winter.' One may be sure they went away satisfied.

While lacking Beatrix Potter's essential economy and matter of fact toughness, Alison Uttley has descriptive poetry. Though sometimes almost too 'cosy' in a back-to-the-burrow manner, she introduces elements of folklore and country magic that make some of her stories nearer to animal fairy tale. The feeling is that if we can see ourselves personified by these humble, country animals, we may find a magic that humans have lost; as when the Hare and the

Hedgehog take a walk together at night to watch the corn grow and argue that the ways of men are beyond them. Why do they have those 'tarrible dazzlers on the motors when there's a bright lantern hung in the sky?' they ask; and when Sam Pig (living with his brothers and sister in happy serenity, far from the farmyard) goes to seek his fortune with a cow, a cat, a dog and a wren, he finds fairy gold which turns into kingcups. And the Old Woman and her Little Red Hen sit and exchange stories with each other, unsurprised and with no feeling of Old Mother Hubbard and the Dog in fancy dress: 'The old woman's tales were about the boys and girls she had known in her long life . . . and the little red hen's stories were about the fairy folk and witches and goblins she had met . . .' Sam Pig and Brock the Badger enjoy themselves even more on Guy Fawkes' Day than many children do. Homely delights, the natural world and country magic combine in a way that is full of appealing charm. If only they could speak and we could hear; if only we could live this kind of life instead of imagining small animals in a lost or hidden miniature world; if only hearing and seeing would not spoil it all* and cause it to vanish.

Stories like these do not work without some relation to what animals are really like, but human intrusion destroys the illusion that the small, busy, delightful world is real. 'Miss Potter' is only there, in the distance, sometimes. The Two Bad Mice play in the doll's house while the owner is away. The same Lilliputian pleasure can be transported into a suburban setting too, admirably illustrated by Frank Rogers's 'Robin Family' series (*Woman's Weekly*, from 1940). Never were birds more human, more birdlike. The Robins live an idealised village/suburban life in Tree Stump Cottage and go to school at Miss Owl's – Athene's emblem can never escape being credited with wisdom, though in the case of Wol it was credit only – and are taught by Mr Rook and Miss Thrush. They go to the seaside for their holidays in the family car and spend the time at Sandhopper Bay with never a human in sight. They do everything that children do, passing through the year in the company of their sparrow, mouse, hedgehog and frog friends in perfect bliss. The Woodland is not quite the country – and village life has fewer

*As hearing and seeing usually do. The Beatrix Potter film is a case in point; people being animals being people gives a strange ambiguous awkwardness to something virtually perfect as it was, untouched.

shopping and sports days – but it gets snowbound, flooded and shows signs of spring and autumn in the usual way. What the Robins *do* has little relation to what they *are* – they're birds, but a human family made perfect, having Christmas, Easter, birthdays and Hallowe'en and doing Good (they look after an Old Age Pensioner, Mrs Woodmouse, a Granny figure perpetually sunny and well disposed, never crochety or awkward). Their world has its own dates, history and public figures (Emperor Penguin and the great soldier General Eagle), and never once do large, awkward humans intrude. Charm almost cloys, but not quite. Mrs Rogers must be the only artist ever to dress a bird successfully. The distinction of the drawings outshines the narrative. The Little Robins – with their tails, feathers for arms and bird toes often thrust into Wellington boots which even make concession to what a bird's foot is *like* – are birds all the time, never distorted, altered or made to look silly. The Woodland may be Shere or Finchingfield or Tunbridge Wells but it has an intense reality which never falters or changes; it is the setting for a rare and successful bird fantasy exactly *like* life but with the tiny, doll's house improvements which make this kind of art so pleasing.

Even more suburbanised is Russell Hoban's *Frances* where the child/animal substitution is so complete as to be unnoticeable. Frances the Badger is a small girl afraid of the dark, tucked up in bed but constantly annoying her parents by coming downstairs and interrupting the television. Why make her into an animal at all? The cosy delights of the Badger household – so like a human one – do remove the situation one or two degrees away from discomfort; some children are afraid of the dark, do dislike being alone. Frances's friendship with the moon, stars, wind and shadows seems entirely natural in this context, as does Tim Rabbit's friendship with hail, thunder and lightning, in Alison Uttley. Animals of their very nature sometimes seem older than we are and essentially reassuring, full of moral as well as physical comfort; and the Badger parents have the trusted solidity of that favourite personified animal – the Teddy bear.

If humans could inhabit their own doll's houses they would be small enough to observe, and even join – what? Few have handled this theme with any kind of realism. The Borrowers and the Lilliputians are not part of the human race; their traditions and customs are their own. S. H. Skaife's *The Strange Old Man* (1930) makes the human characters small enough – by a reducing drug – to live in a doll's house at the bottom of the garden and see nature as it really is. The insects, birds and small animals they meet are not at all cosy, and life is full of peril and excitement. It is impossible to pretend, when presenting a disguised natural history lesson, that the world is anything but strange, ruthless, wonderful, sometimes ugly and dangerous.

However, these animal societies that are happening somewhere in the grass or at the back of the cupboard or in a doll's house are spoiled by human intervention. They really don't need it. The most specialised branch of this kind of story, the Mouse Tale, nearly always includes heroic endeavour against giants – the humans – who have to be natural, real and large. But I include here three stories about small eccentrics who depend on human interaction while still having independent lives – in other words, they are not really pets, but have the delights of miniature living as a strong ingredient, while they use the human world to achieve an eventual fame.

The Packet family in Margaret Baker's *Snails Place* (1970) live in a post-box and have a rather Victorian flavour, full of gentle humour with their old-fashioned, Latin-quoting father and quite literal application to their letters. Though they do not become as famous as Samuel the Snail or Chester the Cricket, they do stow away in air mail to reach America, the sort of thing Samuel would have done had he thought of it. Slowness and small size are no disadvantage to the Packets. Margaret Baker has a fine gift for lending her characters movement and credibility, though they be immobile as snails, tortoises or Teddy bears. It is easy for a child to believe in slugs' and snails' secret lives if he can imagine everything going on just beyond the bounds of sight; that the snails on the garden path are on their way to a secret rendezvous; that the bears propped up outside the grocers are doing it on purpose to deceive one into thinking that they are not out on one of their secret walks, but have just been left there.

Hugh E. Wright's Samuel, in *The Interminable Trudge of Samuel the Snail*, 1936, becomes famous indeed, and the fact that people have *heard* of him becomes the occasional way out in difficult situations. He has only to say 'I'm Samuel', and people help him, policemen do his bidding, though his world is mainly 'the garden' – the same pleasant, orderly microcosm that Sarah Trimmer's Robin family lived in. These funny, lively stories are full of the optimistic, fanciful nonsense of the golden age of radio. Written to be broadcast, they have a surrealistic comedy that can only be appreciated imaginatively and not pictorially. There is social comment too that sets the scene. Houses are being turned into flats and the snail does the same to his shell. Samuel's home is near a wall and his friends are birds and insects. He lets his shell to an earwig (on the attic floor) and a rather military centipede, a Colonel given to 'stalking off to his club' when things go wrong, who likes shooting stag beetles. The comedy is punning and literal. 'It was a very large gun. "Kicks like a grasshopper," said the Colonel proudly. Unfortunately it was very rusty and the Colonel had to take all his boots off, wrap his feet in oily cotton wool and crawl through it half a dozen times to clean it.'

Engaged to take the Colonel on a shooting holiday, Samuel climbs the wall and crosses a road ('If only there were a Belisha Beacon – but there wasn't. "Careless of Belisha," said the Colonel'). Samuel is always being mistaken for knobs – on BBC switchboards, naturally, and also those at the top of policemen's helmets, on one of which he rides to see King George V's Silver Jubilee. 'The Depression' is blamed for mishaps, and at the seaside he meets a gull who is complaining of 'Empire Broadcasts' which fill the atmosphere without a by-your-leave. 'Low waves they call them,' he remarks. 'They are that.'

Samuel – irrepressible, indefatigable as Archy the Cockroach, never at a loss – is sometimes more of a mascot come to life than an animal. True to type, for this is not Archy's New York, there is no real harm or danger. The tide may come in, but Samuel is not drowned. He crosses the road and is not stepped on. He falls from a height and merely bounces. Eating or being eaten is ignored or passed off as comedy:

'One dallies with this and that,' said the Pigeon, and pecked hard at a passing grub. 'Oh, live and let live.'
'But you didn't let him live,' said Samuel. 'That's it – no thought.'
'Oh, but I thought of letting me live,' explained the Pigeon. 'And me being hungry, and he being handy.'

On his journey to London in the heart of a lettuce, Samuel meets a cockney Thrush:

'Hi, I'm Samuel,' said Samuel.

'Nice to know the name before lunch in a manner of speaking,' said the Thrush, 'but I expect you'd taste much the same if you was George.'

'But I'm going to the Jubilee,' said Samuel.

'Oh! That's different. Wouldn't care to go with me – inside?'

This is animal clowning; under the circumstances, it has to be. Chester the Cricket in George Selden's *The Cricket in Times Square* (1960) has, in its way, more reality. There are no houses, shells, burrows or holes – their place is taken by the New York subway, a news-stand in the station at Times Square, and a drainpipe home of a mouse called Tucker who, unlike most fictional mice, is neither neat nor good at housekeeping. His hole is a magpie nest of odd-ments picked up from the subway station: lost jewellery, money, buttons, scraps and bits of food. Nearly all the action takes place underground, and in man-made surroundings.

Tucker meets a cricket from Connecticut who has jumped off a train, and they both become friends with a roving cat, Harry, a fugitive from the East Side who shares the drainpipe with the mouse. The drama and amusement of the story come from the three creatures' adventures with, and observation of, the Italian family who own the news-stand. There is nothing unlikely in the scaveng-ing animals living below ground and existing on scraps humans throw away, or the helpless insect's being carried there in a picnic sandwich. Fantasy only lies in their friendship, their ability to under-stand each other and talk and comment on the humans, and the rosy glow that this imparts to a reality that must have been hard and uncompromising. The unnatural nature of the cat/mouse friendship is, indeed, attributed to non-natural New York. 'In New York we gave up these old habits long ago.'

Chester learns to chirp in tune and play the classics, achieving eventual fame; but eccentrics or stars are in a minority. Homely virtues are the rule and illustrators come into their own, as does Ernest Shepard with *Ben and Brock*, 1965. At first it seems that Mr Badger has risen again, but when one reads instead of looking, it is not so. Mr Brock, marauding, pushing through into the garden and digging up tulip bulbs, is at first much more of an animal than the Toad's guardian and friend. But then comes the clever size equation (used to such effect in the illustrations of *The Wind in the Willows*) and the boy Ben, of about equal height, is following Mr Brock to his underground house and meeting Mrs Brock and learning the family history in one of those cosy burrows that we know so well. The smaller, working-class Victorian kitchen or parlour would appear, to a modern child, to have all the warm, dark earthiness of rabbit hole or badger sett. Sharing this dwelling is the lodger, too, one of the most engaging insect creations; the musical black beetle Mr Pipe, of few words, long hair and glasses. His extra arms help him while playing the organ and other instruments, especially percussion and tympani, and also with composing, as he writes up to four instrumental parts simultaneously – all this while never looking very different from the beetle that got away from Christopher Robin's Nanny. A full-size human policeman does not think any of these characters odd. When his luck turns, Mr Brock ends up in the Royal Enclosure at Ascot, with his wife appropriately dressed. Strangeness and magic have no part in these fantasies; visual pleasure is strong.

'B.B.', Denys Watkins Pitchford, has very similar qualities in *The Little Grey Men*, and other books that deal with river banks. The magic is of a natural kind, the miniature delights exactly described with some of the excitements of the adventurous life that small animals really lead, whether they will or no. Women writers in this genre still like to write the improving tale or slip a moral in somewhere like the gritty grey powder under the jam. Men perhaps find it harder to abandon cops and robbers. The 'Mr Toad' chapters of *The Wind in the Willows* are full of crime, chase, escape and pursuit in cars and trains, and 'B.B.' and Alison Uttley, united in their understanding of what it might be like to live among the grass and wild flowers of field and river bank, show these two characteristic strains. Alison Uttley's neatly dressed Little Brown Mouse and Little Grey Rabbit not only *are* good – they go round doing good. 'B.B.'s *Bill Badger* books, 1958 onwards, indulge in the animal adventure plot that kept Mr Toad on the run, without too much of the strange, disturbing human fantasy that makes the Toad and his friends sometimes too memorable for comfort.

In the beautiful *Little Grey Men*, 1942, 'B.B.' enters into river bank life (with an apology for giving the animals powers of speech) quite as intimately as Kenneth Grahame. The three gnomes who explore the Folly Brook looking for their lost brother are as near to being small animals – voles perhaps – as it is possible to be. There is none of the human parody of *The Wind in the Willows*, no depths, no mysticism, but considerable delight and accurate description of a tiny, enclosed world. The escapes and dangers are from giants – Colonel, Gamekeeper and Pike – and there is astonishing sympathy with the reedy, weedy, watery world of lush growth and dark woods. The small creatures never leave it – as, in real life, they would never leave their natural cover.

But Bill Badger has robust, Toad of Toad Hall adventures with no pretence that the animals are anything other than human stand-ins. The charm of river bank and country living is there, but Bill's battles with his enemies, the criminal cats Big Ginger and Napoleon are pure adventure, and at times unlikely. However, the animal convention has the twofold advantage here of giving the chief characters instant interest and ready-made typecasting, while removing the whole story into a slightly miniaturised world so that the events do not seem quite as impossible as if humans were taking part. Bill

Badger, on his barge *Wandering Wind* on the Junction Canal, is badger enough to scent out his enemies rather than notice them, and his hedgehog companion likes to roll into a ball when nervous. But otherwise, though their barge is smaller and more like a toy than real, they lead human enough lives. The hedgehog Izzybizzy was once a roadmender living in lodgings, and their enemy cats drive lorries (road haulage being the anathema of the canal trade), and go to, and escape from, prison. The towpath has rabbits going to school along it as well as humans going to work. The reminder that on a fine, sunny day the animals enjoy life without a care in the world ('except where their next meal was coming from, or who was going to gobble them up') seems rather a surprise; Bill's routine money worries seem more natural.

There are many similarities to Grahame – the river life, the animals' apparent ability to change size* so that they take lifts in cars and trains, use firearms, join humans in public bars without being unduly noticed or embarrassed. These are all part of the convention that gave Toad's adventures a momentum which, for a while, made one forget the great gap that kept the Mole and Rat outside the human houses in the village one winter's night, looking wistfully in. The lack of female characters is also part of the river bank myth; a spinster weasel called Little Drizzle and the gangster cats disguised as a Mothers' Union outing are mere comic relief. There is a good deal of unnatural fighting with guns, swords, cannon and – it is a watery story – torpedoes; but one cannot forget the heavily armed Rat, Mole and Badger, the gun-carrying sentries at Toad Hall, the armed, pursuing policemen on the train. There are precedents for this sort of thing.

Too much has been written already about *The Wind in the Willows* (1905), and Kenneth Grahame's inability to grow up, for much to be added. The book is a unique blend of many different kinds of animal story in which most of the rules are successfully broken. The river bank idyll, the Wild Wooders who are the awful, multifaced Them, Toad's adventures, the mysticism of the Piper at the Gates – all combine into something that no one who has read it at the right ages ever forgets.

*A perpetual problem, dealt with successfully by Elizabeth Beresford in 'The Wombles' and Michael Bond in the *Thursday* books. Both authors give, and keep to, exact dimensions – no cheating.

Few come to this book in adult life. One always has with this, as with many others, two views, one coloured by childhood, biased because enjoyment was so complete. What I best liked then, I like still, through many re-readings: Mole alone in the Wild Wood menaced by Them and rescued and comforted by the Rat and the Badger whose underground home runs beneath the Wood in many directions and so encompasses it and makes it harmless; Mole's nostalgia for his hole and its eventual discovery by the Rat (these incidents have the adorable ingredient which leads one to build Mouse Towns); Toad's ebullient conceit and quick deflation, only to rise again irrepressibly, and his final modesty, far more effective than any other possible behaviour. I cast myself at once into the story as the Mole and his failures and successes were mine. I did not like, and still do not, the Piper at the Gates and Wayfarers All. Politeness to the author compels me to read them every time I re-read the book, but, immune to their adult appeal, I wished these two odd chapters, which bored me, had not been there.

I had what I now think must have been an intuitive rather than intelligent liking for *The Golden Age*, not usually thought of as a children's book. 'The Olympians' summed up exactly what one felt about the adult Them – that having reached such heights, they could only think of boring things to do. I still think this. The odd part is that when as an adult one reads *The Wind in the Willows* one realises that it is a very strange book: the animals are Olympians, middle-aged men living in what must be early retirement, earning nothing, paying for nothing, doing nothing as becomes animals, yet very much involved with the real world, strolling along roads, eating at hotels, taking part in court actions, all a perpetual Utopian childhood – and like the Olympians, they have not found anything particularly constructive to do. Messing about in boats, singing songs to ducks, taking country walks, indulging in vast picnics and meals full of the poetry of buttered toast – any child could improve on this. Yet there is a fascination in seeing what the adult animals, given a limitless holiday, are doing.

For animals, read chaps, and highly unusual chaps they are. Schizophrenic Rat, childlike Mole, manic depressive Toad and lordly, ill-mannered Badger – they are all rather eccentric, not quite the kind of chap one meets in the human world. Yet perhaps there was some time in the past between Now and 1905 – when rivers

were quiet and deserted, motor cars a rarity and people could live in Jacobean mansions with money to indulge their expensive tastes – when chaps like these could live and flourish naturally. It is a place where sex, money and politics do not exist – they are banished to the Wide World where nobody with any sense ever goes.

The trouble that penetrates this Utopia is all intrusion and consists of things, or people, that upset the perpetual holiday; the doings of Toad and his involvements with the law, the innocent wanderings of Mole, the brief mob-rule of the weasels, stoats and ferrets, threats to the sunny lives of these Edwardian gentlemen easily dealt with and quickly dispatched to their rightful place in the order of things so that even the Toad, traitor to his class, is rendered meek and harmless. In the final pages, when the animals 'take a stroll together in the Wild Wood . . . it was pleasing to see how respectfully they were greeted by the inhabitants'. Their old enemies have been defeated and all is well.

But the book's being a period piece – as it has been since the First World War irrevocably altered the social order of which it is an illustration and an ornament – does not invalidate the strength and many dimensions of the four main characters. How they stayed in one's mind: Badger the father figure doing things 'For Your Own Good', who seemed to own everything in the Wild Wood and to have real, but not titular power; simple Mole who thought more than he spoke; Rat quick and practical, rather condescending (like certain Uncles with a brisk genius for making one feel small and inept) yet with real kindness and an odd, frightening poetic streak and an hysterical cracking point; and Toad, so charming, conceited yet even in his conceit, lovable, like those noisy extroverts with (one's elders pointed out) more money than was good for them, and ostentatious (when that was a sin worse than the cunning displayed in evading captors). They are, as C. S. Lewis says in *Three Ways of Writing for Children* (1959), 'an admirable hieroglyphic which conveys psychology . . . more briefly than novelistic presentation and to readers whom novelistic presentation could not yet reach. Consider Mr Badger . . . that extraordinary amalgam of high rank, coarse manners, gruffness, shyness and goodness. The child who has once met Mr Badger has ever afterwards, in its bones, a knowledge of humanity and of English social history which it could not get in any other way.'

Ernest Shepard's drawings admit one into the small world of river bank growth, hedgerow, wood and burrow, and yet make the purely human action credible. Toad's imprisonment in the Tower of London, his washerwoman adventures and escape by train and horse, where his creator is himself carried away and forgetful of the nature of his hero, are made believable, if charadelike, by a growth in the size of the animals and a lessening of the humans.

A. A. Milne's much-maligned play manages to convey a great

deal of the action of the book, cleverly condensed, admirably capturing the humour but eliminating the numinous elements. Toad is the hero, and the final scene which shows him not at all subdued, but triumphing, has a pleasing rightness that is in keeping with the delightful comedy of such scenes as the trial, the canal bank, the secret passage and the banquet – all much funnier but less memorable than Grahame. The mystery of the Wild Wood has gone – Dulce Domum is reduced to a short soliloquy – the Piper at the Gates is missing (and so is Wayfarers All – indeed the Rat, it can be argued, is more *likeable* in the stage version) but the humour and truth of the animal characterisations are there. However, children should read the book first, or they will miss the quality that no stage adaptation can convey.

8 Lilliputian Life: the Mouse Story

This work of art was a penwiper. It showed a black velvet mouse with beady eyes, lying on a circular mat of leaves of cloth which wiped the pen. The Mouse was the glory of the work. Art could hardly go further than that mouse. Often I was welcomed there to look at the mouse, to stroke it and admire its lifelike eyes and the miraculous likeness to a mouse . . . mice meant much to me as a child, multitudes of little mice behaving like men.

Grace before Ploughing, *John Masefield*

'Supposing' (said the boy) 'you saw a little man, about as tall as a pencil, with a blue patch in his trousers, half way up a window curtain, carrying a doll's teacup—would you say it was a fairy?'
  'No,' said Arietty, 'I'd say it was my father.'

The Borrowers, *Mary Norton*

Mice are small, secret, numerous and usually hidden. They are beautiful and neat and, one must feel, courageous to live with us so closely. Their fur-coated bodies make them endearing and strokeable. Stories about them outnumber those about any other kind of animal: perhaps it is easier to imagine them members of their own hidden social systems and to think that when out of sight they might be a part of a miniature mirror world. Their fur and appearance helps them to win our love, their apparently timorous and desperate courage, our sympathy; and they are easy to 'dress'. It is difficult to visualise hairless or armoured creatures or those with more than four legs in a society that is in any way like our own. Mice have an almost unfair advantage. Under the imagined clothes (and mouse stories are much concerned with clothes and furniture) there is the soft but sexless strokeable layer.

  If you are going to imagine a small or parallel society, mice make useful pawns for its population. No other small creatures are as appealing and versatile, from Aesop onwards, and as new versions of Aesop have always been popular – the Town and Country Mouse story is the one most often repeated – the mice will lend themselves to any fashion and copy the humans of any era, from Robert Henryson's Scotland of the fifteenth century, to the late Victorian England of 'Miss Browne'. Thus *The Mice and their Pic-Nic* written in 1810 by 'A Looking Glass Maker' (Mary Belson) is the Town and Country Mouse brought up to that date, but is also 'An Allegorical tale representing the Manners and Customs of the Present Age'. The mice are members of fashionable and bucolic society; at times, during these pleasing verses, one forgets that they are mice at all. Mr Sleek, the city mouse, is a smooth talker:

> *The rustic assembly were charm'd with his grace*
> *And guess'd London to be a most elegant place,*

where they meet such characters as Captain Frisk and Major Dareall. Twenty mice go to London, travelling in straw bottle-cases; few return from the London season. The manners of the guests are subjected to fashionable jeers:

> *Mr Sleek call'd for silence, and then with town grace*
> *Arrang'd all his guests in due order and place.*
> *With affected grimace, which he meant should confuse*
> *He requested to know 'What Miss Roundhead would chuse?'*
> *Who quite unacquainted with half what she saw*
> *Made choice of cold bacon, while Lady Soft-paw*
> *Roundly tittering, whispered 'The mere country elf,*
> *Prefers eating hog, because most like herself.'*

Sixty-five years later Charles Bennet was giving Aesop the same treatment with his strange, unnerving illustrations of fashionable Victorian London; but here, hand-coloured woodcuts (done, as we are reminded by Harvey Darton, by assembly lines of children with paint brushes) remind the reader that the story is about barns, kitchens, horrific cats and cooks and that the fashionable, well-bred epicures are living as dangerously as mice always do. Their 'society' is unreal; the mice have been 'used' to say something rather bleak, or rather amusing, about human nature.

Beatrix Potter does not 'use' the mice so much as the framework of the fable; 'Johnny Town Mouse' is more a story about different types of mice than different kinds of human. Johnny Town Mouse – in dark coat, and bowler hat – and Timmy Willie (unclothed) are house- and fieldmouse, moving to stay with each other by means of a vegetable hamper (problems of transport in mouse societies are considerable). This of course could have happened, and perhaps did, in reality, as with all Beatrix Potter's stories. Town society is shown to be noisy, dangerous and given to what is now called Conspicuous Waste: 'The continual noise upstairs made him so nervous that he dropped a plate. "Never mind, they don't belong to us," said Johnny.' The country is too quiet for Johnny, who, after his visit to Timmy, quickly returns home.

Michael Bond uses this plot in one of the *Thursday* books when an up-to-date American mouse tries to turn a village shop into a supermarket – at mouse level – and everyone decides that it was better as it was before. But Mr Bond's Mouse Society is fairly secure – there is little peril from cats or humans. More interesting human parallels occur in Ursula Moray Williams's *Oh For a Mouse-less House* (1954). The mouse society here co-exists with the human one – as in Margery Sharpe's *Miss Bianca* books – and is dependent on it, but always in hiding. The story combines a very human situation with the charm of a story such as *The Tailor of Gloucester* in which mice give humans delicate, diligent and multifingered help.

Here, the society is fairly complex in that there are two conflicting armies: a delinquent group of large mice from down the hill who usurp the homes of the house mice and drive them into the church, where the church mice, spare, thin, respectable and hard working, always ready to listen to sermons, give them asylum. The battle between the two sets, involving the Vicar, parishioners, the Vicar's nephew and formidable Mother, is worked out with some art. The church is deserted by humans, except for the Vicar's solitary Sunday sermons. From a protected playground – 'the older church mice realised that whole generations of mouse children had never seen a trap' – it turns into a battlefield: the church mice with their pew and pulpit families and Bible names, and church council or Mouncil, wearing themselves thin with their efforts to tidy up, scour, sew and polish; the huge, wicked invaders, laconic dustbin loungers with their boss, Bucky, trying to get in, and when succeeding, turning the church into a fairground.

Sympathetic but unwitting humans become agents for one side or the other as the siege is waged with attacks, storming, starvation and trickery; the gallant defenders faithful to the last against the wicked mouse Baron. The human plot – a vanished congregation, stirred up and shamed into returning by the Vicar's dragooning mother – becomes insignificant beside the story of the invaders and the brave last stand of the church mice. No characters emerge and there are few domestic details but a strong feeling that the mouse society and its attackers are commenting on the present by living in the human past where the church is a medieval castle under siege. The mouse doings are as archaic as the stone crusader in the aisle and the church is similarly out of date. No message is perhaps intended. Animal societies that are in tune with topical events are quite rare – Michael Bond's *Thursday* again comes to mind.

When mice are not populating a mirror world, sheer charm and smallness take over – the small size often being allied to courage and resourcefulness. Mice are useful characters who, if you have a doll's house, will come and inhabit it for you. At its most crude, the small character is the one who is forever outwitting the larger one, as in Tom and Jerry. More delicately, mice will become actors in tales where miniature life is enjoyed for its own sake. Some, feeling the pleasure of this idea, have used miniature humans for the purpose (*The Borrowers*, *Mistress Masham's Repose*) or invented a different species (Wombles, and rather larger, Hobbits). Where mice are the author's first love one finds such passages as the following, from Masefield's *The Midnight Folk*, 1927:

> *What on earth was happening to the model of the Plunderer? He could see that the water had reached her on the wall: she was afloat. She seemed to be alive with little tiny men, all busy with ropes. No, they were not men, they were little mice, 'water-mice, I suppose,' he thought. Now she was coming across the stream to him; and how big she was, or, no, how little he was; he was no bigger than the water-mice.*

Kay is transported on the model boat with mouse-crew to the Gulf of Mexico to search for lost treasure with a diving bell that has somehow increased to normal, human size – as have the crew – on arrival. There is a strong feeling in this book of animals and toys, all smaller than real, taking a stand against People, and of course the mice are on the right side; they are seldom evil characters. Hunca Munca and Tom Thumb were merely amoral.

Beatrix Potter's mice, drawn from life and greatly loved, have an almost physical reality. Beneath their charming clothes the mouse bodies are there, anatomically correct in every detail, with all the most pleasing mouse qualities and none of the messy ones. They are frugal, particular, busy: Mrs Tittlemouse sleeps in a tiny box bed with her tiny shoes, brush and pan ranged beside her, and all the other rooms and passages that are invaded so annoyingly by stray insects, bees, spiders and beetles, are part of the bottom of a hedge-row, and as real as all the other lairs, holes and burrows that Beatrix Potter drew. One can learn how fieldmice live by reading Mrs Tittlemouse, but there is little room for personality; smallness is all. 'It were too tiny,' as Bruno said, to hold as much as Margery Sharpe gives her far more humanised species. From Beatrix Potter one learns that mice are timid, clean, charming, ubiquitous and wholly delightful as a species, but their minute clothes are a pretty conceit rather than a means of self-expression. The mice on the Tailor's dresser, who bow and curtsey so gracefully in their eighteenth-century clothes, scamper off down their hole in bare fur as soon as the Tailor's back is turned; the clothes are only there while we look at them.

Hunca Munca and Tom Thumb are even more real and natural, with Norman Warne's doll's house for them to rob. In a few drawings Hunca Munca has a housewifely gown to wear – it really belongs to one of the dolls – when she has stolen the doll's house furniture for her own nest. Otherwise these two disgraceful animals wreak havoc in Mouse fashion with the help of human hands and bad temper. Few who have owned doll's houses and pet mice have not thought of combining the two; the inevitable results are shown here – the mice like naughty children, the dolls unchangeably doll-like. The immortal line about the lobsters, the ham, the fish, the pudding and the fruit, 'They would not come off the plates but they were extremely beautiful', is a definitive summary of what all doll's houses are like – appealing to the eye but firmly defeating all four of the other senses, as the two bad mice discover.

Other mouse artists, Ernest Aris and Harry Rountree, gave their creations more personality, less of the mouse *quality*; Rountree's mice drawn for Mansion and Cherry Blossom polish have comedy of a gently human kind. Dressed in clothes of the era 1914 to 1925 and nearly always with shoes that were too large (to show off the greatest area of shine?) they stared with happy pride at each other's reflections in mirrorlike floors and tables. They had the elongated, rather human faces that Beatrix Potter would never have drawn; and yet they are not by any means caricatures. Ernest Aris's children's books – mainly about mice, though other small creatures occur – were written and illustrated about the time of the First World War. The mouse children have a ragamuffin look, rather like the original Bisto Kids, again with clothes and shoes rather too large for them in the children's styles of 1916 – boy mice in rather baggy trousers, girl mice in smocked pinafores. In their field and hedgerow settings they are very 'real', but their eyes are human.* Drawing of wild flowers, moths, leaves, insects and other animals is impeccable and beautiful and the stories have a slightly romantic element quite lacking in Beatrix Potter. Ernest Aris let his mice leave home to seek their fortunes, or a mysterious Good Fairy, or let them be enticed into a dark wood by a stag beetle bent on vengeance – menacingly and accurately drawn but not in the right decade to be the one that frightened C. S. Lewis as a child.

Mouse speed, desperation and courage are distinct from mouse charm, and develop when the mouse society interacts with the human one, the braver mice making forays and doing deeds of great daring, disregarding the perils of humans and cats much in the same way as professional soldiers come to disregard the possible perils of battle. There is a bouncing comedy in the situation which comes out perfectly in the *Thursday* books and with more subtle wit in the *Miss Bianca* saga. Eve Titus's *Anatole* (1956 onwards) manages to combine cheeky thieving with being a human friend – a situation which is not at all unknown. Anatole and his friends are contemporary characters – wherever humans are, there they will be. Their adventures are a comic mixture of fantasy and mouse action. Anatole is an *important* mouse, friend of humans, chief taster at Duval's cheese factory. He changes his apparent size at will, with no questions asked – he and his wife and six children can go on a cycling

*By this I mean that they have cornea, iris and pupil; the effect is a compromise of human expressiveness in a mouse face, and quite acceptable. When this is overdone in the coy, almond eyes of Disney animals, the sinister manic stare of Louis Wain cats, or rather arch appearance of Racey Phelps's woodland creatures who have large eyes with glasses, monocles, human crows' feet smiles, the effect is rather disagreeable.

The Wee Babes in the Wood

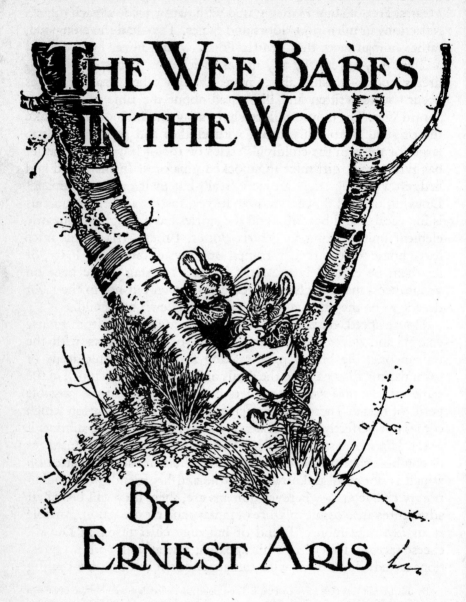

By Ernest Aris

holiday or dash to and fro on their bicycles to round up smuggling criminals. But they can use their small size to hide, explore and listen, and throughout are seldom *seen*. They write notes to the police and live in a mouse village of miniature French houses – a real Snug Town that is somewhere in limbo, or hidden; no cupboards, wainscots or cellars for them. This, to me, has neither one kind of reality nor the other, and for all its amusement has not the true charm of the genre.

Stories which combine the three strains – small size, busy courage and daring and the multitudinous life that makes it so easy to imagine mouse towns or societies near us and yet just out of sight – are the most successful and memorable. Rumer Godden's *The Mousewife*, retold and developed from Dorothy Wordsworth's story of the friendship between the mouse and the pigeon, though short, has all three. The story is touching, beautifully told and has deep human implications. The Mousewife does nothing that mice do not, or could not do, stealing the food from the dove's cage and eventually – her presence tolerated – jumping on the catch so that the dove is free and flies away. The human parallel is not explicit, yet it is there. The mouse is free (mice in stories usually are, even in the *Miss Bianca* books – the bars of her cage are far enough apart for her to slip through) and the dove is trapped. Yet the Mousewife has a routine, cramped, circumscribed existence; there are no cats or traps, but there is no true freedom either. The Mousewife's husband is even worse, because his mind is cramped, too. 'I think about cheese,' he says. 'Why don't you think about cheese?' or 'The proper place for a mousewife is in her hole, or coming out for crumbs and frolic with me.'

The busy little Mousewife, so occupied with foraging and care, ends by having some conception of what the outside world is like through the dove's escape. Freedom, flight, wind, stars, have a meaning that the mouse can guess at, even if she can never experience it. One cannot say that Dorothy Wordsworth, or Rumer Godden have 'used' mice to say things about humans; the mice were there first, and one can read into the story what one wishes.

Mice who do stand out for their individuality and sheer strength of character sometimes appear in other settings; The Mouse and His Child of the unforgettable endurance are really toys and not mice at all; the great Reepicheep is a Talking Beast, one of many;

Stuart Little is notable for being a social misfit and Tucker, of *The Cricket in Times Square*, outstanding for his untidy antique collection and his hidden riches. The mouse stories, about the small hidden society, the courage of its citizens and their minuscule daintiness have a flavour of their own; often characters do not emerge. The quality of Lilliput and the delight of smallness which makes objects increase in pleasure and value in inverse proportion to their size so that a human size is useful, child's size agreeable, doll size delightful and doll's house size a work of art, outweigh the other considerations of Gulliver's first voyage. Smallness is of no particular interest without something to measure it by, and both Mary Norton's and T. H. White's miniature fantasies are in retreat from life of average size, and have to hide from it. Contact with humans is in some way fatal – mouse societies are the same. The People in T. H. White's *Mistress Masham's Repose*, 1947, a colony of Lilliputians living on an island, are self-sufficient until contact with the child Maria encourages them to make use of human artefacts, not always to their advantage. Mary Norton's *The Borrowers*, 1952, experience the same thing. When the precious balance is upset – when Homily, Pod and Arrietty have their home filled with doll's house furniture by the Boy, when the People are overwhelmed with gifts from Woolworths – the relationship has to end and the small retreats from the larger.

The two most notable mouse fantasies, the *Thursday* and *Miss Bianca* books, manage to evade this problem by limiting human contacts – though the humans are always there, and with them great excitement and great danger. Michael Bond, on the whole, shrugs off human society in the *Thursday* books (1966 onwards). The humans are a race of giants known as the Grumblies; but they have thoughtfully provided a world that can be copied. Like the Borrowers, Mr Bond's mice are unoriginal, and very human; yet no other mouse stories to my mind bring out the bright, swift, eager, jerky quality of mice, their fecundity with their enormous ever multiplying families and the inevitable shortness of their lives. There is the casual naming of Thursday's mouse family from A to Z and the equally casual attitude of the mice when some of their number 'go missing'. And the narrative rushes from point to point with mouse speed, mouse energy, while gently caricaturing human endeavour and human triviality; the world is a human one, scaled down.

Mr Bond's comic style and choice of incident has similarities to his *Paddington* books, but the effect is oddly different. The bear is awkwardly lovable and the mice, with similar messy cumulative slapstick, dart like quicksilver and spend most of their time, when not involved in noisy, rollicking action, in shrill conversation, full of Town Mouse wit. Here is a sub-world, or echo of the human one. Forget that it is populated by mice and substitute people and it would be almost as full of action, losing little of its comedy. But, of course, these adventures could not happen to people; or could they? Children would not believe that such a society or village full of characters would do things like trying to reach the moon in a rocket made of tins, go strawberry picking in a coach that is a home-made car and part of a grandstand, stay in a holiday camp that is *really* a prison camp (and not just *like* one, as so many comedians suggest); it is all too unlikely. But make the characters small, and the way is open for a comic copy of life in its more hilarious and exciting aspects. Make the characters *mice* who are traditionally attached to, yet enemies of, people, so that there is a certain state of war, chase and elusiveness, and then the comedy has a different dimension.

The mice copy the human world, enjoy cheeky exploitation of human devices. At times they get their copy right and at times better; sometimes the copy is not quite right in its details, things go wrong and the mouse society is in hazard (their police force seems to be lacking, for one thing; there is plenty of successful crime which is, in the end, put down by ingenuity rather than law).

Thursday, a mouse with far to go (he comes from a home for Waifs and Strays *not* the Church of England Children's Society), is adopted into the Peck family who have children for every letter of the alphabet and live in an organ loft. Thursday is an adventurous mouse with none of the traditional mouse timidity (which is really not true of actual mice – they are bold; and speed rather than shyness is their defence). He leads the Peck family into various escapades which, while being human in nature, do not depend on the real existence of humans other than an ever watchful reference to the giant race from whom the mice get their ideas and sustenance.

Characters are few, action is more important than detail. Mr and Mrs Peck, heads of the family, are almost as unaccented as Mr and Mrs Brown of the *Paddington* books. The *Thursday* stories deal with

6

such aspects of human life as television, package tours, a moon rocket, a floating holiday camp, car-and-boat building, opposition by a gangland racketeer. Why write about mice when what pleases you most – and this pleasure comes through very strongly in the stories – is cars and boats, escapes from death, adventures in gangland and gadgets that work with a kind of slapstick ingenuity? Norman Hunter's Professor Branestawm stories do as much, with no animals at all. The mice's moon rocket made of baked-bean tins cannot do much harm, a supermarket reached through a ground-level ventilation grid is not going to spoil the environment or cause a parking problem in the High Street. And if one has thought of a tiny Show Boat, a minute car, a smuggling racket in cheese, mice seem the right creatures to operate such things; they give the comedy a second layer. They are nimble, bright, dashing, sharp as needles, they bounce in and out of situations which would crush a human or Borrower, such as being dropped from heights, fired from a cannon, shot up on a champagne cork, electrified by a guitar with crossed leads, with what amounts to a cartoon immunity from pain. (Harris's loss of a leg in the moon rocket adventure strikes a false note – and also brings in one of the few human contacts in the saga: 'We'd better get him to the Vet at once.' The mice's casual attitude to loss seems quite natural; Uncle Ponty wears three black armbands at once when three mouse children disappear, but seems otherwise unaffected. The family's Victorian fertility will soon replace those who are missing.)

The style of the stories hurries too fast to avoid the cliches which swarm almost unnoticed in the rush; and who cares, anyway? One wants to see what Thursday and Harris are going to do next. Offending articles, renewed paroxysms and vicelike grips jostle happily in the background. When the car is being built Gleaming Monster happens more than once and one expects, and greets, Nerve Shattering Roar with joy, as from *The Boys' Own Paper*.

However far-fetched the incidents – though always founded on the brighter, more exciting aspects of human fact and fiction – the message is always quite clear: Copy the humans too closely and you will come to grief. Make casual use of their inventions and institutions and you can live happily in your mouse sub-world, untouched and immune, as long as you keep out of sight.* (Uncle Ponty's

*Mrs Frisby and the Rats of NIMH learn the same useful lesson: see postscript.

cautionary tale of the tortoise that crossed the road and caused a car accident, the death of a president and a human war, and then wondered when it reached the other side why the grass tasted peculiar, points this moral rather uncomfortably).

Otherwise, this is the Snug Town inhabited by comic mice, dressed in unremarkable contemporary clothes. The drop-in-uninvited, braces thwacking Mr Peck is a lower middle-class shop-keeper. 'It's all that crowd from the other side of the railway line,' he groans when the supermarket is invaded. The mice help them-selves to 'air power' by an ingenious system of milking car and bicycle tyres. They hitch lifts on human boats and human railways with such comments on the times as: 'In recent years, what with the closing of many branch lines and the electrification of others, the journey had become more and more hazardous, and with twenty children to see across lines and hide away in trucks and carriages often with only seconds to spare, not to mention Grandpa Aristide's wheelchair to supervise, it was no longer the fun-making affair it had once been.' Cats are treated as an annoying crime wave ('Blessed mogs,' said Uncle Ponty).

At one point, the mice discover the perfect way to reduce the humans to less than nothing; they watch them on television. There, in a house which the humans have left unoccupied during a holiday, with the television on, the mice watch the human world made small, ridiculous and shut away safely behind glass. They develop a system of ropes and pulleys to adjust the set and change the pro-gramme, but prefer food commercials and Old Tyme Music Hall. The great success of the *Thursday* books, to me, is, apart from the fun, the 'mouse quality': the dashing, darting, posturing abundance, the shrill enormousness of the mouse community to whom the adventures happen, the sharp answers they give each other, the punning wit, the piling up of incident as events come thick and fast with never a quiet moment. These are not Beatrix Potter's mice, or Dorothy Kilner's, or Margery Sharpe's, but the human life they represent is very different; there is no end to the versatility of this useful species.

Thursday's adventurous masculinity is an exception in the mouse world. Most of the best mouse stories have been written by women, and heroines are the rule. Margery Sharpe's Miss Bianca is a female Pimpernel in a minute, mock-heroic saga of imprisonments,

escapes, the rewarding of virtue and overcoming of villains by
nimble wits, resource, courage and patience – all the traditional
weapons of the weak against the strong. Miss Bianca adds to these
something unique in animal stories and unfashionable as a virtue;
the integrity bestowed by breeding and the discipline of perfect
manners and strict adherence to etiquette. Of course, it is human
etiquette; it always is, even in *The Jungle Books*. Only, interestingly,
is it Animal in that most human story *The Wind in the Willows* where
etiquette is shown to mean non-reference to death, pain, unpleasantness, or even yesterday.

But these are things which Miss Bianca would never mention if
she thought they would distress her listeners. The *Miss Bianca*
stories – *The Rescuers* (1959), *Miss Bianca* (1962), *The Turret* (1964),
Miss Bianca in the Salt Mines (1966) – are adult fantasy, springing
from an original idea, that of a Mouse Prisoners Aid Society, or
MPAS, formed to comfort and cheer humans in dungeons and perhaps help them to escape; one of those self-proliferating ideas
capable of infinite development that gets better and better as it goes
on. The character and exploits of the heroine, the inventive wit of
the narrative, involve one very strongly in such issues as whether

Miss Bianca will ever condescend to marry her humble admirer, Bernard; whether she will retain her office as Madam Chairwoman of the MPAS; the ethics of helping to rescue an unworthy prisoner who may, or may not, have reformed; how Miss Bianca will manage to deal with the two outrageous professors who insist on joining her in the Salt Mines rescue. The likeliness of these adventures on a human level would probably be acceptable in a comic fairy tale; the small size of the mice place them in an almost-real world and compel one to take them seriously. If mice had human brains and lacked a great measure of human original sin, this is how they might behave. One could say the same of Michael Bond's Peck family who behave much as humans do, in miniature; but Miss Sharpe's mice are intensely concerned with human lives. They seem to know everything that is going on and are determined to right wrongs, restore orphans, release prisoners and bring happy endings at great personal peril; without human life, on the usual giant scale, their fields of endeavour would be limited, to their detriment. They are in the position of a healthy young society coping with odds rather than a settled group devoted to in-fighting.

There are two elements in these fantasies that appear at first to cancel each other – but perhaps they succeed in giving them a sort of equilibrium. The mice are very like Borrowers in that their miniature living is full of expedients and the pleasant vandalism (or agreeable use of common objects for extraordinary purposes) that every doll's house owner knows; their chairs are matchboxes, their committee room an old carriage lamp, carpets and pictures are postage stamps and the platform in the moot-hall is a chocolate box, the moot-hall itself is an old wine cask. The mice do not appear to have made anything for themselves (apart from the furnishings of Miss Bianca's exquisite porcelain pagoda which is part of the high life at the Embassy where she lives, rather than part of day-to-day existence). It is all Borrowing, shelf, pantry and cupboard living. But the human world into which they venture from these rather prosaic surroundings is the oddest, unreal, fairy-tale place: long railways and waggon routes lead into barren wastes, the enemies are the Black Castle, the Salt Mine, the Diamond Palace, and their rulers or gaolers – Ruritanian or Bohemian dukes and tyrants, including the most unpleasant cat ever invented, Mamelouk the iron tummed.

In this setting the mice, in delicate human parody, have much play with committee procedure and mouse rivalries – even a dash of university politics. The mixture is enchantingly real and unreal – if only mice did behave like this, the world would be a happier place. In fact, the humanity of the mice is contrasted with the inhuman people; few pleasant humans are shown, apart from the victims – children and poets regarded as friends to mice – who are rescued. The mice are cultivated and educated – the Chairwoman can quote Suckling – and appear to have read *Jane Eyre* and to understand the seriousness of parental deprivation. Miss Bianca's poem 'O flitting form, half-house half-bird' owes much to Wordsworth. Miss Bianca herself, Lady and Poetess, is a rounded character who grows with each story. She is described as silver-white with brown eyes (anyone who has owned a mouse of this colouring will agree that it represents the ultimate in mouse-beauty) but, in her porcelain pagoda in the Embassy, she is the pampered pet of the Ambassador's son. She is a Marie Antoinette who announces, with happy unconcern, that she 'dotes on cats' and seems quite ignorant of the outside world and its dangers; indeed, she faints with shock when asked to participate in the dangerous adventure of travelling in a diplomatic bag to permit a Norwegian mouse to rescue a poet. She sets out uncertainly with her companions, Bernard (loyal but plebeian, 'a short sturdy young mouse . . . he looked rough but decent: no one was surprised to learn that he worked in the pantry') and Norwegian Nils (' "Not a family man, or anything of that sort?" "Not me," said Nils. Several of his friends round the bar roared with laughter'). But breeding tells, or Manners Makyth Mouse. Miss Bianca proves to have nerves and courage enough to inspire the rescue, save the lives of her companions and bring the poet home at last. Her courage and resource develop during the course of the stories. At first she makes mistakes: drawing a picture of a garden party hat instead of a chart, carrying 'only toilet articles and a fan' with her to the Black Castle, worrying about the class differences between herself and Bernard – she is attracted, but could she marry a pantry mouse? Her courage, like human courage, is often mixed with vanity. She does not mix with the fieldmice they meet on the journey, excusing their lack of manners by their evident lack of opportunity to observe the best models, which the fieldmice overhear and resent: ' "No manners indeed!" they chorused. "The

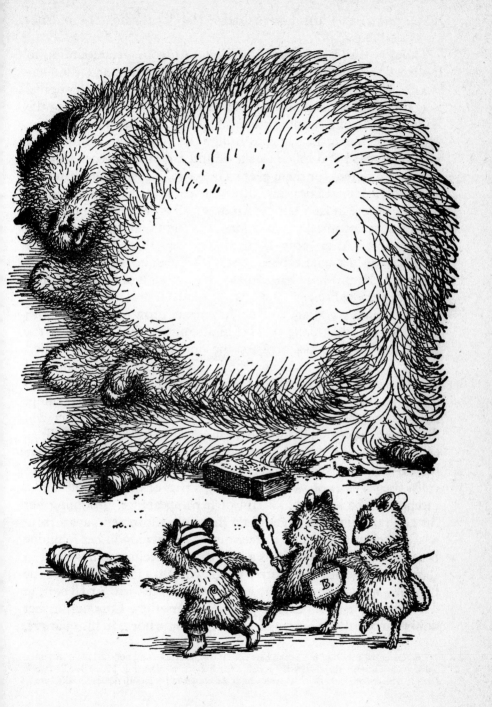

lady says we never learnt no manners! Hands up who goes to dancing class!" '

Though Miss Bianca braves the cat with courage amounting to
foolhardiness she is not indifferent to discomfort and thunder-
storms. Her poem 'Black as the Castle press my mournful thoughts'
is as romantic as *Childe Harold*. Bernard's greatest feat is scaling the
body and face of a sleeping gaoler;* he functions on a lower plane.
Miss Bianca never manages to bridge the class gulf. 'Fond as she
was of Bernard and much as she admired him, their backgrounds
were too different for them ever to be more to each other than they
were now.' Her relationship with Bernard remains platonic and is
a strong theme in later books: for ever will he love, and she be fair.
Miss Bianca becomes, in fact, a kind of Virgin Queen, exquisite and
unattainable. (Afterwards, Bernard graduates from the pantry to a
bachelor flat in a cigar cabinet, but it is no use; he is one of nature's
doormats. Even Miss Sharp admits that, though of sterling worth,
he lacks personality.)

Miss Bianca's courage and achievements grow with each book;
in the second, she thinks nothing of attempting the conquest of the
Diamond Castle alone, save for the doubtful help of the Ladies'
Guild, who are soon routed. She is often in desperate straits and
always the faithful Bernard is there to help. On later journeys – to
the Salt Mines for instance – she is better prepared for travelling.
Daring and fearless, she is also the mistress of perfect tact and
diplomacy, never saying a hurtful word or permitting her feelings
to overcome her. She restrains tears lest their effect should give
her an unfair advantage, her exquisite manners enabling her to
enlist the services of a colony of bats, a pair of bloodhounds and a
racehorse. She is always careful of her appearance, grooming her
fur and polishing her silver chain (her only adornment, apart from
a lace fascinator worn on a river outing), knowing in her feminine
heart that to look beautiful is a help towards feeling courageous. In
short, Miss Bianca is a perfect gentlewoman. Her handling of the
famous – and perhaps touchy and sensitive racehorse Sir Hector, in
The Turret – is a model of polite conversation. Conquering her
doubts about the etiquette of visiting a single horse in his quarters,

---

*'Where beardstubble gave place to bare flesh it was like traversing polished rock.' An inter-
esting gloss on what the centipede probably felt like when traversing James Bond's face in
Dr No; whereas one only hears 'Now it was at the corner of his mouth tickling madly,' etc.

Miss Bianca – offering her almost invisible visiting card – talks about fame. Sir Hector replies, and they continue with delicately Japanese self-deprecation, apologising for the inability of each to offer a chair to the other with the perfect good manners of natural, and trained, courtesy. They end with quotations from Cervantes and Bacon.

The French Ambassador was heard to say of Miss Bianca, as she bowed gracefully among the wine glasses on the dinner table: '*Je n'ai jamais rien vu de plus joli.*' She is a Queen among mice, as unforgettable as Reepicheep (perhaps the only mouse worthy of her hand? But Reepicheep is somehow as celibate as she is virginal; and that is part of the charm of both.)

Garth Williams – the Rembrandt of animal portrait artists – shows very mouselike mice, quite different from his portrayal of Stuart Little, or Templeton from *Charlotte's Web*. The character of each individual is beautifully evident, from serious, earnest Bernard, to old Caerphilly, the Professor of Geology, who has lectured to an empty hall for several terms. They are amiable and endearing. The humans – apart from poets and children – appear gross by comparison. The cat Mamelouk is a creature of nightmare, not only conceited and greedy but dirty and dishevelled. Garth Williams draws it with a flat, Persian face – the type of cat face that is nearest to human. The effect is very evil, with its shortened snout and heavy brows. Garth Williams is good, too, at crowd scenes (all mouse stories should have at least some crowd action) and at 'borrowing' improvisation; the Ladies' Guild busily at work knitting, with their tea urn made from a Kodak film capsule, the Moot Hall audience, the scene in the Norwegian tavern. He draws no clothes, apart from occasional hats. They are not necessary – neither author nor artist needs them for characterising – not mice like humans, but intelligent mice.

9 Only Toys

I . . . turned to Archibald, my safe old bear
Whose woollen eyes looked sad or glad at me,
Whose ample forehead I could wet with tears,
Whose half-moon ears received my confidence,
Who made me laugh, who never let me down.
I used to wait for hours to see him move,
Convinced that he could breathe.

'Summoned by Bells', *John Betjeman*

A toy or pet is by close association a semi-human object. When you give it a voice it takes on an identity that can be strange, wonderful, frightening and quite unsupportable; Chester the Cricket with a voice only understood by the cat and the mouse is infinitely preferable to Tobermory who demonstrated the impossibility of a voice without a conscience. The voice has to turn the creature into some kind of human, even in Malacandra or Narnia.

Human is what the child wants his toy or pet to be, the substitute friend or brother, like himself but exempt from all the dreary rules attached to childhood and growing up, the eternal confidant or companion, steadfast and unchangeable. Stories about pets that speak are as old as Dick Whittington or the talking horse Falada, but those about toys that 'come to life' are most often of the kind that fathers and mothers tell to children in order, as C. S. Lewis mentions in *Three Ways of Writing for Children*, to give one particular child what it wants. They do not date back much before the Victorian Age and the time when childhood began to be considered in isolation and regarded in sentimental or romantic fashion. How many little girls have always spoken to their dolls and answered for them? But it is not until Hans Andersen in 1846 that you get a story like *The Little Tin Soldier*; and in nurseries, the gradual additions of strange characters to the more conventional 'human' families – toy animals, the Golliwog and that indispensable piece of nursery furniture, the enduring Teddy Bear. Adults made the toys talk, and they became a child's companions on magic adventures.

The children in Sarah Trimmer's *History of the Robins* were taught to feed the birds and be kind to them, as Tom had to be kind to the caddis worms. Talking toys too can give a story a certain moral ring; one must be kind to objects or possessions and the screw is turned when they prove to be human after all. Bad brother breaks his sister's doll with the excuse that Toys Can't Feel. Night comes and the toys come to life and of course they can feel and sometimes take a nasty revenge in a place where they are powerful and children are not (Rupert has this experience several times and once with Freudian additions in Mary Tourtel's *Rupert and the Wooden Soldier*, 1928. The style is long lasting). In fact, Toyland becomes a recognisable place for fantasy happenings and sometimes retribution from F. Anstey to Enid Blyton.

F. Anstey's *Only Toys* (1903) has a toys' vengeance theme and more interesting experiences of doll's house living, which turns out to be as awkward as Hunca Munca and Tom Thumb found it. Torquil and Irene, transported to the place where toys are real, find their own doll's house a very inconvenient place to be – the food is inedible, the drink not what it seems, the fire won't burn and the kettle won't boil. The dolls have a stiff hierarchy as wooden and artificial as themselves. But few toy stories exist without human interaction. Toys have owners as pets do and in Toyland toy and owner meet on equal terms. All animals speak, whether 'real', carved or stuffed; it is a place that everyone recognises, with wooden trees and animals out of the Ark, always dreamlike, an after dark playground where nothing goes really wrong – one always wakes in time.

Quite the most interesting and unusual Toyland was written about by, as might be expected, E. Nesbit in *The Magic City* (1910) – the only book, as distinct from her short stories, where she deals with talking toys. Nesbit children usually do not need toys – they are too busy having imaginative adventures by other means. Like F. Anstey's Torquil, they might remark that toys are 'a babyish pursuit . . . except when they are exact models of things'. The Magic City, or rather series of cities, is a place that can be entered only by those who have helped to build it with books for bricks; and it is populated by creatures and people that have been put there, or have managed to escape, out of the books from which it is made. H. R. Millar's drawings give the city that slabby, Babylonian/Aztec look of any structure made of books, ornaments, chessmen and dominoes. The story has that odd, logical but numinous quality shared by *The Enchanted Castle*, when the children who enter the city find that it is greater inside than out and has a history, prophecies and laws that seem to be older than its creators. That the dragon outside it is a toy with a winding key does not make it any less fearsome; but it is still dreamlike – and one never dies in a dream. The lions in the desert that the children encounter are Noah's Ark lions, but fierce and predatory. These lions are killed, and when dead are found to have turned to wood once more – a dreamlike easing of otherwise intolerable consequences. Indeed, talking animals are never killed – it would be too much like murder. *The Magic City* has an interesting approach to the problem of eating – usually shelved, ignored, or by-passed in toy and pet stories – in suggesting that there exists a race of expendable animals which can be hunted and eaten without any trouble with one's conscience. They are not only expendable but nameless and vaguely mass produced by toy makers who do not credit children with enough intelligence to recognise the 'exact models of things' which Torquil wanted: 'They get weary of copying nature and begin to paint the animals pink and green and chocolate colour which in nature is not the case. These are the chocmunks and vertoblancs and the pinkuggers. And presently the makers get sick of the whole business and make the animals any sort of shape and paint them all one grey – these are the graibeestes.' The hunt goes out and secures a blugraiwee, a pinkugger and half a dozen graibeeste, returning home to its sandcastle with great pride and pleasure.

There are two dogs in this story – a pair of dachshunds who talk to each other like husband and wife. The story ends with Caesar chasing the Gauls into a volume of *De Bello Gallico* from which they escaped when a building, whose wall it formed, was knocked down. *The Magic City* is as full of invention as anything that E. Nesbit ever wrote – it almost suffers from a surfeit and the plot is breathless. But the strange, twilight atmosphere of being, so to speak, trapped inside one's imagination, however willingly, is unique. For some, it will always be rated with *The Enchanted Castle* as the best of the Magic books.

S. G. Hulme Beaman's *Toytown* is an interesting contrast; it has many of the same ingredients but the total effect is one of a cosy kind of comedy. The wooden toys on the playroom floor have become suddenly lifelike in a manner that copies an English village of fifty years ago, and the only magic is the kind used by the Magician – more than half a party trick. There is the same Mr Noah – but in Toytown he is the harassed zoo keeper of Ark animals who walk and talk and behave rather like delinquent children. *Tales of Toytown* (1928) and the broadcast plays that were *Children's Hour* favourites for nearly forty years show a toyland that has a particular, daylight reality about it. Author and artist in the same person created the human and animal characters visually by carving them out of wood and making drawings of the models so that these creatures were literally like Pinocchio, articulated toys that came to life. Broadcasting gave them voices so comically idiosyncratic that they became visual again in a way that radio sometimes manages better than television or the pages of a book.

S. G. Hulme Beaman's drawings are always of a Noah's Ark kind. Everything has a cubed, block-like perspective and pleasing, solid, wooden appearance; animals and humans seem to have stiff limbs that work with cotter pins and heads that twist jerkily from side to side but cannot nod. The look of restricted movement does not make them unreal, but gives them a kind of racial similarity, living in a little enclosed world, more than anywhere else the place that has no hurt, crises (other than comic) or disorder (other than that of all the toy soldiers being knocked over at the end of the battle; the signature tune that the BBC used for the series was particularly apt). Early *Toytown* stories did not include all the characters that children came to know so well – these developed in the telling – but always Toytown was a place where human and animal oddities of nursery translated to village life mingled in a hierarchical society of which the Mayor of Toytown was titular head. The various institutions under his rule were the Town Theatre, run by Punch and the Marionettes, Farmer Giles's farm where Larry the Lamb lived, the Railway, the 'Dog and Whistle', the Constabulary with Ernest the Policeman, the Low end of the town with Peter Brass and his pirate friends, all 'desperate characters', Mrs Goose's Sweetshop, Captain Higgins and his soldiers, the Ark and its inmates. There was also Arkville, a rival town. The animal characters, behaving like rowdy schoolchildren, mostly live in the Ark, ineffectively controlled by Mr Noah who is constantly getting complaints about them. But the two main characters, Larry the Lamb and Dennis the Dachshund (the latter developed from the original dog character, Toby, of no particular breed) gradually became the prime movers of the various plots – early stories have very little about them, later ones a great deal more.

It is difficult to tell how much the voices of Derek McCulloch and Reginald Purdell contributed to these two characters; no one who heard them can ever forget Larry's bleat and Dennis's growling Germanic transpositions. Dennis had the ideas – the guileless Larry helped to carry them out and act as a front by seeming more innocent than it was possible to be. The population of Toytown treated both with, at times, considerable restraint, defending them against the accusations of outsiders such as the Mayor of Arkville. From the start Larry, a lamb who has 'nothing to do but grow up' has plenty of time to get into mischief, but his method is to appear small, helpless and 'wee': 'my little hoofs are awkward for holding a pen. I never could manage it' – the 'a' sounds impossibly lengthened, tremulous and appealing. When he rushes into the Mayor's parlour disturbing the Mayor, who is usually asleep or playing noughts and crosses, all he can say is 'Oh Please, Mr Mayor, Sir.' The reply is always a benign 'Take your time, my lamb, take your time', while Dennis, wily and thoughtful, fills in awkward moments with remarks like 'A lovely day it has become, perhaps?'

The characters, behaving as toys might, are as delightfully predictable as toys with built-in solidity and reactions and words to match. Mr Growser (in early stories merely 'The Old Gentleman') is the real uncrowned king of Toytown, always appearing in a crisis, always referred to, grudging in his approval at last. 'Ought not to be allowed,' he shouts. 'They should be Ashamed to look me in the face! As one of the oldest and most respectable citizens of Toytown, I tell you it's disgraceful!' Mr Growser pops up like a well loved Jack-in-the-box, always with the same disgruntled roar.

The Inventor's fondness for gunpowder, complicated sausage machines or vast mouse traps, the Magician's high-class spells, Ernest the Policeman's ponderous 'speaking as an officer of the law' and his universal remedy for all law breakers – taking their names and addresses – Captain Higgins's remarks always addressed to himself – 'Your Worship and Gents all, I says to myself, 'Iggins I says' – these characters, when pressed, always returned the same

bleat, grunt or squeak like friends who never changed, whose pre-
dictability was a perpetual delight to witness. As J. B. Priestley
remarked of some comic characters* 'They seemed to realize . . .
that much was expected of them, and so they lived tremendously
up to themselves, piling it on like comedians in the third act. Every
time they popped up, they were better than ever. As if they *knew*.'
Among these adult drolls, so closely identified with the voices of
Ralph de Rohan, Ivan Samson, C. E. Hodges, Reginald Purdell,
Frederic Burtwell, Derek McCulloch, Arthur Wynn and Mary
O'Farrell, Larry and Dennis lived like favoured naughty children,
stage managing events in which the Mayor's statue turned green, a
'portable' radio set was wheeled to and fro between Arkville and
Toytown trying to catch elusive broadcasts, the two rival mayors
peppered each other with the Inventor's darts which waggled in a
mistaken duel. There were few troubles other than the rudeness of
the Ark animals, an occasional highwayman and a harmless dragon.
Larry and Dennis were always forgiven ('One mud pie. Or was it
two? Only little mud pies and the mud was not really squa-ashy.
It wasn't the sort that spre-eads.')

The disgraceful affair of the Mayor's statue was the first broadcast
I ever heard – in my grandparents' then rather progressive house
which had wires round all the picture rails and two sets of head-
phones dangling in each room. It could not have been a more
agreeable initiation.

Toyland is a very useful place for magic adventures as well as a
comic copy of life. Children when admitted can be taught useful
lessons (usually about tolerance) and the toys themselves are by no
means always virtuous, as Kathleen Tozer shows in *The Wanderings
of Mumfie*, 1935. Dennis and Larry are toy versions of real animals,
but Mumfie the elephant is very much a toy with no relation to an
animal at all; the stylish and dated illustrations by the author remind
one of a vast-eared Dumbo in the land of Oz. Mumfie's Toyland is
populated by talking animals and dolls, a place in which such creatures exist before they are 'born' or go into Santa Claus's sack. The
atmosphere of the story is rather like one of those moral games of
snakes and ladders, or ludo where the virtues of cleaning one's
teeth led to the Ivory Castle and neglect to Giant Decay. The toys
and animals in 'Mumfie' do end in a fairy-tale castle where they are

Delight, 1949.

given a party by Father Christmas, who remarks: 'I often wonder why you toys are all so eager to go down to earth – it's a toss up what sort of children you'll belong to – but here you all come, year after year, clamouring to be chosen.' Quite stern advice follows: be good and you will be happy. Black Beauty was told the same thing. The passivity of our stuffed or woolly friends seems to be a positive virtue – they must be obedient, must not push forward, must put up with bad treatment and remember their parents; clearly toys and pets both have a feminine role to play.

Once 'born', Mumfie's adventures in the human world include a wartime story of great period interest (*Mumfie Marches On*, 1942) in which the Elephant, still with his scarecrow friend meets some evacuee toys and eventually joins the Home Guard. In 1942 the war was serious enough. The idea that an invading army could be trapped and caught by a toy elephant (even with Winston Churchill's help) including the enticing of Hitler with cream buns, seems a feat of fairy-tale optimism; but as children's *ITMA* style comedy the story is successful enough. Life had to be full of jokes about invasion, including literary ones,* the War of Nerves, the blackout, ice-cream men looking like Mussolini and fifth columns turning out to be lamp posts. Mumfie and the Scarecrow are given lines like: ' "Scarecrow, what is a Territorial Ambition?" . . . Scarecrow frowned thoughtfully. "Well, a Territorial is a volunteer soldier, so Territorial Ambition must be when he wants to be an officer" ' and 'Hitler can never quite get over how dreadfully offensive he is going to be in the Spring.'

Mumfie's tactful visit to 10 Downing Street is not without parallel – various animals and creatures constantly assault reality by meeting the famous: see The Wombles and the Queen, Albert and the Duke, Mary Plain and Uncle Mac, The Birthday Unicorn and the Cabinet, Pete the Parrot and Shakespeare, Pooh and the King of France.

That toys and their human owners should be able to enter adventures together is a dream that most children have. Adults can appear to make it come true by hinting that after dark, or in some other dimension, child and toy can live together on equal terms and

---

*Such as Peter Fleming's *The Flying Visit* in which Hitler, following the example of Rudolf Hess, parachuted into East Anglia to try to win the war by himself.

have experiences of which the child has only to say 'remind me' and the adult story teller will unfold the adventure before his eyes – as A. A. Milne did, or anyone who has united child and bear. The best kind of stories are sometimes personal ones in which one has one's own part to play and can be brave and resourceful with animal friends who are always there, always dependable, repaying all the love that has lost them their fur, eyes and ears, and blurred their features. Roger Lancelyn Green describes this process so perfectly in *The Land of the Lord High Tiger* (1958) that the story – a blend of magic adventure and fairy-tale characters that have come to life from other sources – is never quite as interesting as the doings of Roger and his musketeers, Leo, Squit the squirrel, Foxy and Sir Timothy the Lord High Tiger who lives on the chest of drawers.

Sir Timothy and the other animals 'had never learned to talk quite properly. This did not matter very much, because Roger always knew what they were going to say and very kindly said it for them. Some day, he was sure, they would all learn to talk by themselves, just as he did.' The animals, like Chester the Cricket, think and the child speaks. The wonderful moment comes when the animals do speak alone and the magic country becomes real, the clocks chime, the Tiger growls, the imaginary friends are true. 'And was I in the story?' asks Christopher Robin. Of course he was, in the place where toys and animals could talk and he could hear. Winnie the Pooh's celebrity exists outside the story in that quotations from *The House at Pooh Corner* (1928) and *Winnie the Pooh* (1926) by A. A. Milne are almost as literate as those from *Alice*, and proof that one had had a certain kind of 'correct' childhood. But in

When Pooh was Very Young – *an early Pooh illustration*

person, he stays in the enchanted place – the Hundred Acre Wood, never entering the real world as Mary Plain, Paddington, or the Pushmipullyu do. Pooh, the most famous bear ever created, made his first appearance not under the name of Sanders, but that of Edward in *When We Were Very Young*, worrying about his weight and girth (though E. H. Shepard's drawings show him as smaller and thinner than he afterwards became) and wearing the shrunk and armless coat meeting rather painfully across his chest with one button. The bear models that Shepard used – his son Graham's Teddy, and the real Pooh – are both thinner than the Pooh of the two story books.

A bear character is never inconsiderable; no Teddy bear takes second place in the toy hierarchy. He is always King, the first in a child's affection. As Pooh progresses his rotundity increases, his legs and arms shorten, his back becomes humped (a rare characteristic only seen in vintage bears and never on modern ones), his head pokes forward as if in deep thought. He is the first famous fictional bear and all the others owe him something; his size, his fondness for honey, ponderous *naiveté* and occasional flashes of brilliance have left their mark on other lesser bears, real or toy; and there is no question about Pooh's reality. His adventures in the Forest and Hundred Acre Wood spring as naturally from character as the happenings in any real life.

All the personages in the Pooh stories have houses or burrows or the corner of a thistly field and Pooh makes up verses as he 'stumps along' which remain unappreciated by everyone except author and reader. The appearance of each animal – as in all toys – gives its character, and in contrast to the human world, things are always what they seem. Brisk motherly Kanga, mournful, sarcastic Eeyore, timid Piglet who needs reinforcement from his friend Pooh even to make a decision, bright optimistic Tigger, pedantic Owl and efficient Rabbit are all what their faces and bodies have made them. Shepard's drawings underline this; and character dominates toy. Even Piglet – who starts out in preliminary sketches as fat and happy looking with short ears and a pig's face – grows small and wistful with ears that can blow in the wind and turn pink with emotion.

The solemn facetiousness and rather artful simplicity (very much the same note is used in *The Magic Roundabout*) and ponderous use

of capitals may mar the stories for some: ' "Nothing," said Pooh, "as long as *we all three* say it. As long as we all three say it," said Pooh, "I don't mind," he said, "but I shouldn't care to say 'Aha' by myself . . . by the way," he said, "you are quite sure about Kangas only being Fierce in the Winter Months?" ' But the individuality of Pooh, Piglet and friends is at times uncomfortably and sadly life-like. Eeyore's sarcasm, made sharper because he is unlucky and unpopular – or thinks he is – is something unforgettable because one recognises it, as one does all the others; Owl, the pretentious scholar, his reputation resting on long words and a mythical ability to spell; Rabbit rushing here and there making lists, Army fashion, too annoyingly public spirited to leave anything alone; Tigger, brash and gaudy, the unclassifiable foreigner who doesn't know the rules; Kanga, Mother, Nanny who always knows best and squashes one's remarks with cast-iron illogicality as does Christopher Robin's Alice with her 'Sure to, dear, but it's time for tea.'

Most Teddy bears since Pooh seem to have been born middle aged, plump and dependable; Pooh's direct descendant is Alison Jezard's *Albert* (1968 onwards). Albert is part of a real world made rather sweeter than usual – a home fit for toys to live in. His simple adventures have a pleasant charm, as old fashioned as the watch chain after which he is appropriately named. At a first view, Albert seems to begin the era of the working-class Ted with his cloth cap and East End basement flat at 14 Spoonbashers Row, with none of Pooh's whimsy or comedy, and none of his poetry, either – but this is not quite the case. In their way, Albert's flat and Pooh's house have the same cosy antiquity, and Albert's doings, lacking Pooh's quirks and individuality, are those of Christopher Robin turned toy and out for once without Alice but behaving in exemplary fashion all the same.

Margaret Gordon's illustrations for the *Albert* books emphasise this admirably, see opposite page. Albert has no clothes other than his checked cap, with a best one for Sundays. His simple rounded limbs are purposefully toylike, his changeless expression that of all the Teddy bears one has known, new from the shop, without the 'twist that denotes character' mentioned by A. A. Milne. But should a Teddy bear walk and talk, should he live in a basement flat of his own, *this* is the toylike room that he ought to live in. Above all Albert is domestic and spends his happiest hours sitting in his basket

chair gazing round his room, lovingly itemised in nearly every story, always 'sparkling clean, the brass knobs polished'. His curtained front door, sailing ship picture and geranium in its pot seem out of a child's favourite room in a doll's house. The things he does – shopping in Petticoat Lane, helping at the docks, riding on a fire engine, joining the chimpanzees' tea party, kicking off at a football match are just the things, more or less, that a small child would like to do but cannot because he isn't old enough. Luckily most small children do not realise that by the time they are old enough they will no longer want to do them. Albert – with his middle-aged sexless independence, his childlike simplicity and toy mascot attraction which bring him instant love and attention – is able to combine innocence and experience, have his cake and eat it in a way which must be everyone's envy. He doesn't toil or spin but is always 'helping' – he is loved wherever he goes, has no relations to tell him not to, can eat what he likes and grow stout, adding to his pleasing rotundity with no conscience at all.

Who would not long, at times, to be such a bear, wearing his cloth cap in bed, hibernating through nasty weather with never a bad dream, in all the innocence of a time when all the adults were kind and children good, when horses liked pulling carts and donkeys were pleased to take one for rides and said so – a time that never really was but which one thinks one remembers, properly inhabited by bears, because humans on their own would mess it up, as they do.

Toys talk under certain conditions; they may be real only to their owners – like Teddy Robinson – or only to other toys or animals – like Russell Hoban's mice – act like humans at all times and to everyone – like Mumfie or Albert – real in a special, separate existence – like Pooh – or real after dark – like the Lord High Tiger. Margaret Baker's *The Shoe Shop Bears* (1963 onwards), belong in the last category, and are real when no one is looking; but their stories achieve a balance or harmony where credulity is never stretched and the human world co-exists with that of the bears, who like most Teddies are bound by various ties of love and need to human children and cannot live without them. Perhaps these are the most believable and touching bears of all. Old and well worn, they sit in their basket chair in the children's part of Mr Shoehorn's shop 'for the comfort, amusement and edification of juvenile customers during the fitting of their footwear'. This is their work, and they are proud of it. Again, as in all bear stories, the ingredients are cosy like the bears themselves. The cathedral city, old-fashioned shops, kindly bishop, grocery and church cats and the eager, hard-working child assistant in the shoe shop, Polly Trinkett, are all friendly without being bland. Events are happy and sad but always likely and credible and the effect is one of great harmony. The strangeness of a talking toy, which sometimes distracts, is quite missing; children and bears never talk to each other.

There is here something of the sadness that all toys have. The bears' characters and their relationship (they *are* and yet are *not* a family, like Rumer Godden's *Doll's House* dolls) are wonderfully suggested; large, threadbare Boots, the father figure, expensive and old, his fur brushed carefully forward to hide his worn canvas, is solid and knowledgeable and dependable. Slippers, the mother, too worn and mended to be beautiful, is kind and much loved by children. Like most mothers, she has an obsession: it may be laxatives or wet feet or too much reading in bed tires your eyes – but hers is Moths and she worries constantly over moth prevention with horror stories unvoiced at the back of her mind. Little Socks, jaunty and plushy, won at a shooting gallery on a choir outing, is the mischievous baby.

After dark, the bears tidy the shop like elves, read the shoe catalogues and exchange news with cats from other shops and the cathedral, who come in by the skylight. The bears take their jobs very seriously and have their ups and downs – frowned on by a new manager, they work their way into a window display, are almost thrown out and leave the shoe shop by climbing into a parcel for the Bishop's Christmas tree. They are again rejected by unfeeling adults because they are battered and worn, but are comforted by the Bishop's own bear, Chesterfield, who dated from the days when bears were an expensive novelty. The theme of the helplessness of toys, and the constant wear that life gives them, is always present; as quirky as people and as subject to the battering of time, they can only live if loved and wanted. A later episode is very reminiscent of Hoban when it deals with a large collection of toy animals thrown out on the town dump by accident or design, and rescued by the bears and given eventual good homes. In Russell Hoban's America these are clockwork creatures; in England they are stuffed, feathered or knitted. But always there is the message that life without love is nothing. The shoe-shop bears in their adventures always strive to remain together: 'We'll fasten ourselves together with that string they use to keep the beach shoes in pairs. Everyone will know then that we're meant to keep together as a family set' and Chesterfield has the final word about Teddy bears with his remark – uttered between the dozes of old age – 'You'll find there's always someone who needs you. It's not good looks or being young that matters, but what you can offer from your heart. A bear's job is just to be there, ready to receive all the affection that's offered, and to give it.'

C. Walter Hodges's beautiful illustrations are of the detailed kind that send one from picture to text and back again in confirmatory delight; character shows in every toy, from the Bears down to Woggles, the car mascot and the vaguely knitted Boston who, even himself perhaps, was not quite sure if he was meant to be a dog or a cat. Bear expressions are almost fixed, just quirky enough to give emotion and feeling to faces that have lived and been marked by age and wear.

Perhaps the most perfect blend of fantasy and realism is that achieved by Joan G. Robinson in the *Teddy Robinson* books, 1955 onwards. Teddy Robinson's life is limited to that of his owner Deborah, and he lives in a real world of 'I said to Teddy and he said

to me', or of Christopher Robin's Binker, 'I have to do it for him.'
He moves when Deborah moves and stays where Deborah puts
him. His adventures are those of a toy who has thoughts and makes
remarks, but is quite unable to move or initiate action. To Deborah
he is child, bear and friend. ' "Poor boy," she said. "I expect you're
tired: it's time for your rest now," and she laid him down flat on his
back so that he could look up into the sky,' whether he liked it or
not.

In Deborah's absence, Teddy Robinson can talk to blackbird,
snail, tortoise and kitten; and to Deborah he makes short, simple,
acquiescent remarks. Each loves the other wholeheartedly and their
lives are totally shared – in many ways Teddy Robinson is the most
'natural' bear of all. His personality reflects Deborah's in the ageless
way of well-loved toys, and his adventures are those of getting lost,
left behind (on a sandcastle) and forgotten (in a tool shed), placed
for sale in a shop window, thrown into a tree by 'a boy who ran
round the garden shooting at people who weren't there until they
were all dead', bouncing on a piano while it is being thumpingly
played at a party, playing the games that one insists on one's toys
playing too, being turned into pirate or Indian, or sent to the toys'
hospital. 'Been here long?' he says to a horse. Like Pooh, he is
given to sitting – on a window sill – and *thinking*, and like Pooh he
makes up occasional rhymes to pass the time, the long boredom of
not-being-played-with:

> *Toddy Robinson looked out*
> *On the Feast of Stephen*
> *All the stars were round about*
> *Some odd ones and some even.*

His excited behaviour at his own birthday party, showing off – why
is it always at one's *own* party one behaves in such an appalling
fashion? – consists of actions and positions in which he is *placed*.
Who has not made his toys play tricks, as it were by proxy? He
moves his head from front to back, stands on it, falls on to the table
and off his chair. As the 'Lords of the Nursery' sit silent and disconsolate waiting for John boy, so Teddy Robinson has no existence
apart from his owner. His life is hers and without her he is, like
Feste who needed laughter and occasion to rouse him, dumb. Forgotten in the tool shed he sits in a bicycle basket while a spider

weaves a web from ear to toes. There is no sadness in these delightful books for the very young, but one can't help feeling that toy
neglect is child neglect, and there is an odd pathos in toys' feelings
– when one of them is forgotten, lost or hurt, the hurt belongs to
the owner, too.

The toy that becomes real as a kind of reward for virtue (forti-
tude?) or as the result of great love has a legendary feel about it, as
old as Pygmalion, as moving as a good fairy tale ought to be, when
life, love and forgiveness and understanding spring out of trial and
self-sacrifice. The best toy stories have this quality in a manner that
pet stories cannot convey; pets are self-limiting, toys share a creative love that makes them sometimes more than human. Pinocchio
on his travels, hard but perishable wood longing to become a boy,
the toy soldier steadfast to death, have an innocence about them that
is childlike, full of pathos. All toys are like this; however humble,
they have power and magic. Whether they are greatly loved or lost
and broken, they are still the prettiest dolls, or horses, or bears in
the world. Ursula Moray Williams's *Adventures of a Little Wooden
Horse* (1938) has this power in a great measure. The Little Wooden
Horse goes on its long pilgrimage to find a fortune for the master
who made it. The feeling is that of fairy tale, but one has only to
believe that the child's toy can move by itself on wheels, speak and
be answered, and the quest becomes sadly real; perhaps not as
hideously so as that in *The Mouse and His Child*, but real enough.
The Horse meets good and bad humans and animals, is exploited,
battered, loses limbs and head, makes and loses several fortunes in
its tramplike wanderings, is loved and rejected, used and thrown
aside in the manner of all toys, suffers and enjoys from moment to
moment in the manner of horses, and sadly and hopefully looks
before and after, as humans do.

Toys are made to be loved, yet what they seem to do is endure
hardship with patience and steadfastness. The Little Wooden Horse
in its ups and downs sees itself rejected in favour of cheaper metal
toys, is sneered at because it is simply and plainly made, is ill-used
by spoiled children, loses its beauty, its sight, its head, and in the
human world joins barge horses, pit ponies (who oddly, have a very
closed sort of Union), circus performers, seashore donkeys and race
horses. It is always ready to offer its services for money and is often
exploited because it is willing, strong, and does not eat. Toy and

horse combine in a story of courage, strength and love as the horse labours for its distant master in the face of impossible odds and losses. The horse has a heart and tears and can feel hurt. It carries its fortune in its hollow body, rolling, galloping and swimming, full of life in its wood. Even in the sea with its head gone, it can think and almost despair, always endure. The simple sadness and joy are of the same nature as that which makes *Black Beauty* at times a book almost unbearable to read; the fairy-tale elements, the Princes' and Princesses' horse race, the wedding of the old toy maker, give the story a more distant quality that is less directly sad but no less moving. People are loved and rejected, exploited, grow old and lose their beauty; no one who reads the book can fail to think about human nature. It compares with Gerda's quest for Kay.

Russell Hoban's *The Mouse and His Child* (1969) is such a strange, haunting and distinguished book that it is very difficult to classify. It is about toy mice, yet the clockwork father and son move through a world in which small animals act out human dramas. The happy ending does not dispel the lingering sadness of the clockwork pair, the father doomed to travel forward through the world and the son (who is joined to him) backwards. Helpless when they are not wound up, unable to stop when they *are*, they are fated like all mechanical things to breakage, rust and disintegration as humans are to death. Hans Andersen with the clockwork nightingale and lead soldier, Kingsley with the fate of the lost doll, Collodi with the strange quest of the puppet who wanted to be a boy – all tell of the human sadness of toys, which is something that adults see, and one wonders if children really enjoy *The Mouse and His Child*. As an adult, it is impossible to read it unmoved.

The mice are searching for the things that people want: happiness, a family, a home, self-winding freedom, from their bright morning in the toy shop at Christmas to their ending on a bird-house platform by a railway line, near the town dump. There is a glimpse of shining perfection as the toys – the mice, elephant, seal and doll's house that come so largely into the story – wait on the shop counter to be sold. The mice dance in a circle when wound. The doll's house is inhabited by wonderful papiermâché models talking in scraps of newsprint, and is an enviable mansion with every detail exact, one of those American country houses whose adjectival accompaniment is always 'decaying' and 'Southern' as if they have to end up in Tennessee Williams land. And indeed, this one decays and suffers as doll's houses, and some real ones, often do. To be bought is to be born. For four years the mouse father and son dance under the Christmas tree, always put away in their box until, pounced on and broken by a cat, they are thrown away. Repaired by a tramp who can only make them walk straight, they follow an endless road, tramps themselves, finding their way into a place like Cannery Row only far more sinister – the town dump ruled by the exploiting bandit Manny Rat, the underworld king who wears a greasy dressing-gown and lives in an old TV set.

The rat is hideously real, always foraging, exploiting everything it meets, using old clockwork toys to fetch and carry, mending them just enough to keep them going like abused and broken-down horses, running sordid sideshows that offer and give nothing, and taking his profit from their wretched owners, miserable beetles and crickets.

' "Come on," snarled someone, "keep it moving, you."

' "My spring's gone," came the tinny reply. "See for yourself – one end of it's sticking out of my chest. I'm done." ' The toys do their best, but 'All their trades and tricks were gone; the best that they could do was plod ahead when wound, and that not very well.' When broken, they are casually murdered for their spare parts which are used to repair others.

The chief supporting characters in this strange nightmare are 'Frog', a figure of destiny who inhabits an old glove and makes his way with herbal remedies and fortune telling, a philosophic musk-rat, a terrapin who is a thinker, scholar and playwright, two crows who run an experimental theatre company, a kingfisher and a bittern, both helpful characters represented as do-it-yourself expert and a solitary bachelor fond of fishing.

Likeness to the human world is both satiric and symbolic. The mice are sent to rob a bank by the rat; the chipmunk behind the counter pushes 'the alarm twig' and a badger guard eats the rat. The mice get involved in a territorial war between shrew armies with battle cries of 'ours' and 'onwards'; weasels casually eat the shrews; owls catch the weasels. A recurrent motif is an old empty dogfood tin with a picture of a dog in a chef's cap carrying on a tray another dog in a chef's cap. The mouse father's heart is his clockwork centre. He has patience, courage, sad endurance. The child, with less clockwork, has room for dreams of family and home – 'I want the elephant to be my mama and the seal to be my sister and I want to live in the beautiful house.' In their hopeless quest, the mice somnambulate through impossible tasks, like Tess in the potato field. They pace the Crows' stage in an incomprehensible play ('the meadow isn't ready for this yet'), they are harnessed by the muskrat to a saw device for felling a tree, which takes all the winter, they fall to the bottom of a pond. Their physical disintegration is a persistent theme. When they do at last find the doll's house its fate has been that of many real ones. It has been ravaged by fire and 'become in its romantic ruined state a trysting place for young rat lovers, then a social and athletic club'.

When the house is finally reclaimed and re-inhabited by the battered toys (who will never look new again) they live in an Edward Lear assortment: duck and kangaroo, owl and pussycat all associate happily; even the dreadful Manny rat reforms – after one relapse when he tries to blow up the house and all in it – and with an arrangement of reciprocal springs, makes the two mice as self-winding as they will ever be.

The reality of this strange, fragile little group living lives that are half-clockwork and half-soul is painful. One wonders how long the house on the pole will last, how long the springs will exist without rusting, how soon the freight trains will shake down the bird table. As a story of courage, endurance under impossible odds, love and self-help, it is loaded as heavily as *A Peep behind the Scenes*. One is meant to shed tears at the right places, but the sadness is often unexpected, the wit sharp and true. The central characters leave all the rules behind. 'They're almost animal-like,' yell the audience as the Mouse and his Child plod over the stage. 'Ugh', says a hawk who tries to eat them. 'You aren't part of the balance of nature.' Tin caricatures, thinks Manny Rat at the end of the story, were they becoming animals? Over all, a jay flies screeching headlines to the world, an iteration of facts like a chorus, surface observation, often lurid and inaccurate: WINDUPS CRASH IN DUMP, he calls, NO SURVIVORS. Human life is tragic, human love indestructible.

The path of every toy is always downwards. Though they share with humans apparent death (by smashing) and strange resurrections (by mending), they do not, like humans, have a high noon.

The Velveteen Rabbit (Margery Williams, 1922) has once again the theme of the toy made real and immortal by love. The Rabbit is quite new. Bright and plushy he comes to the Boy at the top of a Christmas stocking, at the peak of his physical perfection, and 'for at least two hours the Boy loved him'.

When such creatures are given thoughts and emotions, how can they be other than tragic? The wonder is, that humans are not the same. The only way out of the difficulty is to turn toys into cheerful ageless beings such as Larry the Lamb or Winnie the Pooh, neither of whom lives in a real world at all, but in some place where a small boy and his bear will always be playing. But the fairy-tale satisfaction of this short, perfect allegory would not be valid if the rabbit were not part of a child's real life. The allegory is about human love and human childhood. At first neglected by his owner, the Velveteen Rabbit turns to an old and shabby fellow toy for comfort – the Skin Horse tells him the great secret that to be greatly loved makes a toy become real. Together the pair watch mechanical toys come and go, breaking their mainsprings and passing away.

' "By the time you are Real," says the Horse sadly, "most of your hair has been loved off and your eyes drop out and you get loose in the joints and very shabby." ' The Rabbit finds the idea melancholy: he wants the prize of life without the decline that goes with it. But, like all of us, there is nothing that he can do. Almost by chance, and just because the Rabbit is there, during a long illness the Boy begins to love him and at the same time old age begins to set in. The Boy recovers at the seaside, the Velveteen Rabbit is thrown away (how callous, in stories, some of these Olympians are), and his past flashes by: 'he thought of those long sunlit hours in the garden – how happy they were – and a great sadness came over him.' But the magic has worked; he has become real. 'He might have sat there a long time, too shy to move' – but wild rabbits appear and he knows that he is one of them. From the wood he looks back at the Boy in the garden, to whom he can be a friend no longer, with love and gratitude, and runs away at last, unnoticed, forgotten, and alive.

It seems as difficult to write about toys without saying what happens to them, as it is to write about humans without mentioning death. The Mouse and His Child on the town dump, Leotard and the Ark in the 'grim big box . . . in which so large a portion of our past and our personality lay entombed . . . awaiting the carrier of the morning who should speed them forth to the strange, cold, distant Children's Hospital, where their little failings would all be misunderstood and no one would make allowances.' They all come to some sort of end, like the Tin Soldier, brave to the last. Friends, children, alter egos, toys' power is magnetic and real. When a toy is an animal image, to give it animal status, as the last three books do, is almost to give it the means of grace the hope of glory; human consciousness expects no more.

10 If only they could speak: the Pet Story

Their psychology, their means of communicating their motives, actions, hopes and fears in all that follows must be rendered in gross human terms – because we know no other way.

Dudley and Gilderoy, *Algernon Blackwood*

Pets, like toys, are friends, confidants and helpers, the comforting resource for children, between them and the grown-up world of parents or others who arrange their lives, or the reality outside home that may sometimes be too painful to be faced. A pet animal can be anything, anyone, any sex, young or old as needed. Dolls with their more defined humanity seldom fill the bill. Masefield's *The Midnight Folk* (1927) and *The Box of Delights* (1935) deal in toy, pet and wild animals as a child's allies or enemies. They are delicately humanised as belonging to the after-dark world when creatures talk and the day light rules become vaguer and less well defined; it is a kind of dream country and yet intensely real. Everything that happens after dark in *The Midnight Folk* belongs to a new, different set of rules which are shut off when Kay wakes up; yet everything is remembered and leaves its mark. The quest for treasure – once trusted to Kay's Great Grandfather and lost by him, now searched for by Kay – is not a new theme. But the manner of the telling, the atmosphere of witchcraft and the strange, nostalgic feeling that the past is not remote at all but co-existent with the present, is reinforced by Kay's discoveries and by the long memories of servants, sexton, the magician Abner Brown and the spirits he calls up and the animals – cats, foxes, bat, otter and owl. All these have an indefinable longevity and the freedom of attic, cellar, underground passage, and the lost secret places of the countryside. There is a unique blend of treasure hunt, magic and animal lore.

In Kay's adventures at night, Nibbins, the black cat, takes him here and there by hidden passages in the old house 'Seekings'.

Nibbins talks as naturally as if he were another boy, but knowledgeable and mature – in and out of black magic which he takes
with a shrug and a warning that once *into*, it is difficult to keep *out*
of. They meet Rollicum Bitem the fox, characterised as a spry,
gamey, nimble poacher, always one jump ahead of the law. The
other house cats, deeper into witchcraft, are enemies; they talk to
witches and real, human poachers, as naturally as if they were all of
the same species. In both *The Midnight Folk* and *The Box of Delights*
the commerce between human and animal is as natural and serious
as if the adventure stories were being told without any extra dimensions in which brazen heads recall the past, portraits speak from the
wall, or mice man a model ship to take one to the Gulf of Mexico.
Kay, having swallowed the witch's invisible mixture, walks unseen
through the Herefordshire woods at night, watching rabbits play
and witches plot.

The curious but convincing blending of magic and reality, of
animals' human identities and changing sizes, extends to Kay's
devoted – but absent – band of helpers known as 'The Guards'.
They were his 'toys of bears, dogs, rabbits, cats, horses and boys',
removed by authority 'because they will only remind him of the
past' – the dimension that the witches are trying to erase from his
mind. Well they know the power of toys to resurrect it. But these
toys have power enough to carve their names on the wall as a perpetual reminder. They include oddities such as Robin Pointnose,
Eduardo da Vinci, P. Dogg, Horse and Petter Horse – and 'Jemima,
Maria, Susan and Peter' who all appear later as children in *The Box
of Delights*. One is never told what the Guards look like, though
Rowland Hilder's illustrations to a later edition of *The Midnight Folk*
make an attempt at interpretation. Robin, P. Dogg and Horse are
animal toys become real, and at the end they bring the treasure to
Seekings in a procession of toy carts. Edward – a soldier, a military
bear? – in his 'coat with the piping down the edges' makes remarks
like 'Ha, Kay, We've jolly well got the treasure for you' in, we are
told, 'his usual extravagant way'. Restoration of the treasure, and of
the past, is made by talking animals and toys without any suggestion that, in the future, Kay will grow up and they will cease to talk.
Always, among the Midnight Folk, Kay will be free to have them
as equal friends.

The most memorable of the animals Kay meets is the disreputable Rat, a cellarman – 'I never done nothing against no young ducks, nor I didn't neither not against no chicks. I lives in a cellar and I does a bit in the dustbin' – vivid, Dickensian, unforgettable and human, his gait, gestures and phrases having that human conviction where author and reader forget that he is animal. In *The Box of Delights* he turns traitor, reports to Abner and uses his nephew for the same purpose. His animal nature is by-passed to such a degree that, like the Toad's, it matters no longer, nor is it noticed:

'I make so bold as to present my nephew, Master Abner,' Rat said. 'Make a reverence to the gentleman.'
'What's your nephew's name?' Abner asked.
'Oh, he answers to any name,' Rat said. 'Alf, or Bert, or any name. He ain't earned a name better'n one of these.'
Alf Rat came forward and seemed much abashed at having to speak in company. Kay thought that he had seldom seen a more hardened young villain: he was pleased to see the brazen face now confused, the eyes downcast, sweat starting from the brow and the cheeks flushing and turning white by turns.

The reader does not have to be told about clothes, or upright stance. When Rat suddenly eats a piece of bacon rind with a quick sideways nibble, it comes almost as a shock.

Kay's friend, the delectable cat Nibbins, acts and speaks like a rather older boy, and his intelligence is equal, if not superior to Kay's; if pet animals could talk, they would probably have few thoughts to fill out their words. T. H. White's setters, both portraits of his much-loved Brownie, mostly think in images. Kipling's Aberdeen terriers, Boots and Slippers, bark in breathless sentences and monosyllables and their thoughts, though clear enough, are limited and few. We think humanity into objects we love because we know no other way of loving them better; but however fond one is of a dog or a cat one knows about the simple brain that makes speech impossible, while not excluding a kind of rough logic. The talking pet can only become delightful in a fantasy; it becomes terrible if you give the animal the speech equipment of a logical brain without the moral equipment, or conscience, that tells him how to use it. H. H. Munro's Tobermory is such a one, demonstrating the impossibility of speech without reticence; it says exactly what it is thinking all the time. When talking pets are seen as

7

simplified, amiable humans, as in Dr Dolittle, the results are quite
different. H. H. Munro, never, one feels, liking the humans he talks
about (though children are sometimes exempt), chooses a cat – the
animal which, like the satirist, has apparently the best symbiosis
with humanity and the least need for it – to be the subject of Mr
Cornelius Appin's experiment in animal grammar. Mr Appin, while
concerned with communication, only wants to teach, not, as Dr
Dolittle does, to learn. The first words the cat utters are 'I don't
mind if I do', to the consternation of Lady Blemley's house-party
guests and thereafter, his cold, all-revealing honesty makes the
prospect of the humans' co-existence quite intolerable. *They* manage
to be civilised by never saying what they mean; the cat either has
not achieved polite hypocrisy, or scorns it; it has learned speech
without rules, communication without silence, and the joke is on
Clovis Sangreal and Bertie Van Tahn.

Tobermory talks like a disembodied intelligence, or a brain without love, and the second twist of the joke is that that is what his
owners – and most of the other Saki characters – are *really* like.
Maeterlinck in *The Blue Bird* (1909) is kinder, and perhaps more
truthful. When the Cat and the Dog show their souls at the turning
of the diamond they are simple creatures, very like their child
owners – or seem so, at first, until the Cat reveals unexpected depths
of cunning self-interest. The Dog jumps on, and embraces everyone, his barking speech unable to express his tumbling emotions
quickly enough, yelling 'Good morning, good morning, I love you,
I've kissed everybody, oh grand, I'm going to frighten the Cat!' –
Who, quieter, going up to his mistress, says with ceremony, 'Good
morning, Miss – how well you look this morning.'

The Cat's contempt for the Dog's noisy idiocy grows with every
word he utters; and it is the Cat who promotes the conspiracy of
the elements, animals and trees against the children to stop them
from gaining the Blue Bird, and so (they fear) knowledge and power.
The Cat is a double dealer, fawning on the children, but ready to
betray them in contrast to the Dog who leaps into danger with
foolhardy bravado, always ready to defend the little god he loves,
ready to give up his life and his secret soul too, without question
At the end, when the animals' souls return to their bodies and
they are dumb as before, the Dog howls in parting, promising
everlasting goodness, tricks and perfection, if only he is allowed to

talk – while the Cat, in farewell, only says 'I love you both as much as you deserve'. It is impossible to give a dog a character as anything different from man's devoted friend; but cats are more equivocal. Sometimes it is difficult not to resent their apparent success, and they are good or evil according to their creator's feelings. While Mary Tourtel never portrayed an evil or unfaithful one, other writers are not so sure; perhaps Kipling was right, and cats are neither for nor against us, but both or neither, as they wish or feel. As characters they have great possibilities and depths that few writers, with the possible exception of Paul Gallico, have made use of. Their long history of connection with witchcraft has suggested tales of magic cats such as Barbara Sleigh's *Carbonel*, 1955, or, in a more down to earth setting, Rosemary Weir's *Pyewacket*, 1967; and their urbanised versatility (dog stories are more usually about country life) is categorised unforgettably by T. S. Eliot. Most of the cats one knows are typecast in *Old Possum's Book of Practical Cats*, 1939. They are Gumbies, or Jellicles, Rum Tum Tuggers or Macavities or like one or other of his feline varieties: Criminal, Old Thespian, Railway, Conjuror, Oldest Inhabitant, Pirate, or just the kind that sits about for ever. Their psychology is placed, wittily and firmly, among the humans whose lives the cats share; the only difference is one of size and shape, though even appearance is doubtful, from Growltiger, baggy at the knees, to Bustopher Jones with his well-cut trousers of impeccable black. The message is that these are cats we should be proud to know, described in verse so pleasing that it demands to be *said*, from the Rum Tum Tugger's jogging perversities to Growltiger's Kiplingesque ballad and the intricate jazz rhythms of Mungojerrie and Rumpelteazer.

Karel Capek's original *Fairy Tales*, 1933 in England, contain 'The Dog's Tale' and 'A Long Tale about a Cat' as might be expected from the author of *Dashenka*. While the Cat is a silent, enigmatic symbol rather than a character, 'The Dog's Tale' is a delightful account of the growth of Jim the puppy and what it feels like to be a youthful, imaginative dog, with just enough humanity to appreciate a kind of dog-mythology. From Jim's puppy days, when he could only count to two and mixed up his legs, he is taught how to bark by the groom and learns to look after his master's farm. But coming home alone one night he has a vision; he sees 'lovely white dogs, absolutely white, almost transparent, and so light that they

didn't even shake the dew from the grass – they danced and chased each other, or fought and ran after their tails, but everything was so light and airy that not a single blade of grass moved beneath them.' They also had no smell and did not scratch; and when the moon rose they lifted their heads and began to howl and sing softly and sweetly. Jim was moved to tears.

At last they speak, and Jim learns how the dogs lived in Eden and begged for a God whom they could smell, and were given Adam. Presumably this experience changed Jim for ever; his religious conversion was complete. Capek's animals are, for themselves, at the centre of creation; however Godlike man may appear, they regard him as a creature placed on earth specially to feed, amuse and care for them. This view comes out very strongly in 'Fairy Tales for Dashenka to make her Sit Still' (*I Had a Dog and a Cat*, 1940) and in the Cat's remarks about his master in the same collection: 'He is not beautiful because he has no fur. Not having sufficient saliva he has to wash himself with water. He miaows with a gruff voice and much too often. Sometimes he purrs in his sleep. Open the door for me.' Pets' Master-worship is clearly ambivalent.

The most convincing attempts to enter a dog's being and find out what his soul is really like, have been made by Kipling and Jack London and are among the author-and-animal identification stories in another chapter. But another very telling effort is made by T. H. White, who loved dogs so much. His faithful Brownie has a part in that strange book *The Elephant and the Kangaroo*, 1947 – the fictional story of the building of an ark from an Irish barn turned upside down – which has a cast of real people and animals. Brownie's thoughtful remarks are much to the point, if muddled in approach (rather like the educated foreigner that Michael Bond makes Paddington). 'Captain' in *Mistress Masham's Repose*, 1947, is Brownie again. Captain's world revolves round dogs, and humans take second place:

Poor Cook, thought Captain, I must be kinder to her. She makes a splendid pet. How faithful she is! I always say you can't get the same love from a dog, not like you can from a human. So clever, too. I believe she understands every word I say. I believe they have souls, just like dogs, only of course you can't smell them. It is uncanny how canine a human can be if you are kind to them, and treat them well. I know for a tact that when some dogs in history had died, their humans lay down on the grave and howled all night and refused food and pined away. It was just instinct, of course, not real intelligence, but all the same, it makes you chink . . .'

His thoughts do go on in a rather metaphysical way and later he mistakes the Lilliputian schoolmaster not for a child, but a puppy: 'He sat down carefully on the basket and arranged the School-master on his stomach. He prodded him with his nose several times, to shovel him into the right position.'

T. H. White's comedy only slightly exaggerates the possibilities of dog *persona*; the dog needs no speech, and thinks in an emotional flow, translated into words, for the benefit of humans who need them. But the best, and most happily convincing account of the speech of pets – and all animals – is *The Story of Dr Dolittle*, Hugh

Lofting, 1922. The whole series of the *Dolittle* books is based on this main idea, giving rise to another; first, that all the time from the rise of civilisation to now, the birds and the beasts had speech among themselves and were waiting to be understood by the first human with the luck, sympathy and application to study their languages; and second, that this outstanding human should be a doctor – not a vet – who is tired of, and disillusioned with, treating other human patients and is ready to turn to animals instead. Hugh Lofting wrote as many *Dolittle* books as Arthur Ransome wrote about the Blacketts, Walkers and Callums – but unlike Ransome's work which progressed with each novel, the first *Dolittle* book is the best. It is one of those perfect books without a word too many, and later ones tend to be lengthy and tedious, with dull spaces between incidents which have almost the perfection of the original, but are not built up with the original logical crescendo.

The action springs, as it should, from character. John Dolittle is an animal lover to the exclusion of humans. He alienates his sister by the 'rabbits in the pantry, white mice in the piano, squirrel in the

linen closet and a hedgehog in the cellar,' beside the more conventional pets of duck, dog, pig, parrot and owl. When his human patients desert him, Polynesia the parrot is the link by which John Dolittle makes his great discovery – she talks both human and bird language and is the Rosetta Stone by which the Doctor finds his true mission in life. His excitement at the discovery is as great as that of Newton or Archimedes: ' "Tell me some more," said the Doctor, all excited; and he rushed over to the dresser drawer and came back with the butcher's book and a pencil. "Now don't go too fast . . . this is interesting – very interesting – something quite new. Give me the Birds' A B C." '

Something quite dazzlingly new and simple is what *The Story of Dr Dolittle* is. The first moment of human-animal communication in human terms of words and grammar (wonderfully caught and illustrated by the film) is as strange and marvellous as the animals giving strength to Arthur's arm when he pulls the Sword from the Stone, or the meeting of Ransome and Hyoi in Malacandra.

After the Doctor has realised the possibilities of his discovery,

the story that follows is as neatly, sparingly logical and amusing as Edward Lear or Lewis Carroll.* The joke – or is it a joke? – is that the animals are not only much nicer than most people, they are also more intelligent than many of them. This is not new, it happens in Gulliver, but Hugh Lofting makes the point in a good-humoured and delightful way:

> '*I'm a pretty quiet creature as a rule,*' *said the horse* – '*very patient with people – don't make much fuss. But it was bad enough to have that vet giving me the wrong medicine. And when that red-faced booby started to monkey with me, I just couldn't bear it any more.*'
> '*Did you hurt the boy much?*' *asked the Doctor.*
> '*Oh no,*' *said the horse.* '*I kicked him in the right place. The vet's looking after him now. When will my glasses be ready?*'

Satire is gentle. The Doctor's domestic pets, the owl, duck, dog, pig and monkey are, on the whole, more sensible than the wild animals he meets – the monkeys and rather stupid lions in Africa, the wild birds and animals and circus performers in England. The Doctor, on his travels round the world like a modern St Francis/Robin Hood, righting various wrongs that have been done in the animal kingdom is, of course, in an impregnable position; most saints are. With every animal and bird on his side, he cannot lose; and as an Animals Liberation leader, he does have some very good ideas; teaching the animals to read and write and communicate at a distance, upholding their rights in the human world, releasing captives, curing the sick, reuniting 'families' and perhaps best of all, founding an animal reserve or sanctuary on a mysterious island off the coast of Africa that humans are guaranteed never to visit.

The animal characters that help him are brisk, natural, uncorrupted, with only the gentler human failings – the pig is a little lazy, the duck a trifle fussy, the delightful cockney sparrow Cheapside ('Ullo, Doctor, 'ere we are again! What-O! The old firm') a shade conceited; but it is the humans who are villainous, stealing, fight-

---

*Hugh Walpole's original foreword calls the book, 'The first real children's classic since *Alice*.' One might compile quite a list of such works. Why *Alice* is always the criterion, no one knows; but claims have been made for *The Hobbit*, *Winnie the Pooh*, *Peter Pan*, *The Lion, the Witch and the Wardrobe*, *The Wind in the Willows* and others. You have to be good to qualify for a Since Alice, but why not Since *Tom Sawyer*, *Emil and the Detectives*, *Black Beauty*, *Treasure Island*, or even *The Butterfly's Ball*?

ing, capturing and exploiting. As in Kästner's work, if the world were in animal hands, it would all go right, and Doctor Dolittle is the only human in history saintly enough to have noticed this fact. One has slight unease when the animals copy humans by developing institutions of their own – running their own post office (much swifter and more reliable than the GPO), writing their own magazine (full of true-life confessions and advertising: 'For hire, dogs' bones, suitably matured') and even opening their own shops and bank accounts ('With great dignity the King of Beasts strode into the Animals' Bank, deposited ten pounds and received a special gilt-edged cheque book from the bank manager himself – who also made a short speech').

It is all too human. As developing nations are supposed to copy the worst institutions of the richer ones, one fears the animals will enslave themselves to the things that seem most humanly dreary and inevitable; work and money and trade and rules and prisons. But uncorrupted, they are apparently incorruptible; this really is a glimpse of a brighter, kinder world. Though dog, owl, duck and pig cook, clean, do shopping, lock up and perform human acts with various degrees of dexterity, they help their human friend with superhuman powers as the dog smells, the owl listens, the eagle sees (*The Story of Dr Dolittle*, chapter 18 onwards) and his bird friends circle the earth with news and messages. Never are the grosser human values absorbed or upheld.

'Gosh, how lovely,' murmured Gubgub (as a cormorant brings pearls from an oyster bed).
'Pearls before swine,' giggled the white mouse. 'Tee, hee!'
'How uneducated you are,' snorted the pig, turning up his snout.
'Ladies before gentlemen, swine before pearls!'

The sad thing is, that there is only one John Dolittle; the rest of us never learn. When the Royal Meteorologist is sent to Fantippo to find out how the Doctor gets his weather reports, he returns, saying, 'He hasn't any new instruments at all. The man's a fake. All he has down there is an old barge and a whole lot of messy birds flying around.'

The Pet that achieves notoriety or fame – like Samuel the Snail or Paddington – has, in a way, become human by its own efforts and so to speak, pulled itself up by the paws. The delights of being a human-voiced pet are many: you can act and speak like a spoiled child and escape neatly from the consequences; you are seldom disciplined or punished or sent to school or encouraged to be your age or do anything painful. In fact, you do not grow up at all. This is fine if, like Paddington, you settle for a comfortable sexless middle age. But Paddington's great forerunner, Mary Plain, becomes fixed, like Baby Jane in an appealing female toddler stage with child star precocity and capacity for keeping in the centre of the limelight. There is a sad truth behind the fantasy. Bear cubs as pets are round, cuddly, endearing, and like the food that children like – in zoos they may become spoiled by too much attention.

Mary Plain – Gwynedd Rae: *Mostly Mary* and *All Mary* (both 1930), *Mary Plain in Town* (1935) and many others – like Samuel, Chester the Cricket and Mr Toad, achieves a kind of fame which gets her out of trouble on various occasions (one feels that broadcasting went to some animals' heads in the thirties; Samuel and Mary had only to show a BBC pass and they were allowed to go to the heads of queues and mingle with the great on public occasions like the 1935 Jubilee). Mary is half a real bear, half a child, never a toy like Pooh or Albert. Gwynedd Rae admitted at the beginning of her first book about this heroine, that she knew 'nothing whatsoever about bears' real lives and habits', but as long as her stories deal with the happenings in Mary's home – the bear-pit at Berne – the bears' doings are truthfully and amusingly observed and reported and what goes on is given a human meaning without any distortion of bear character and behaviour. The bears – four generations of them – live in a pit divided into 'rooms'; and their dens, open at night and shut during the day, are their only privacy. All their adventures are open to the sky and to the spectators. In the morning 'Friska, the mother bear, was busy getting all the bowls clean and ready for breakfast . . . she licked them all with great care and then gave them a final polish with her paw' – why not? This may be just what a captive bear does.

Mary leaves the bear-pit in her fairy-tale dreams. But the transition from the pit to the outside world via the Owl Man with whom she is able to exchange remarks is achieved quite naturally by her being taken out for walks with collar and lead – gradually Mary is growing into domestic pet, thence into human child. Taken out to tea she is first treated like a clever dog, then she talks to her hostess, shakes hands and says thank-you-for-having-me; this is the beginning of a different type of adventure. The humour is partly bearlike (Mary has adventures on a farm with ducks and other animals), but there is also the naïve humour of a foreign five-year-old who can behave, in human situations, with animal freedom: a pet who can talk, with the manners and privileges of a child. Mary has, like Paddington, the best of both worlds and the children she meets are sometimes envious. Dressed in her 'bathing drawers' and sailor hat (both optional) she can walk round London with the Owl Man eating éclairs and meringues (her favourite food), and everyone she meets is charmed and attracted. She wins a prize at the Crystal Palace exhibition and crowds greet the train on her return to Berne.

Spoiled by adulation and all too human now, she pretends to be ill to attract more attention, gets measles in earnest and goes to a children's hospital; everyone is confused by her identity. Her delightfully topical adventures in 1935 include the inevitable visit to the Jubilee, a broadcast with 'Uncle Mac, Elizabeth and Barbara,' and a visit to the cinema to see Disney's *Three Little Pigs*. The accompanying film seems to have had an A certificate, but as Mary was with the Owl Man it cannot have mattered. Her remarks must have annoyed him: 'Why has he got black hair on his chin? Why is she taking her dress off? Who's that in the bath? Why is he squeezing her neck like that and why is he putting her in a trunk?' At this stage Mary's bear nature disappears entirely and she goes to a dancing class, to a kindergarten, numerous children's parties and takes to writing verse. Her cinema visit, help with conjuring tricks, hospital antics, capacity for eating and two birthdays a year have many similarities to Paddington, her natural descendant, and her allegiance to Friska and the twins has echoes in Paddington's loyalty to his Peruvian Aunt Lucy. One's consciousness of the characters' animal origins has to have the occasional jog or they would turn into Shirley Temple and William Brown.

Perhaps the greatest oddity about the bears of Berne is St Bruin's Day, a kind of ursine Christmas or Shinto festival at which the bears honour their ancestors and take gifts to the oldest. Where is the cross bear, Harrods? the Owl Man asks, and is told, 'She's gone to live with St Bruin because he wanted her. We didn't.' Bears are unsentimental creatures, and so are many children. At times, in the *Mary Plain* books, it isn't easy to tell the difference.

The two last works in this section use Man's familiars, or best friends as subjects for novels, giving a sly view of human society on the way. The theme of Algernon Blackwood's *Dudley and Gilderoy* (1929) is that the co-existence of pets and owners is a pleasing joke in which it is difficult to tell who is the winner and who the loser. It is a curious, unworldly comedy about a cat and a parrot with the added humour of the parrot's volubility – he can, and does, express himself, but unlike the great Polynesia, is not listened to. He lacks his Boswell, or Dolittle.

The story of a friendship between cat and bird, apparently unnatural by human standards, is a real attempt to enter and examine the souls of both, but also uses the relationship to comment on humankind and to parody stories about the friendship of unequals; each of these opposites supplies what the other lacks. The bird, neat, beautiful, erudite and immobile, is complimented by the cat, a shaggy, ugly Tom, silent and resourceful. Together they elope, take a train to London, find a new home, are advertised for and at length reclaimed. They are a Pickwick and Sam Weller in the way they fit, a pair of confidence tricksters in the lofty way they treat the humans upon whom they depend; and one feels that perhaps all pets are like this, their secret lives bearing little relation to their actions. The parrot, Dudley, feels towards people a kindly pity, the cat Gilderoy, a slight disdain, but they talk to each other in thoughts that humans – who have to converse in set terms – do not, and in spite of Dr Dolittle, cannot, understand:

Purring, and a parrot's gurglings, since they refer to another order of experience, remain, for humans, undecipherable . . . gesture and attitude, the shaking of a feather, the twitching of a tail or whiskers, the cock of head or angle of neck, the flick of an ear, even the movement of agile claws and toes – these largely took the place of clumsy words. Thus, while Dudley and Gilderoy now gazed into one another's eyes, apparently uncommunicative, they were actually exchanging ideas of this high, but above all different order.

While Dudley can talk to humans using his Old-Man's voice, his Vicar's, Mother's Patient, Childish, Librarian's or Sailor's voices, his speech, larded with Latin tags, swear words or old-fashioned phrases like Anyhopedoctor or Abaslesboches does not 'mean' anything. But to his friend Gilderoy, he speaks of his great Life's Work his feelings about his owners, his slight disgust at the cat's sex life, appetites and irregularities with half-human, half-bird comedy:

'I for my part,' he now observed, 'am chaste.' It was offered as a statement of indubitable scientific accuracy.
'By what!' asked Gilderoy without looking up.
'Stet,' said Dudley sharply, believing it to be a snub, then slipping into the confused gabble in which it was his aggravating way to say extremely interesting things too softly to be audible. Two words alone emerged clearly towards the end: habeas corpus, which he considered even more annihilating than 'stet.'

Together 'the creatures' understand and manipulate the humans – as, one feels, pets often do – producing the effects and events they wish, partly because in them instinct and reason appear to be perfectly balanced, partly because to each other they cannot lie or dissemble. To humans they do this all the time, but their consciences are each bare to the other in a world which seems both above and beyond, the human one; and from this lofty height they regard humans – so oddly moved by print, so often calmed by Latin – as accomplished, at times lovable, but on the whole a minor kind of animal. In its oblique way, and for all its domestic comedy, this is as penetrating an animal study as *Black Beauty* or *Thy Servant, a Dog*, and unrivalled in its physical description of pets well known, well loved and perfectly understood.

Similar in quality but far removed in time and manner, *The History of Pompey the Little*, Francis Coventry, 1751, is a mock-novel of a delightful kind, and must be the first ever dog book. It appeared in the same year as *Amelia* and *Peregrine Pickle*, and gently uses the adventures of its dog-hero to comment on human life, and novels, of the day. It contains interpolated 'tales' to relieve 'tediousness' and 'urges the value of fiction as a mirror of the times,' as John Cleland said in the *Monthly Review* of that year; it was thought at first, that he had written the book himself.

Pompey, a small spaniel, son of Julio and Phyllis, is conceived during his master's visit to a courtesan, born at Bologna in 1735 and taken to England. Throughout his life, 'born to be a herald of love', he witnesses the amours and intrigues of his many and various owners. There is comment in the narrative on various aspects of a dog's life too – ill-treatment by servants who are kind only when the Mistress is present (a favourite theme of early animal stories), a married couple who quarrel over their pets, children who do not know how to treat them, women who lavish too much affection, owners who are drunk, neglectful or cruel and a blind beggar who is kind. Through all his vicissitudes, Pompey maintains a kind of alert, amused dignity, human enough to appreciate, animal enough to be dumb. In Lady Tempest's household 'He quickly became a great Admirer of Mr Garrick's acting at the Play-House, grew extremely fond of Masquerades, passed his judgement upon Operas and was allowed to have a very nice and distinguishing Ear for Italian music.' What he could have said 'If he could have Spoken' or 'If he could have Written' is of course told in Pompey's thoughts which he keeps to himself, only exchanging opinions with a learned and philosophical cat called Hopson whose sister Mr Gray commemorated in 'a most elegant little Ode'.

His life continues with various owners from the rich to the poor and industrious: with the beggar, and in an ale house and with an undergraduate at Cambridge. His gay and jaunty courage leads him through many amorous exchanges ('No modern love can in the Nature of Things, last above Three Days') and 'Little Parties of Innocent amusement' at last back, like Fanny Hill, to his first love – Lady Tempest. His death is recorded by a monument which mentions that, in 1749, he was gathered to the Lap Dogs of Antiquity; and the lack of religion, politics and moral teaching contributes to the gaiety of this pleasing and fascinating story. Pompey's debating on the Summum Bonum with Hopson, as they sit on a pair of open books, is the perfect picture of an educated dog and cat; Pompey can also pick out other educated dogs by the way they enter a room. He dies in serene old age. This lighthearted, ironic, picaresque dog story stands alone.

11 The Rupert Stories of Mary Tourtel and Alfred Bestall

'Oh, mother, mother!' Rupert sobs,
'My heart is full of fear
You'd save me from old Gruffenuff
If only you were here.'

'Rupert Gets Captured', *Mary Tourtel*

Take a fairy tale from Grimm, one of the more exciting but less grotesque – say, 'The Golden Goose' or 'The Frog Bride' or 'Rumpelstiltzkin'. Add to this some of the glamour of *The Arabian Nights,* some of the magic and mysterious qualities of the *King Arthur* cycle and some of its knightly heroism. Add a homely taste of folk tale. Blend these ingredients very smoothly. Dilute the effect by a contemporary setting or framework. Express the result in drawings of beautiful, accurate detail, with no cartoon facetiousness, and then ration the dose to a picture a day, ensuring that addicts will always demand more – and you have the Rupert Bear adventures of the twenties and thirties, and some of the reasons why he enjoyed, and still enjoys, such success and popularity.

That Rupert should be one of the most enduring animal characters of the last few decades seems at first rather odd, as there is no reason for him to be a bear rather than a child or a youngest son. But he was made in the days of Pip, Squeak and Wilfred, the Bruin Boys, Bobby Bear and Teddy Tail and in a children's picture story in a national newspaper it must have seemed natural to have an animal hero. However, his nature was, and is, ambiguous, and here again is part of the secret of his enormous appeal. Children can identify themselves with him in all that he does, as he was always rather more a child than an animal, for all his Teddy bear look.

Like Sexton Blake, his adventures have no end but continue as the work of different authors.* November 1970 marked Rupert's fiftieth birthday but he has not aged at all. He has changed a little and, on the whole, grown younger and been brought gradually up-to-date, while still keeping to a rural and fairy-tale setting. There seems no reason why Rupert should ever end; his immortality is perpetually renewed as his adventures continue on television and in annual form, and three generations of children have enjoyed them and asked for more.

Rupert has slowly evolved from animal to person as his reality grew in the telling; he passed from animal-toy into boy, like Pinocchio. Today he is entirely a boy. But during his long life he has inhabited a strangely changing place that is always a serious world – unlike that of his early contemporaries, Pip, Squeak and Wilfred, or Tiger Tim – never really an adult one such as the world of Flook and Rufus. Rupert's setting when it had reached its final form of Nutwood and the surrounding countryside, had no towns, no cities. It was populated by animals and people in about equal numbers, none of them ever noticing that there is anything odd about the others. All behave and are dressed in human fashion. The animals often give the stories a different dimension without being used as plot material. Apart from the obvious Robber Wolf and the occasional dragon, they are seldom 'bad' characters – this is reserved for 'human' humans, dwarves, wizards and witches – and here the Rupert tales resemble C. S. Lewis's Narnia.

Characters that have their main life in drawings might be expected to have adventures with plenty of incidents but weak plots; but this has never been the case with Rupert. His originator was Mary Tourtel, a talented artist and the wife of a sub-editor of the *Daily Express*. She gave Rupert too much plot rather than too little. Rupert was born on 28 November 1920 with a story called 'Little Lost Bear'. The inspiration was perhaps Goldilocks and Red Riding Hood combined. Rupert lived in a small cottage in the middle of a wood. He went out into the wood, got lost, naturally, and in the course of his wanderings met many of the characters that Mary Tourtel was to keep in all her stories. He eventually returned home again to a triumphant reunion with his parents.

This plot was the basis of every Rupert story that Mary Tourtel wrote, and the basis of many of the stories of Alfred Bestall. From

*Currently Frederick H. Chaplain and Alex Cubie.

the very first comes the odd, anomalous situation that this appears to be animal land; yet there are a few people in it, and the animals are all of mixed types – wild animals (Bill Badger), tame ones (Algy Pug, the Rabbit Twins) and an African elephant (Edward Trunk). They are all dressed, of course – in animal land human clothes are the rule rather than the exception – but apart from that, Mary Tourtel's animals are almost exactly half-humanised. They are not as non-human as Frank Rogers's Little Robins, where one can almost see the bird bones under the cloth. They walk upright as humans do, but the parts that *show* are animal – space is left for tails and horns. The one exception is hands and feet: the former have human fingers and the latter fit neatly into boots and shoes. But even so there is the Wise Goat who consults his magic books and writes letters with hoofs, and Edward Trunk whose hands are elephant's feet, adapted.

Among these creatures Rupert is, at first, part animal, part toy. The drawing suggests a real bear: he has a long snout, large head and small body. He is given a furry outline. In Mary Tourtel's earliest stories – 'Rupert Gets Captured', 'Rupert and the Robber Wolf' – there are lines on the head which might indicate the joins where a toy's head is sewn together. Yet the face is wild-bear shaped and is given quite a lot of expression; looks of fear and dismay are shared by Mrs Bear, who at one point goes weeping to the Wise Goat.

'Rupert Gets Captured' already has the basic plot, and the basic quatrains which jingle on in ballad style:

> *Come boys and girls, all you who like*
> *To read of Little Bear*
> *Begin today and you will find*
> *What he will do and dare.*
> *He goes out for a morning run*
> *Not meaning far to roam;*
> *How little does he know his fate*
> *Before he next sees home.*

Later in the Rupert saga these words would have been unnecessary. Rupert's fate was so monotonously terrible that one wondered why he went out at all, and conversely, why his parents ever bothered to worry. But here he is, bowling his hoop along. It goes in through the gates of a castle: Rupert follows, and is captured at once by the Ogre Gruffenuff's soldiers – toy soldiers, quite clearly made of wood (in later Tourtel stories they would certainly have been either animals or real men, more usually the latter). The ogre, realistic, gross and frightening, puts Rupert in a cage to be fattened before he is eaten. A robin, not dressed (few artists dress birds convincingly – Frank Rogers's success here is unique), talking to Rupert in animal language, flies off to Mrs Bear, who goes at once to the Wise Goat, a reliable character and magician who rescues Rupert again and again, often coming in at the end of an involved plot when all other help has failed. Mary Tourtel shows him in many stories living ascetically – a hermit in a bare cottage with simple wooden furniture, a stone floor, books ink and paper, and a mysterious box like an early crystal radio set apparently wired up to some point in the ceiling. It has knobs and dials and a hooded 'viewer' in which the Wise Goat can see at a distance, though not, apparently, into the past or future. It is a mixture of the magic and the mechanical and is about the only piece of machinery Mary Tourtel ever showed, apart from vehicles (planes, and a very occasional bus or car).

In 'Rupert Gets Captured', the Wise Goat calls on two of Rupert's friends to go to his aid. These are a monkey and a golliwog and are real toys – they are discovered in a play-room with a doll's house in it. They have fixed expressions. The monkey is sewn together and has visible cotter pins in his joints. They saw through the cage, but Rupert is recaptured and put in a dungeon. A mouse, dressed (the temptation to humanise mice is irresistible), tells the Wise Goat again, who sends for the Rabbit twins, Rex and Reggie. Burrowing tactics fail; Rupert is imprisoned in a high tower. Swallows take the news to the Wise Goat, who informs a wandering group of balloons (these 'air balloons' are not always on Rupert's side: in 'Rupert and Margot' they treacherously carry Margot away), who rescue him from the tower on an aerial raft. The ogre sees the escape and falls from his own ramparts in an effort to catch the balloons, breaking his neck. Rupert is restored to his rejoicing parents.

This simple story was to be repeated again and again in different forms – the capture, imprisonment (with considerable anxiety and duress – Rupert shown crying in the cage, standing with bowed head between his gaolers), and the rescue.

Early stories include Rupert and – the Robber Wolf, the Magic Toyman, the Wooden Soldier, the Black Dwarf, King Pippin, the Little Prince, Margot. In 'Rupert and the Black Dwarf' – with a simple plot of capture and rescue – the twists and turns of the escape have an ingenuity worthy of the inmates of Colditz Castle or Stalag Luft III, involving disguise, shape-changing, memory, tunnels and animal help through the use of animal language. Rupert is bilingual, and it is assumed that all animals share the same non-human speech, unlike those in Dr Dolittle. Rupert's eventual success owes a good deal to resource and courage; he is never shown as a helpless victim.

As Mary Tourtel continued, the plots improved. At first Rupert seems to be involved for no particular reason – he is trespassing, or happens to meet a witch that doesn't like children or who has a personal grudge (this happened when his activities in bringing witches and ogres to their fate became well known). But later, Rupert is seen as a rather odd, small, hero figure – only Rupert can solve some particular problem, find the remedy for some enchantment, or restore the missing princess. He is seen to be in a special position, to hold some almost magic powers that ordinary people haven't got, notably by being half in the animal world and half out of it. In 'Rupert and the Enchanted Princess' from the mid-twenties, Mary Tourtel's best period, Rupert is pounced upon and carried off (a familiar beginning) by a huge heraldic bird, and taken to a king who has lost his daughter; perhaps Rupert can find her. He has been called upon as a last resource. Here there is a story with elements of Grimm, as are many of the best; Rupert is the youngest son, or the person least likely to succeed. Even the king is disappointed at seeing him. He sets out on the quest, laughed at by the palace guard, until he gets his first clue from a dog and a cat who at last can tell that the Princess was stolen by witches. This tale concerns the completion of a series of tasks, each depending on another; at last the Princess is found to be growing in the garden of the witches' castle, in the form of a flower. *But* the castle is guarded by a dragon *and* a time must be chosen when the witches are asleep *and* which is the right flower to pick? This story has great suspense, cleverly maintained. One feels genuine anxiety for the outcome and there is a rare trace of humour (not a strong point with Mary Tourtel) – the dragon is fond of riddles, to which Rupert has to find the right answers.

Mary Tourtel had no scruples about borrowing a good fairy tale from another story teller or from a folklore source. As well as Grimm, her best stories have echoes of *The Arabian Nights*, Perrault and Dickens and are interspersed with real-life adventures such as 'Rupert and his Pet Monkey' (immensely popular) or 'Rupert and Algy at Hawthorn Farm'. To this peak period belong 'The Old

Man of the Sea', 'The Magic Har', 'Prince Humpty Dumpty', 'The Circus Clown', 'The Wood of Mystery', 'The Wilful Princess' and others. In all these stories invention is unfailing and marvellously maintained, suspense holds to the end.

In 1931 Mary Tourtel's husband and collaborator, H. B. Tourtel, died. He may have acted as a restraint on her plots which thereafter became more elaborate, and Rupert appeared to be made unhappier by the straits in which he found himself. Perhaps the witches were no worse – quite the most unpleasant is in 'Rupert in Trouble Again' 1928 – but there seemed to be more real-life evil characters, and the effect on children must have been to give them serious concern for their hero. Magic, the Wise Goat and poetry fade, replaced by mere action. 'Rupert and Bill's Aeroplane Adventure' involves a black prince, gorillas, cannibals, white hunters and at least two plane trips – there and back. This is boys' adventure material and out of character for Rupert as he was.

Later work shows a decline. The fairy tales still went on but they became patchy and involved. A feature of the later stories is that the pictures are no longer self-explanatory and require long, rather boring verse conversations to help the plot along, delivered by static characters, running to several episodes. Perhaps by 1935, even if she had been able to continue to draw (failing sight brought her retirement), Mary Tourtel had had enough of Rupert.

The verses that accompanied each picture were so much a part of Rupert that one cannot think of him in prose. They were neither exceptional nor very poetic, often being marred by archaisms such as e'er, and e'en and 'twas and descried. They jingle quietly on for ever like Tennyson's Brook and are only noticed when they are impossibly bad, with jerks, inversions and suspensions, i.e.:

> *Said Little Bear to Puss: 'Perhaps we could find out some way*
> *To escape the witch and get from here – 'when they heard a voice say:*
>   *'Nay*
> *I told you to go straight home, you know, that day you rescued me:*
> *And now there's no escape for you.' How surprised were they to see—*
> *The Little Mannikin stood there. 'Perhaps I can help you'*
> *Said he to Little Bear: 'Tell me just what you have to do.'*

This all makes sense and scans, if you are nimble. But usually the verse is simple, short, adequate and quite pedestrian.

Where the sister witches sleep, one stirs
In restless dreams she moans,
Then wakes up: 'A Stranger's here,
I feel it in my bones.'

With very few exceptions, the poetry lies exclusively in the drawing and the ideas which, at their best, combine the strange and haunting qualities of the best fairy tales one knows and an intense reality which fairy tales often lack. 'Once upon a time there was a woodcutter with three sons' may be happening in Bohemia or fairyland or anywhere, but when we see Rupert and Edward Trunk roasting chestnuts by the fire on a winter's day we know that the place is Nutwood, England, not too far from London, the time about 1928. There are two armchairs of the period, one with loose cover. There is a high hob grate and brass fender. The very high mantelshelf is decorated with a frill, the front door opens straight into the room, bellows and coal scuttle are shown, real and inevitable. It is not only an idea of what a country cottage ought to look like but an image of rooms and objects that have been, and still survive, recognised with delight. And one knows that something wonderful is just about to happen.

This is the start of one of Mary Tourtel's best stories – not perhaps the best plotted, but quite the most original. The old woman who knocks at the door has lost her graddaughter, who has gone out to look for a cat. Tracks in the snow lead to a hole high up in a tree. Rupert helpfully climbs the tree to look and finds it is hollow; iron rungs lead down inside. He climbs down and jumps to the bottom only to find that it is false. He falls through twigs and leaves into another country – not an underground region, but an island where it is always summer, ruled over by the Old Man of the Sea, a terrifying Triton dressed in seaweed which also seems part of his body.

This story owes nothing to Grimm, or any other source. The only fairy tale to which it can be compared is C. S. Lewis' *The Lion, the Witch and the Wardrobe* which has a reversed situation of summer-into-winter, and a wicked queen. The Lewis story is cleverly plotted and beautifully and movingly written; the 'Old Man of the Sea' has the simplest of plots but is beautifully and poetically drawn. The setting is strange and haunting; the Old Man's palace, the rocky island with its maritime pines on which the little girl is kept a prisoner, reached by a spidery aerial ropeway, the Old Man out hunting with his seal pack, the Fairies of the Earth and Sky who eventually drown the Old Man for a thousand years, the wintry woods above, and on a homely note, the wonderful tea in which everyone joins (Mary Tourtel was superlative at depicting meals) make this story memorable.

Mary Tourtel's drawing was characterised by its great clarity and simplicity, allied to attention to detail. Nowhere is there a fuzzy, indefinite line. One fault is that the pictures occasionally have a static, rather two dimensional cardboard quality; another could be that little is left to the imagination. But more often the effect is that the imagination is stimulated. There are delights such as the house in the tree where Margot lived, the rabbit princess who loaned her miniature coach drawn by tiny ponies with mouse footmen, the village grocer's in 'Rupert and Bill Keep Shop' which might have come straight out of Cranford. What could be truer than the cottage interior in 'The Magic Whistle': the hob grate with its ovens, iron candlestick, oil lamp, calendar on the wall? Nothing is scanty or hurried, all lovingly described in line. The pony trap in this story is accurate in every detail, the stag which appears later is a proud and beautiful animal.

Mary Tourtel's attention to detail cannot be faulted. Her notebook, it is said, recorded a gallery of objects which she observed from day to day and which she thought suitable for inclusion in her stories. They can be seen now as a faithful record of life in the twenties, from the decorations in the Black Dwarf's garden – pilasters bearing Art Deco elephants balanced on balls – to the cottage interiors, the clothes, the plane in which Rupert stows away in 'Rupert Gets Stolen' which has basketwork seats and curtains at the windows, the few cars, train, taxi and bus. Even the period costume has a twenties flavour, now as noticeable as the hairstyles in Korda's *Private Life of Henry VIII*. All the fairy-tale quest stories have period settings, usually in some vague part of the Middle Ages. One can tell when the plot is about to begin when Rupert meets a character dressed in Robin Hoodish villein costume, often almost on his own doorstep. This odd fact is not usually noticed by Mrs and Mrs Bear, who are absurdly trusting.

In the all-animal story 'Rupert and Bill Keep Shop', the animals lend great diversity and interest, and act so humanly that their heads are not disguises but character masks. One by one the customers come in. The kangaroo is a bouncy character who wants a ball of string and muddles up everything the shop can offer, without buying. The lion is rather poor and old, with a weak chest. The kindly elephant, who wants 'a little snack of biscuits – bring a tin', is apologetic about his appetite and dates the story at a time when biscuits were sold by loose weight and not in packets. Mrs Fox accuses Rupert of cheating and goes off quietly without paying. The busy, black-suited, townish little rat tastes every piece of cheese. It is interesting in this tale, which must gratify every child's wish for being left in charge of a shop for a day, to note Rupert and Bill's success, whereas William, in the same situation, has anarchic failure. The period charm of this story is very great; it deserves a place beside 'Ginger and Pickles', or 'The Pie and the Patty Pan'. Every detail of the little village grocery is shown; the eggs stacked in a wooden crate, the hams on the shelf, Badger's Tea at two shillings (per pound?), sweets in open trays on the counter, a huge barrel-shaped block of margarine cut with a small shovel-shaped scoop. At the end of the day they count the takings in silver, notes and gold.

In only one story does Mary Tourtel appear openly to recognise Rupert's double nature. This is the curiously sad 'Rupert and the Circus Clown', a balanced vice-versa tale, the Little Dorrit of the *Rupert* saga. Rupert is kidnapped by a clown, to become part of a travelling show. He finds the animal cages at the back of the circus, and the animals all warn him that eventually he will become as they are. They seem to recognise him as an animal and tell him in their own language what his fate will be. They have sad, realistic faces. Rupert escapes and there is a semi-magic episode in which he meets one of Mary Tourtel's nastier witches and most bizarre and frightening dwarfs; the witch keeps him chained up in a dog kennel. At last he meets the clown again, now with a Toby dog, out of work and hungry. They join forces and clown and dog perform in the street while Rupert passes round the hat for pennies.

Liking Rupert was considered, at my school, as babyish as believing in fairies, but addicts took no notice and swapped the yellow books secretly, unashamed. To me they gave the feeling that outside one's very own front door (our house was Rupert's cottage grown larger) the adventures would happen, and Rupert, always the crusader on the side of right, would find his way home in the end. Some children obviously found the real-life stories more satisfying, but in all of them there was something unique that compelled serious attention; perhaps it was that they took themselves so seriously.

A rather grim element is nearly always present in the fairy tales which at times may have been disturbing to a child (it obviously disturbed editorial policy on the *Daily Express* and may account for Mr Bestall's lack of witches), but its presence keeps Rupert from being a pet or a toy and gives him the role of hero. The same kind of threat is often present in Beatrix Potter, and does not appear frightening, but part of life. In Mary Tourtel it is sometimes strangely overdone. The rather gross ogre Gruffenuff is definitely going to eat Rupert. So is the Sandy Whiskered Gentleman going to eat Jemima Puddleduck, but she is mercifully ignorant of his intentions. In 'Rupert's Mysterious Flight', one of the tasks King Toucan gives him is the recovery of a pearl from a pit of snakes and crocodiles; he only just escapes in time. In 'Rupert in Trouble Again' a sadistic witch puts him into a cage which is hoisted up 'for ever' to the battlements of her castle by her unpleasant 'family' – a toad, a wolf, a dwarf and a raven. Rupert is soon rescued, but one hopes children did not know that medieval prisoners died in such horrific devices. This witch is punished and dies at the end of the story – she 'falls to her doom' off stage. Her wolf too is killed by a dog. One does not witness the death of Gruffenuff, though one sees him fall from his own castle wall.

But to balance this, there is so much enchantment; so many stories that have a magic and poetry all too rare in children's books of this particular era. There is the moment when Rupert and the Wilful Princess, playing in the old castle, find the mysterious locked door. The Princess has to turn the key – but what is inside? Only broken lumber. Among the old toys is a rocking horse on which they both climb – much against Rupert's wish, but the Princess, characterised as a determined, rather unpleasant little girl, insists. As it rocks they find they cannot dismount and the horse flies through a window to a giant's castle where they find that they themselves have become toys: justice, poetry and strangeness all together. There is the moment when Rupert, waiting in a room in a

castle on a strange island, sees The Magic Hat – his only transport – float past the window, carrying away the gnome who brought him. And in this story there is an enchanted garden, from which no one returns, containing mysterious clues for escape in a winged horse, a golden butterfly and a caged bird. And best of all perhaps at the end of the *Black Dwarf* story is the search that Rupert and Bill make to find the place in the forest where the dwarf was changed into a twisted tree. They can never find it.

> *Thus was Merlin bound for ever by enchantment, so they say*
> *In an oak in Broceliande Forest in good King Arthur's day.*
> *There are tales told by poets of nymphs and sprites who dwell*
> *Within the trees which children here 'twould take too long to tell. –*

And there are all the other mysterious gardens and forests and sea-shores and castles, with the true taste of romance about them, drawn with a beauty and invention that is an unusual and sustained achievement.

Alfred Bestall changed things, though he did his loyal best not to. Taking over a character – indeed, a whole mythology – created by someone else, is a difficult, nearly impossible task. Mr Bestall's drawings, from his first Rupert story in 1935, copied Mary Tourtel's style as closely as they could with 'Rupert and the Smugglers', a deliberately unoriginal adventure where continuity was all. Rupert the dependable figure had to be the same and the pictures, two a day, each story lasting about five weeks, were also deliberately and modestly unsigned. The effect at first was of a curious anonymity. The bear had not appeared to change in essence – the careful placing of his 'dot' eyes and his occasionally permitted smile gave him expression, his clothes were as they had always been – yet even a child could tell that his surroundings were drawn by a different hand. Those tortuous quatrains were lacking, and there was something about the shape of the body . . . Alfred Bestall was gradually rescuing Rupert from the odd sadness that had clouded the end of Mary Tourtel's enchantment. The proportions of his body were becoming more youthful, his activities more varied, his expressions less stylised. Though occasionally during Mr Bestall's thirty years of drawings for the *Daily Express* Rupert shed a tear because he was lost, he never cried with terror because he was going to be imprisoned, tortured, killed and eaten.

Some of the magic went, and so did all the witches, but Rupert's adventures continued and do so still. The Second World War reduced him in size and allowed only one picture a day – Winston Churchill once crowded him off the page and he disappeared in respectful mourning for the deaths of President Kennedy and Pope John. His annuals have appeared from 1936 with five, or four, stories in them – usually one reprinted from the paper and the rest new – in full colour, with Rupert in red and yellow, the fields and forests of Nutwood glowing in pea green and copper beech. Mr Bestall's talents, at their finest in his end papers and covers for the annuals, have given Rupert a new dimension of charm and pleasure.

Rupert himself, always the sort of small boy that parents would be happy for their son to be, continued to formula, but of course it was a different one. Carefully kept were Mr and Mrs Bear, unchanged as all good parents should be: Mrs Bear's dress still ankle length, Mr Bear with pipe, bow tie and plus fours. Bill Badger, the Twins, Podgy Pig, Algy Pug and Edward Trunk continued agelessly – though Edward and Algy now have far more humanised faces than Mary Tourtel gave them, and Podgy has turned from a greedy country oaf into a rather likeable character with a worrying

Mama who slightly spoils him. Others have been added to the Nutwood population: Billy Goat with his Granny, Bingo, a dog characterised as a resourceful and rather intelligent small bespectacled boy, fond of dangerous experiments with chemistry sets, Gregory Guinea Pig, Rastus the country mouse, Podgy's rather annoying girl cousin Rosalie Pig, Lily Duckling, Pong Ping the Peke, and some new humans – the three Guides (drawn from life) and Rollo the gipsy boy. Margot, still the Kate Greenaway girl, makes brief appearances, but there are fairy-tale characters too such as Simple Simon, Mary Mary and Tiger Lily – not a Red Indian from the Never Land, but the Chinese daughter of the Conjuror, a useful magic-making character who lives in a pagoda-like tower.

The rhymes had gone. Rupert was more everyday, and less like a ballad character. Verse reappeared in the annuals, but prose rather than jingles suited Mr Bestall's creation. Rupert's friends kept their oddly old-fashioned bow ties and Eton suits – the most obvious differences were those of mobility and speed. Rupert appeared at once more agile and spry, and so less of a victim and less helpless. He has undoubtedly been socialised. To begin with he was very much an 'only' child, having adventures that took him on solitary quests. Mr Bestall turned him, in many stories, into a member of a group of assorted boys and girls who seem to meet on their village common, play games together and have adventures often only slightly blended with magic and the unusual. The village settings have expanded from Mary Tourtel's detailed views of corners and edges and parts of things – perhaps the result of her poor sight, one seldom saw much of the village shop, of Rupert's cottage, or a really wide vista of village street. Mr Bestall gives views of field and wood, the Nutwood lanes and cottages and church, even quite modern lamp posts are there as if the whole place had grown larger. Once Rupert's cottage opened straight on to the lane. Now, with growing affluence the old cottage is no longer typical even of an idealised village. It has been expanded, and given a hedge with a respectable front garden in which Mr Bear potters in rather suburban fashion. The proportions of the cottage have changed too – though the furniture and the curtains are still more or less as Mary Tourtel left them when she moved out, the whole place has subtly grown, and the kitchen is almost up-to-date. Mrs Bear once cooked on a range; she does so no more. Rupert's bedroom has more furniture, and the sitting-room is large enough for a sizeable children's party.

The village setting is very real, with Constable Growler patrolling the streets and the children playing on the common. No longer can a mysterious cobbler come to the front door with magic boots in his pack, or strange men in medieval dress go by on horseback, ready to kidnap bears to be toys for a prince. When floods appear, they do not lead Rupert to the wicked gnome who imprisoned him in his enchanted garden – but instead, Rupert does brave deeds of rescue with a raft and a rope bridge ('Rupert and the River Rescue', 1959).

Far more of the Bestall stories are about real-life adventures in all of which Rupert shows courage, resource and initiative: in fact considerably more of these qualities than most children would be able to muster. Rupert explores caves, rescues animals, climbs cliffs and finds his way home from various difficult situations, such as being taken away from Nutwood in the wrong train or wrong bus, being lost in strange country, or floated down a river or out to sea in a boat. Mr Bestall introduces more 'real' crooks, burglars, outlaws and villains than Mary Tourtel ever did. They menace Rupert and occasionally capture him, but never for long; the more usual formula is for him to uncover their plans by careful observation and inform Constable Growler in good time – as in 'Rupert and the Fishing Rod', where Rupert's catching an apparent poacher leads to the recovery of the Squire's stolen silver.

But more common are the fantasy stories involving Rupert, his friends and parents in semi-magical situations happening in and around Nutwood where magic objects are found ('Rupert and the Diamond Leaf'), strange trees grow up suddenly between the floorboards ('Rupert and the Backroom Boy'), or Rupert discovers an animal underground railway beneath the human one ('Rupert and Ozzie'). These events are extraordinary rather the terrifying, and the Bear parents treat them as such, showing surprise and interest rather than alarm.

Mary Tourtel, though she wrote during the days of the classic detective story, did not make use of the technique for Rupert. His mysteries were those of being launched into the unknown. One of Mr Bestall's favourite plot devices is the genuine mystery, or fitting together of clues to make a finally revealed whole. A typical example is 'Rupert and the Diamond Leaf', in which Rupert sees a bush, a Botanist, a strange bird, the three Girl Guides and Lily Duckling. The events are connected as Lily eats a berry from the plant, and *flies* over the Guides' skipping rope: The Plot is resolved as Rupert, eating a berry also, flies to a tropical island and thence to the bird kingdom (ruled by King Toucan, a borrowing from Tourtel) and learns that the flight-inducing berries are grown in Birdland to revive weary messengers. One has been dropped on Nutwood common by mistake. Rupert is flown back to Nutwood (by bird), the plant is uprooted and the secret kept safe – 'humans' must not be allowed to fly.

On the face of it, this is a more original story than any of Mary Tourtel's. It has a puzzle that is eventually solved, and a most unusual idea; but it lacks the Tourtel suspense and enchantment. Rupert is frequently removed from Nutwood to strange kingdoms under the earth or in the sky or over the sea – indeed Alfred Bestall has always shown considerable ingenuity in getting his hero out of his home environment and into Bandit country: the Far East, Pagoda land or distant islands with odd, Mongolian rulers. But these places, when reached, have no numinous qualities; there are no magic quests, no feeling of strange dooms and imprisonment for ever. No doubt this is deliberate. Mary Tourtel's speciality – her really frightening witches – are no longer acceptable agents for adventure. Instead, Alfred Bestall has his own speciality: the semi-magic Conjuror, the unpredictable Old Professor with his dwarf servant, the Inventor, who can be relied on to produce unusual effects with pipes and retorts and substances that change the properties of matter so that magic can appear to be used with the escape clause of possibility. Magicians and enchanters exist, but they are not a dominant species. Appearing more often are those wayward botanical creatures, the Elves of Autumn and the Imps of Spring, who provide interest by making underground mistakes so that the seasons change, the wrong plants come up and bushes, flowers or trees assume animal life.

To summarise, many of the Bestall stories are involved with science fiction of a sort. Even the imps and elves have their gears, dynamos and experimental laboratories underground, and machinery – beautifully drawn and apparently workable – is often the agency of strangeness and excitement. Rupert no longer lives on

the edge of fairy tales and enchanted forests; but – as in one of
Mr Bestall's finest, 'Rupert and the Sky Boat' – a factory for making
lighter-than-air metal appears in the depths of a wood, sucking in
clouds from the upper air and eventually floating away because its
product has become lighter than itself. (Mr Bestall's ingenuity is
considerable; Rupert and Margot, in a lighter-than-air boat, have
to use their wits and their weight to beach their craft.) The story is
nothing if not logical, and so are others; Blue Moon or a Mare's
Nest are exactly what they sound like; a 'monster' in a wood turn
out to be a donkey carrying double panniers. While Father Christmas is often lost or at his wits' end and having to be helped, or
while there are a few toys' vengeance stories and a few crafty fox
and greedy pig adventures, for the most part Alfred Bestall's obess-
sion with flight brings the most unusual and delightful semi-
scientific arrangements with birds, balloons, rockets and flying
machines of all kinds.

Rupert has wisely stayed away from topical realities. He visited
the Queen's coronation, but that has been his only trip to London.
He got lost there, and his pleasing journey home on the animals'
under-Underground was one of Mr Bestall's inventions which one
wishes were true. It is rather surprising that Dr Dolittle never
thought of it.

Rupert's Animal Land has never had many rules. Characters have

been changed or introduced when needed, while trying to keep continuity. In Nutwood animal children have animal parents, but the human population of the village has grown – the hippos and dogs and chimps who were once the servant or working class (used by Mary Tourtel as shop assistants, footmen or bus conductors) are giving way to humans. There is no animal conservation – the various species are just plainly on the wane and are not being re-placed. As for Rupert and his friends, Alfred Bestall has humanised them to the degree that one imagines he would rather draw human children and turn Rupert Bear into Rupert Brown. In this series, humanity has won by achieving boyhood. Perhaps we should all give up pretending.

12 The Tables Turned at the Zoo: Mowgli and Stuart Little

The Lion has a tail and a very fine tail,
And so has an elephant, and so has a whale,
And so has a crocodile, and so has a quail –
They've all got tails but me.

'In the Fashion', *A. A. Milne*

In the Du Maurier cartoon *The Tables Turned at the Zoo*, various animals stare at, feed, or merely tease, two unfortunate men in cages. The fashionable realism makes the picture, to me, very uncomfortable. The animals are feeding the humans with the sort of food they like – the Disneylike elephant in the foreground dressed as a little girl holds out a bottle to the emaciated, miserable-looking man, and a lion is passing to the other man something that looks like a pork chop on the end of a cane. A dog pokes an umbrella between the bars. Various dressed birds and monkeys have the advantage of being able to climb and fly, so as to get a better view. the animals are very well dressed – notice the Gladstonian collars flattering the long necks of ostrich and giraffe and the design of ornamental people on the ostrich's cravat.

Like much of Du Maurier's work, the picture is not amusing in itself, but the idea *is*, or is not, depending on what is read into it. It may mean that there is nothing to choose between the caged and the onlookers, only clothes distinguish them – rather like the Fougasse cartoons that used to hang in the monkey house at Regent's Park: 'How would you like it if *your* cousins poked *you*?' It might be a plea to uncage everything that is caged, or it might be intended to show the public how silly it looks to the animals. Whatever view one takes it must be agreed that there is a moral there, and that it was probably great fun drawing it. You cannot

THE TABLES TURNED AT THE "ZOO."

transpose creation by fitting intelligences into the wrong bodies without making some conclusions. The people are the ones that are most unhappy. This is true of Mowgli and Stuart – they are both *boys* with one foot in the animal kingdom, but the paradox is overt and the stories are about misfits. Is Mowgli a boy at all, or is he a wolf-cub? And above all, which does he *think* he is? And Stuart Little, born in the shape of a mouse, has awkward doubts; he thinks he is a boy, but his appearance leads everyone to think otherwise. For neither of these characters is there any happy ending.

The longing to cross the gulf between the human and animal worlds is present in everyone who writes animal fantasy, and is the prime motive for so doing. *The Jungle Books* and E. B. White's *Stuart Little* are unique in that they have bridged the gulf, found the situation impossible and have had to turn back and break the bridge behind them. Mowgli and Stuart are both outcasts and lead lives that are psychologically and physically perilous. Befriended and rejected by both animals and humans, they are strange Peter Pan figures without any real place in the world, suspended between human and sub-human. Of course, if such stories are written in an exactly lifelike way they would be about horrific or miserable monstrosities, Caliban figures – such as the occasional wolf, bear or antelope-child adopted and cared for by animals which when captured and tamed, live miserable, inarticulate and short lives – or the sub-species that every human and animal in Narnia is warned about, the 'nearly human but not quite', or the 'was human once, but isn't any more'.

In *The Jungle Books*, Kipling, 1893–4, the Jungle is on one side of the gulf and civilization, such as it is, on the other. Kipling makes the leap in the exploration of the man-joining-animals theme (wish fulfilment in so many of us) by reversing the usual order and making the Jungle the important place, containing an advanced animal society which is difficult to join and in which it is as difficult to live. The humans in the stories are unimportant supernumeraries living uneasy lives on the Jungle's outskirts, or in clearings that seem to be hardly won and easily lost. The English fade into the background. 'White men' are indeed only mentioned (apart from 'In the Rukh') twice, as some distant authority, responsible for Indian welfare but of no relevance to Jungle life.

The Jungle is the real world. It is described as a place of great beauty, delight and variability, with its forests, rivers, pools, hills, rocks and cold lairs, or places in which the humans have been once and are no more. It always seems to be growing larger, as if the victorious animal kingdom were on the advance. No towns or streets eat up this India, for the animal habitations threaten and destroy what man has made. The Indian villages are described as primitive places: the adults are ignorant, priest-ridden, bigoted and cruel; there are a few groves of sugar cane and herds of cattle managed by children. Mowgli himself, the wolf boy, is a figure of powerful, mythical qualities. He represents the very essence of the longing that humans have to experience animal life, to participate and to understand, to go back to the garden of Eden where all animal life was innocent and good and Man was the leader. Narnia is such a place, and so is the Jungle of *Tarzan of the Apes*, where all the 'good' animals come to the Man's aid when he is in danger, or threatened by the 'bad' ones. Here, Peter Pan has a Wendy; Tarzan and Jane live an idyllic life in the Jungle before Tarzan is discovered to be a millionaire, well able to live an idyllic life outside it.

Narnia has rules of its own and, while closely involved with talking, reasoning animals for plots, is not really *about* them in the end, and Tarzan is merely a potent and exciting fairy tale. But *The Jungle Books* have an immense amount of realistic detail that impels the reader to take the situation seriously. One never pauses to think that the situation of a boy, brought up among animals and able to communicate with them, eventually emerging as their leader, is impossible; it has a kind of logical poetry in its triumphant reversal. Mowgli, who grows into an almost godlike figure, is not, in himself, particularly interesting It is his predicament which holds the fascination, and the nature of the society in which he finds himself, which, by true reversal, turns out to be so much more complicated than that of the Indian village from which he came

It is a vast society; belonging to it would appear to be almost as difficult as belonging to the whole human race at once, something which humans find impossible, even in part. All the languages and battle cries and passwords of the animals have to be learned and remembered, otherwise peril is ever present Even so, there is danger from non-comformists and sub-species such as the bees, the wild dogs, monkeys and snakes. The rules and signs and exclusions are endless and the slightest mistake may mean death, for this uneasy world is a serious, dangerous place and though its societies are ordered, they are not civilised. It is as though we are shown a number of armies engaged in skirmishes in a vast, unseen, limitless country; or the largest, yet most exclusive public school imaginable with its rules and prohibitions, head boy, prefects and renegades. Mowgli is in the position of the new boy who works his way up the school to become head boy, and eventually to leave, with scenes of nostalgia and regret for his youth and parting from his school friends and masters; or of the new recruit who rises steadily through the ranks to become field marshal, and then, in an unlikely fashion, leaves the army for civilian life while still in his prime. Beside the discipline of the Jungle, *Stalkey and Co* does not seem to be a school story at all, but a tale of anarchy and practical joking which, in the 'real' Jungle, would not be tolerated for a minute (but here boys are among other boys, and the conflict is different). The Jungle is essentially a place of rules and order, and *The Jungle Books* are *about* rules and order, and about the outsider who learns to conform and to pass on to a different (and, one feels, lesser) kind of society. It becomes even more obvious that the Mowgli stories are partially disguised school or soldier stories when one thinks of the way the Scout movement took them over. Telling children that they were wolf cubs ruled over by a female Akela was a way of persuading large numbers of little boys to do something useful all at the same time – as if no solitary boy ever did anything useful – which is what the school is supposed to do for bigger boys, and the army for men.

In contrast, human laws are given no place. Humans are poor things who live in sordid dwellings like traps and haven't even the ability to build beautifully any more. Their city and temple are ruined and deserted, whereas the Jungle is organised and powerful, capable of battle and revenge – the animal vengeance theme is very strong and happens overtly in 'Letting in the Jungle'; it is silently present most of the time. The theme of sin and retribution is only secondary to that of proving the new recruit or new boy, progress from youth to maturity, the leaving behind of the natural, careless, unclothed, unburdened time of childhood. Neither theme really belongs in the animal world. Animals don't, in real life, take revenge; but of course 'nature' occasionally does, or seems to do so. The initiation of the new young creature to the tribe happens only in a minor degree. In linking these themes Kipling has not only shown a boy among animals, but has made his animals more human than the villagers; he has turned his animals into men. Bagheera, Baloo and Kaa are three Colonels, Akela a General, Shere Khan a wayward leader who tries to make malcontents join his mercenary band and so usurp the leadership. The mass of the wolves are the privates in the army into which Mowgli, when a baby, is bought

BAGHEERA WOULD LIE OUT ON A BRANCH AND CALL.
'COME ON, LITTLE BROTHER.'

for the price of a bull to the accompanying password, 'Look Well O Wolves'.

This phrase really does sound like the verbal equivalent of a wolf's howl. The wolves' parliament or council rock may be just such a place as wolves will use to congregate on moonlit nights. Packs have a pack leader, as any student of animal behaviour will know. But for the bear, the tiger, the panther to be present at such meetings, and for the python to be on friendly or speaking terms with all of them is not animal behaviour at all, and demonstrates that these animals are something more. The Law of the Jungle – taught and administered by Baloo, the schoolmasterly bear – has a certain relationship with things that really happen and is a kind of externalising of instinct. It expresses as a set of rules the things that animals do anyway:

> *The Jackal may follow the Tiger, but, cub, when thy whiskers are grown,*
> *Remember the Wolf is a hunter – go forth, and get food of thine own*

There follow other things – about fighting and the division of food (which read like Konrad Lorenz in verse) and not waking the jungle before midnight and the wolf's lair being his castle – which partly relate to instinct and partly do not; but it is an army of men that has to have rules, not an army of animals, because men can think of reasons for disobedience.

Why was not Mowgli suckled by a bear, an antelope, or an animal of solitary habit? There is a precedent for the wolf-boy but any solitary parent would have spoiled the central idea of *The Jungle Books*, which are about joining and belonging, and which unfold as a rather beautiful but sad saga of growing out of one kind of society into another.

The Biblical formality of the animal speech – with its 'thees' and 'thous' which approximate to an Urdu idiom, the solemn names and use of the words Little Brother for Mowgli, including him as part of the tribe, not of wolves alone but of all animals – gives every utterance great dignity. All wild animals have this naturally, but to do them justice, the Indian villagers tend to talk in the same manner. They say so little, however, that their speech is of less importance than their actions, whereas the animals make quite long speeches to each other, reinforcing the rules by reiterating them until 'By the bull that bought me' and 'By the broken lock that freed me' become like a solemn poetic refrain. 'We be of one blood, ye and I,' said in the right accent is the password for all the Jungle creatures. They are never slangy and seldom make jokes. The most they do is join in gentle sarcasm: Is there anything in the Jungle too little to be killed? asks Baloo, giving reasons for teaching Mowgli the Jungle Law. 'That is why I teach him these things and that is why I hit him very softly when he forgets.' The ponderous way in which the animals tell each other everything that everyone knew already in the manner of men making afterdinner speeches or statements of policy is a staple ingredient of a certain kind of romantic epic. Some of the solider characters in Tolkien do this; it is similar to a pre-battle exchange of heralds and formal messages, and its use gives a warlike, epic feeling, as well as a hint of remoteness. Even Mowgli learns the trick:

I go from you to my own people – if they be my own people. The Jungle is shut to men and I must forget your talk and your companionship : but I will be more merciful than ye are. Because I was all but your brother in blood I promise that when I am a man among men I will not betray ye to men as ye have betrayed me.

The Council Rock is the place for this; in pack or army there has to be a place for parliament or trial or court martial at which leaders are chosen, opinions stated and opposition silenced. This meeting place recurs and is often the scene of dramatic action, especially the theme story 'Mowgli's Brothers' which contains the acceptance, ageing and proving of Mowgli, and his revenge – not so much on Shere Khan personally, as on the untamed, lawless part of the Jungle that he represents. Mowgli's rejection by the wolves, his turning from the Jungle to the village to be accepted as a man, his real revenge on Shere Khan in 'Tiger Tiger', are all a matter of Law and logical negotiation, as was Mowgli's original crossing of the man-animal gulf by being 'bought' by a pact between animals. And the same inexorable rules eventually turn him out again. The wolves' parliament is a skilfully dramatic device for externalising laws that, although they seem manlike, are real and natural and can never be broken. The laws are, as animal instincts are, a built-in system, learned and taught without question. Only Mowgli himself ever doubts, or tries to disobey; and he is the man-cub, the outsider, though unwilling. Tabaqui the jackal brings the dawn of unease into his life by suggesting that he is not in the right place, but naked and human. It is the wise, proud, gentle Bagheera who reminds him that men and animals can never really meet, and that in the end, as he returns to the Jungle from his cage in the king's palace, so 'thou must go back to men at last, to the men who are thy brothers'. The tears that come unlooked for when Mowgli leaves the Jungle for the village, seal his fate; no animal can laugh or cry.

The origin of *The Jungle Books* may have been, as Roger Lancelyn Green suggests, Kipling's reading of a certain page of *Nada the Lily* which gave the image of the wolves on the council rock; or even further back, in James Greenwood's *King Lion*, 1864, or *The Bear King*, 1868, each telling a story of human intrusion into the animal world, which Kipling read when he was a boy at Southsea. The Lions in the first story were Freemasons and the Monkey tribe against whom they are having a war, were conceited and wicked. The uneasy nature of the Bandar-Log shows them to be imitation men.

The tragedy of *The Jungle Books* – and of the reverse situation, the story of *Stuart Little* – is that the gulf cannot be crossed properly or permanently, and that Mowgli as a man is so greatly inferior to the boy-wolf-cub. The situation is made more poignant by turning Mowgli into a semi-godlike figure, or noble savage, and making the men so mean, superstitious and unworthy. The Bandar-Log show the way by demonstrating the contempt that the Jungle has for the human qualities that they display. Perhaps it is not until the work of Walter de la Mare that monkeys are treated with dignity and poetry. Kipling's Bandar-Log alter one's feelings about monkeys – and the human types they represent – for ever. Feckless, irresponsible children, they have all the faults of a bad imitation: they are faithless, tell lies, cannot concentrate or achieve anything, live from hand to mouth, plunder, do nothing with the hands that are so different from other animals' paws except meddle and spoil, and are so conceited that they can find no fault with themselves. Always there is the implication that *this*, in some measure, is what men are like. The monkey tribal system is the opposite of that of the Seeonee in that it has no laws, no rules, no language. The Bandar-Log quarrel and fight, torment other animals, always trying to be in advance of fashion, making absurd speeches to each other to say so. They are neither man nor beast. The story in which Mowgli is carried off by the Bandar-Log to the ruined city represents Mowgli as being sinful and disobedient. He has to be rescued by his three friends, the python, panther and bear, who are as admonitory with Mowgli as the Rat and the Badger are with Toad when he is having one of his more foolish turns. Bear and panther become quite emotional when Mowgli is at last rescued, but that does not stop Bagheera from giving Mowgli a sound beating to remind him not to do it again.

It is inevitable that the Jungle, or corps of superior creatures, should triumph over both Bandar-Log and the Indian village of primitive, lowly men. The tragedy of Mowgli's having to rejoin the men in the end is similar to that of the hero vanquished by weakness (his love for his human mother?). The weakness is his nakedness or manhood; one must, in the end, leave the school or army. On the way, Mowgli's victories are powerful – over Red Dogs, over the bees, Shere Khan and other wolves. Inside the village, his behaviour is that of a rather noble animal trapped in a zoo; or, as the tables are turned by the story, a man trapped by monkeys. The men's tales – particularly those of the boastful Buldeo – are shown to be childish nonsense which Mowgli can understand, see through, and treat as ridiculous. He sits among the village elders like Jesus in the temple, wiser and more mature than they.

Mowgli's contempt for men is complete and vocal: 'Men are blood brothers of the Bandar-Log: all they do is talk and play with their mouths', boasting, making up stories, eating and drinking and blowing smoke, acting in a generally foolish and inexpert way. His vengeance on Buldeo and the villagers is as swift and sure as that on the tiger, but his attitude is inescapably ambivalent.

'Who is Man,' says Bagheera, 'that we should care for him – the naked brown digger, the hairless and toothless, the eater of earth?' but he is silenced by Mowgli's stare, before which his eyes must drop. Mowgli cannot, even in vengeance, kill one of his own kind, But he cannot acknowledge that he *is* a man: threatening Akela with a knife when he is called one, yet turning on the wolves when they offer to attack and kill Buldeo, saying 'Am I to give reasons for all I choose to do?'

'That is Man,' 'There speaks Man,' mutters Bagheera. Mowgli is neither one nor the other. He is fatally divided and will never fit.

He has a curious immunity from human beliefs and superstitions and a curious loyalty that takes him towards the human and not the wolf mother in the end. The psychological depression that attacks him in 'The Spring Running' is something that the animals don't feel and cannot understand, apart from Bagheera's acknowledgement, with great sympathy, that it exists. Even Bagheera fails to understand the depth and imperative urges towards vengeance on the men that compel Mowgli to plot the obliteration of the Indian village – a vengeance that, had Mowgli identified himself completely with the animals, would not have taken place. All the animals, the flesh-eaters and the grazers, join in plundering and spoiling, led and driven by Mowgli and the elephants, until the village is no more and the men have fled. Even Bagheera murders three horses. Though no humans are killed, they see their houses demolished by Hathi the elephant in an orgy of destruction.*

This story ends the *Mowgli* cycle; the theme of retribution has come to its close and all that remains is for Mowgli to move on from the hierarchy in which he has been such an apt pupil and at whose head he stands. The unbearably poignant 'The Spring Running', 1895, the last *Mowgli* story to be written, tells of Mowgli's goodbye to his friends. Animal-like, they have grown old while Mowgli is still in his prime. With most humans and animals, for this reason alone, the parting is inevitable. The story is almost a poem to the Indian spring, as Mowgli sings, leaps and swings through the jungle of which he is now the master, afraid of nothing that lives except for the inexplicable human shadow that follows him everywhere and cannot be shaken off. In all his alternating rejections and homecomings he himself must make the final choice and part from everything that he loves most. He does not know what he wants, or what he has outgrown, but realises instinctively that he has reached the end of careless happiness and the beginning of adulthood, and that however much he wishes it, man and animal can never meet. However much Mowgli tries to convince himself that he and the wolves are of one blood, they are not so.

*" "The outer wall bulged, split and fell, and the villagers, dumb with horror, saw the savage, clay streaked heads of the wreckers in the ragged gap." This is very similar to the horror of the teachers when Aslan revenges himself on a progressive school, whose garden wall he casually pushes down, sitting in the gap with his back turned. *The Silver Chair*, C. S. Lewis. In each case the event is used as a powerful image of good triumphing over evil. The only vengeance ever taken by humans on an animal is, of course, when the animal is corrupt, which happens rarely – Shere Khan, Shift the Ape in Narnia.

Kipling had, it is suggested by critics including Orwell, a neurotic strain, a hunger for cruelty and blood; but you cannot write about animals without mentioning that nature has arranged that they kill each other. C. S. Lewis almost manages to do this in the *Narnia* books by altering 'nature', but when animals have completely human status, problems of cannibalism arise. For those that are almost, but not quite humanised, the problem is more difficult: 'the kill' is mentioned and various second-class animals such as deer and buffaloes (Graibeeste? Vertoblancs?) are expendable and un-named. Treating the animals as soldiers in a just war overcomes the problem to a degree and in the adventures in which the author doubles back in time – 'Red Dog', 'The King's Ankus', 'Kaa's Hunting' – this is what happens. In 'The Spring Running' wolf fights wolf; and in 'Red Dog' a wholesale war of tribe against tribe is planned and carried out in a manlike way with logic, strategy and eventual slaughter. At Akela's death, Chil the Kite eats his body (naturally) but the deaths of wolves and red dogs are dramatic in human and not Jungle fashion.

Mowgli and Bagheera have no need to deplore the deaths in that Pardoner's Tale the King's Ankus for the evil that caused them is very apparent, and is present in the animals too with the almost political cries of 'North are the vermin', 'South are the lice'. Only in C. S. Lewis's *Malacandra* is there perfect, peaceful co-existence with humorous toleration, and even there the Hrossa are allowed evil creatures to hunt – the Hnakra.

The Jungle animals are allowed to believe that there is evil in killing. The story 'How Fear Came', or 'The Water Truce', is a conversation piece between the old elephant Hathi and other animals who discuss a creation myth that deals with the fall of the animals through the first murder – that of a buck by a tiger – the meeting of Man and Animals and the beginning of flesh-eating and enmity. This intelligent discussion of animal mythology (and part excuse for animal deaths) balances the men's talk in the village, which is outrageous and comic.

But the most overt reference to animal war comes in 'Her Majesty's Servants' which changes the army animals into extension men. Here, they inhabit not an opposing world, but a sub or re-flected one, and are oddly enough far more like animals than would appear to be the case. The story is a link between the real, Viceregal

Army, and the armylike procedure of the *Mowgli* stories. It has affinities with the Wart's visit to the mews in T. H. White's *The Sword in the Stone* in which birds of prey are cast as officers in a messroom or club, with strict rules of conduct, etiquette and obedience. In 'Her Majesty's Servants', the animals take on partly the characteristics of their owners, and partly a nature made up of the tasks they have to do. The story is about barrack-room gossip, and the main characters are camels, mules, a horse, bullocks and an elephant. They talk as soldiers do – or might do if surprised in the dark among strangers. They are a little boastful and identify themselves by names, number and function. Their simple and slangy exchanges are very different from the solemn talk of the *wild* animals. Clearly, contact with men has made them manlike in a different way, even when the rather silly camels and young mule are being merely childish. Their oaths and remarks are human enough: 'Why the pickets didn't you stay?' 'Oh that's quite another set of new shoes,' said the Troop horse; 'On your hind legs!' squealed Billy, as two horses rear, preparing to fight.

This curious story, overheard and understood by its author because 'I knew enough of beast language – not wild beast language but camp-beast language,' shows domestic or tamed animals in action in a very different manner from those free, honorary acting Colonels of the 'real' Jungle, Baloo and Bagheera. The army animals have few thoughts beyond what their masters have taught them, vigorous and amusing though these thoughts are. They are soldiers at one degree removed, limited by function and understanding only war. Few of them – horse and mules – remember a time when they were not in the army. Their delight is to obey orders; the mules like to be loaded and led by a driver over difficult mountains and ledges. The camels like to lie down and form a hollow square, the bullocks to drag the heavy guns to the firing line, the horse (which seems to be of officer rank) to answer to its rein. Compare its jocular remarks – 'The man was lying on the ground and I stretched myself not to tread on him, and he slashed up at me. Next time I have to go over a man lying down I shall step on him – hard' – with the gun bullock's dull insistence that 'There is only one way of fighting'.

But they are all soldiers. A young mule remarks at one point, 'What *I* want to know is, why we have to fight at all.' 'Because

we're told to,' said the troop horse . . . 'orders' said Billy the mule
. . . 'Yes, but who gives the orders?' said the recruit mule; and when
it was told that men did, it asked who gave the orders to the men.
One supposes that Her Majesty gave the orders to the men; like
soldiers, the animals grumble.

This does not happen in the Jungle; no one asks who made the
Jungle Law. Its operation is too obviously both useful and expedi-
ent, too patently it illustrates the workings of cause and effect:
Don't kill Man or you'll get Mange. The strength of the Wolf is
the pack, Sorrow never stays punishment, Keep your temper and
above all, Obey. However disciplined the human army with its
animal accompaniment, the Jungle army is stronger, because the
Laws are written in the soul, nature knows no questions, and
defaulters die.

The first *Mowgli* story, 'In the Rukh', 1890, shows the end before
the beginning – Mowgli as a young man, still part of the Jungle,
powerful and beautiful, inquisitive about the Englishman into
whose piece of forest he has wandered, eventually settling to take
a wife, becoming a ranger and accepting the inevitable pension.
The effortless ease with which Mowgli appears and disappears,
drives animals about, communicates with them and causes them
to come to him as if by magic, makes the 'civilised' narrator appear
crude and bumbling. Mowgli is perfect, godlike and so obviously
superior in intelligence and power that if one does not think of
The Jungle Books in which his boyish, animal-nature is stressed, he
seems both formidable and slightly annoying. Normally, as Muller
the head ranger remarks, such animal-reared outcasts die young;
but Mowgli is not at all normal. Neither, of course, was Tarzan.
These gulf-crossing stories voice a deep and constant human wish
and give it mythical form, powerful because it is all taken so seriously. To me, *The Story of Dr Dolittle* and the Warts' adventures with
Merlyn are no less powerful because they are lighthearted and there
is less blood about; the animals themselves are gently satirised. But
it is a theme that never really dies or disappears. It is interesting to
see H. H. Munro's inevitably sinister treatment of the Nature Boy
idea with its flippant overtones; Gabriel Ernest, lesser than and
different from Mowgli, is a conscience-less animal in human form,
voicing his thoughts on eating child-flesh with an accuracy that is
not of course believed in by his human listener. Like Tobermory,

who voices impossible cat's thoughts in human words, he has to disappear. Saki's humour is black. Man and wolf exist in one psyche in his world to terrify and destroy; Mowgli's wolf nature is one of order, love, loyalty and joy.

As Mowgli leaves the animal world for a life among men, *Stuart Little*, E. B. White, 1945, leaves, by implication, a society – the human one – in which he cannot possibly fit, to find his true love, a bird. There is no evidence that his quest will be successful, though Stuart's story ends on a statutory note of hope.

This sad, moving fantasy about the human-animal gulf is melancholy in a way that *The Jungle Books* are not; wherever Mowgli goes, he manages to conquer his surroundings with some degree of success, whereas Stuart's story is one of inevitable failure. Like Mowgli, Stuart's troubles start at birth. He is no orphan mouse who has lost his parents and been adopted by a human family, but a human soul in mouse form. The book is about his tragic dilemma – it is neither an animal story nor a human one, nor does it fit into the 'mouse' category, though it has some of the characteristics. It is a unique tale of a social misfit, and is not 'like' anything else, unless it might be the tale of the Frog Prince in modern dress, told by the frog. It is full of the minute compromises with which small Borrower, or Mouse, characters live. Stuart has affinities with Thumbelina, Tom Thumb, Little Maia and Walter de la Mare's Miss M (*Memoirs of a Midget*, 1921). Like Miss M, he finds himself different and has to learn to adapt to circumstances as Mowgli does.

The story is, as is appropriate to its later date, less sure, more fantastic, sadder, shorter than the *Mowgli* cycle, and just about as inappropriate for children in its implications as *The Jungle Books* are right. *The Jungle Books* represent a world where fantasy is agreeable, a basis for games and imagined adventures into which one might perhaps, long to enter; but who would want to be Stuart, or to contend with a world which is both hostile and too large? It is as if Gulliver were lost for ever in Brobdingnag without hope of return. Stuart was born, one learns, in the usual way, the second son in a New York family. 'The baby,' we are told, as if in a shocked whisper, 'looked very much like a mouse in every way. He was only about two inches high.'

Mr and Mrs Little accept their unique offspring in much the same manner as her father and mother accepted Miss M. Like Miss M, Stuart is precocious and could walk as soon as he was born; like Miss M, he is proud of his fine clothes – Miss M watches her 'fine puffed scarlet' dress and slippers in the mirror, and Stuart has 'a fine little blue worsted suit with patch pockets,' as Mrs Little soon sees that for this sophisticated child baby clothes are inappropriate.

His bed is four clothes pegs and a cigarette box, and he at once begins the compromise life with all its shifts, escapes and stratagems that his smallness brings with it, helped out by his mouse-body which, in its miniature neatness, is more able than a human one. The sadness is that, like the animal teachers with Mowgli, his parents and brother try so hard to make Stuart into a man; even the doctor is called in to see if he can make Stuart grow, but his body will not let him. The doctor, remarking that it is very unusual, certifies him as a mouse, with a temperature of 98·6 degrees, and departs. Stuart tries hard, helping his full-sized family in every way appropriate, searching down the drain (in person) for a lost ring, retrieving ping-pong balls, pushing keys on the piano (from the inside) when they will not play, with other bizarre and random acts that seem to have the sad oddity of fact rather than fiction. The Littles have a mouse in the family in the same way as the Browns, in the *Paddington* books, have a bear, but in one case the results are happy and hilarious, in the other they are frightening and melancholy. Tom Thumb's qualities that helped him through his chequered life – sharp wits, a strong voice and courage – are not entirely shared by Stuart. His parents have to spare his feelings by eliminating the word 'mouse' from the conversation and from

nursery rhymes. They worry about a mousehole and whether Stuart
will wish to go into it, one day: 'After all, he does look a good deal
like a mouse,' says Mr Little to his wife.

Stuart's home life is a series of problems, as for a handicapped
person. He developes devices for turning on lights and taps, for
washing himself. Like Miss M, he has encounters with the family
cat Snowbell, to whom he talks – presumably in cat language – as
easily as he manages human words in his mouse throat. He is formal, in a precocious, adult way – the way in which an only child
might be who has not lived in a child's world at all. When rescued
by his human brother from the inevitable narrow escape from
death he announces: 'It was simply an accident that might happen
to anybody.' He is a liability to the Littles to be treated and handled
as carefully as a haemophiliac, and as inevitably he escapes from
the apartment to a series of hair-raising adventures, as sadly straight-
faced, and in the end as toughly invulnerable, as Buster Keaton.
Philosophy comes to his aid, tragedy stalks him. 'I'm not tall
enough to be noticed,' he remarks, comfortingly to himself, but
adds: 'yet I'm tall enough to want to go to Seventy-second Street.'

There are some odd anomalies in his dealings with the human-
sized world. A bus conductor asks for his fare; he talks to people
sailing boats in Central Park. The idea of mice manning toy boats,
so dear to Masefield, is as beguiling as that of mice living in dolls'
houses, and Stuart's adventures in the schooner *Wasp* have epic
qualities and a delighted audience. Throughout, Stuart is his courteous self, debonair and full of courage.

His love for Margalo the wren is the central theme of the story.
Stuart rescues the homeless bird from Snowbell, enemy of birds
and mice. Mouse stories are not kind to cats who usually appear
as bullies and sneaks, and Snowbell seems to be both. There is a
very cold logic in the way Snowbell discusses the oddities of the
Little family with a friend. With casuists' arguments they decide
whether or not Margalo should be eaten, and Margalo's flight
Northwards begins Stuart's unending quest to find her. Packing a
strand of his mother's hair to remember her by, he leaves her for
ever as Mowgli left his wolf-mother. Stuart, an American, drives
his car, a present from a dentist friend who sees him off, equipping
him with clothes and accessories from a doll's shop.

'People were inclined to stare at him.' But Stuart drives bravely

on into rural America where he takes over a teacher's job for a day. Stuart's predicament is that of any literary misfit from *Childe Harold* onwards – and of many misfits in real life too. Star-crossed yet intelligent, he struts and drives his way through life with hope and courage, nimble and gifted. His school lesson is a model of progressive moralising on the subject 'If I were chairman of the world' with the children doing as much talking and acting as the teacher, experiencing for themselves the evils of stealing and 'being mean'. In many ways, Stuart is as complete a success as his size and appearance will allow; but his unhappy sex life underlines his sad realization that the human world will always reject him.

Why does not Stuart meet, and fall in love with, another mouse? The truth is that he is the only human mouse in existence and has to face the full misery of the Frog Prince with no hope of a transformation. Still in quest of the wren Margalo he meets Miss M instead, a young lady called Harriet Ames who is no larger than he. Her father made a fortune from doing impartial favours to both sides during the civil war; perhaps her small size was a judgement. Stuart courts Harriet Ames, writing her a letter on engraved notepaper in a fully human way, in the manner of a diffident suitor who has something to be ashamed of: 'My only drawback is that I look something like a mouse. I am nicely proportioned, however. Am also muscular beyond my years.'

The date with Harriet that follows goes wrong in the classic manner. The toy canoe he has bought in which to take her on the river leaks, the weather is not good, he wakes with a headache, his shirt becomes wet under the arms, he tries, and fails, to affect an English accent to impress her. The event ends in disaster and his miserable sulking drives her to leave him.

At last he resumes his quest and the story ends with his driving off – not into the sunset but Northwards. The poem to the North, which, in its feeling, is so similar to the end of 'The Spring Running', is spoken by a telephone repairman whose work takes him as far as roads and wires will stretch. Mowgli, at the end, knows that he is not a wolf. Stuart has no such consolation. This sad, haunting – some critics have called it sinister – book tells the story of an outcast who must always remain so. Neither human nor animal worlds will have him, though his unalterable opinion, that birds migrate North, gives him at least a chance of finding his lost love. Perhaps in America the North means loneliness, peace, nature untouched.

Garth Williams's drawings show a neat, thoughtful, spare, adult-looking mouse. This talented artist's animals are all attractive – even the unpleasant ones – and no two look alike. Many of the *Stuart Little* illustrations are drawn from a human point of view, showing, as befits the story, Stuart as a minute dot, or small, desperate and unnoticed as he tries to board a bus, walk down 72nd Street or ask for his petrol and oil to be checked at a filling station.

13 If only we were they: the humanised 'Nature' Story

This time the now tiny Wart felt his toes shooting out and scratching on the floor. He felt his heels rise and stick out behind, and his knees draw into his stomach. His thighs got quite short. A web of skin grew from his wrists to his shoulders, while his primary feathers burst out in little soft quills from the end of his fingers and quickly grew. His secondaries sprouted out along his forearms ... Wart looked quickly at Merlyn, ducked his head between his legs and had a look through there, rattled his feathers into place, and began to scratch his chin with the sharp talon of one toe.

The Sword in the Stone, *T. H. White*

We can only guess at what animals are really like – an early dog story, *Keeper's Travels in Search of his Master*, Augustus Kendall, 1798, gives the dog an heroic and sympathetic part to play without any attempt at feeling what it is like to be a dog. Dogs and cats, farm or semi-domestic animals are near enough to observe, familiar enough for their identities to be imagined. The ironies of Pompey the Little are not very doglike, but Keeper's adventures, or those of Tommy Trip's 'Jouler', are in their way natural enough. Dogs are nearly always 'good' characters in moral tales, or victims, like Good Dog Tray, of human ill-treatment, or shining examples of faithfulness and animal sagacity. The inwardness of dog, cat, or horse, the desire to describe what its life is really made of from the inside, seems to have occurred to no one. The best that could be imagined was to put a human self into the animal with results that were moral, stiff, sometimes unhappy. The method has a brilliant success in a novel like *Black Beauty* but brings with it special pleading that is morally suspect. Dorothy Kilner's Nimble, the mouse, tells in the first person something of what a mouse's experience might be, almost by accident, almost in spite of its author, who intended a different kind of book. R. M. Ballantyne's *The Dog Crusoe*, 1861, is an interesting transitional book, describing a dog's adventures entirely by what is happening to its master, from the puppyhood to the maturity of both. It is objective, yet has extraordinary sympathy with its animal co-hero. As a portrait of a dog it is vivid and stirring, and very real. The dog is bigger, stronger, more beautiful and faithful than others of his kind, but his intelligence is good without being super-canine. His master, Dick Varley, trains him with patience, and as Crusoe learns at last to retrieve, Dick 'sat down on a rock and whistled with glee at having fairly picked the lock and opened another door into one of the many chambers of his dog's intellect'. There is no pretence that 'many' means human, or multidimensional, although the author remarks that Crusoe could speak. Crusoe speaks with eyes, nose and tail, and Dick does a lot of sitting about on rocks, having one-sided conversations with his delightful friend, for Crusoe, like most natural dogs, is pleasing, obedient, moral, full of simple love and loyalty. A bad dog is often an unhappy dog – see *Finn the Wolfhound*, A. J. Dawson, 1908, or Jack London's *White Fang* (1905). Crusoe's love for his mother Fan, and affection for his adoring friend Grumps are expressed by 'soft barking, in every imaginable degree of modulation', but to a human, it overflows into attractively old-fashioned words: 'Are you happy, my dog?' 'You're a stupid fellow to ask such a question; however, it's an amiable one. Yes, I am.'

Kipling's bold attempt at the expression of what being a dog might feel like, turns the dog into a simplified, four-legged human and gives the reader the feeling that, like Dr Candeze's Field Cricket, the animal has taken up its pen and written a diary; yet here, if anywhere, is the truth about pet dogs. The book – *Thy Servant, a Dog*, 1930, has dated, like the popularity of the Aberdeen Terriers it talks about, but its quaint embarrassments are those that such dogs both feel and give: 'We rolled before Feets, asking not to be pushed into Empty Places. I did a Beseech because I were not comfy.' The strength of the story is in the documentary exactness with which the dogs' behaviour is chronicled. Crusoe's life is similarly well described, but he does not speak to the reader as Boots does, in such a manner that Boots's self, his personality and being express themselves in a unique blend of dog grammar, dog interpretation and comprehension. To Boots the world is a place shared by humans with unquestioned power, full of interest, unfolding moment by moment to his short consciousness: 'There is walk-round-on-toes. There is Scrap. There is Proper Whacking. Master says: "Sorry! Awfully sorry! All my fault!"' and 'At morning-time Adar unties and brushes. There is going quick upstairs, past Cookey and asking Gods to come to brekker. There is lie-down-under-the-table at each end, and heads-on-feet of Gods. Sometimes there is things-gived-under-table." '

This impressionist account advances the dog's intelligence by a degree or two, to give it power to speak; and one has to admit that as such the speech has an odd conviction about it. Grammar is strange. The tenses are fleeting. Boots mostly uses the present tense of any and every verb, his occasional past tenses are oddly formed: 'We have found him by own dust-bin. We said "Come back and play!" But he wented off.' It is partly *Sylvie and Bruno* baby language,

Nurse said: "Oh, what shall I do—I do?
My legs are wobbly."

slightly abhorrent; but Boots's brisk honesty and racy flow of minute to minute anecdotes is not in the least babyish. Analysed, his grammar is wild and his spelling odd (perhaps this is mistaken as it draws one's attention and speculation to whether the dog is supposed to be writing or not); he spells cupotea, dretful, Adar, normous, stoopid, hisself. But this is the way he *talks* (one supposes) to other dogs, or to us, or himself, and it is a copy of human words that he has heard, or picked up, or sometimes made for himself, developing phrases into nouns in the manner of Longfellow's Red Indians: 'Was one time when leaves-was-all-on, Shiny Plate came up strong and made-sing. We played Rattle Chain till Adar loosed.'

He makes composite verbs, leaving out the smaller parts of speech altogether, and forms nouns such as Kennel-that-moves (car) Smallest (baby), Sleep-hunt (dreams). Being sick is described as 'I unhad all which was isside me'. His word for thought, or idea is a concrete noun, Rat; abstractions are beyond him. 'When we are bad, there is Sugar. When we are good, there is Whack-whack. That is same rat going two wrong ways . . .' Crying over spilt milk is 'Worrying dead rats'. It is as if one were listening to language being made by a brain that has more ideas than words in which to express them. Boots's vocabulary is small but his word combinations are vivid and expressive. Within his limited capacity his narrative flow never falters. It is only interrupted by occasional prods of memory. He knows no seasons or times, is only conscious of events following one another with good times and bad, and of his friendship with Slippers and Ravager the hound. To them and all other animals he talks non-stop. To humans he does the same, but without communicating; I said, loud; I singed. *Their* talk he hears, interprets and copies in such a lively way that he does not, cannot, win unfair sympathy in the way that Black Beauty does because he is a 'dumb beast'.

With the cocksure hopefulness of the bright, short-legged animal he is, Boots only wishes to please Own God and to grow, somehow, into a hound like Ravager. The scene at the end of the book where Ravager dies and Boots looks for him everywhere in every place that they have been before, is genuinely touching; the dog's limitations are suddenly no longer funny. Everyone knows that dogs can experience loss and sadness and the impossibility of communicating consolation reminds one that the gulf is still there. It is a pity that

I am very little small mis'able dog. . . . I do not understand.

the flavour of Boots's life seems outdated and at times awkward; it is one of the most telling and intimate essays into animal psyche ever attempted.

Anna Sewell's *Black Beauty*, 1877, the most famous and best-loved animal book of all time, stands out as a landmark. It is perhaps the last of the moral tales, the last great first person narrative in the Listen-to-my-life style. It is not quite as original a work as it appears to be; Arabella Argus had already told the story of Jemmy Donkey, and there are cab-horse incidents in George Macdonald's *At the Back of the North Wind*, 1871 – in its way, a far more unusual work, but of less popular appeal. But Black Beauty's vicissitudes have the truth of something experienced and there is no fantasy relief – unless you count the oddity of a reasoning, communicating horse. The world-wide popularity of Anna Sewell's book must be attributed not to its campaigning fervour for kindness to horses, but to the narrative itself. It is such a good story, full of incident, character and suspense, rousing intense partisan feelings about the clear-cut issues of good and bad. It imparts information so effortlessly that even the reader who knows nothing about horses and is not even particularly interested in them is at once involved and ends with as much horse-lore as if he had been studying a rider's and driver's manual.

That the book was written as a moral tale or tract is certain; copies of it were given away to drivers of railway vans, and in America to drivers, grooms and stablemen, on a vast scale. Anna Sewell was very much influenced by her mother, a prolific and successful writer of tracts and moral poems about suffering children, brave parents and the evils of drink. The whole tone of their family life was one of moral uplift and helping the poor – indeed, Mary Sewell, Anna's mother, appears to have been rather unhappy during the short periods of her life when she had no poor to help. Anna, permanently lame and often ill, overshadowed by the active and indefatigable Mary, bore a troubled life with great courage and patience, which is what Black Beauty does. It is impossible to think of this horse without seeing the author incarnated, and thinking of a human soul imprisoned and dumb. The animal autobiography gives the speechless a chance to speak to humans, and the convention is that the animal *can* communicate somehow. (One has to forget ideas about *how* the story was written; they will arise, even in authors' minds, when the Field Cricket is given a pen and oak leaves to write on, or Boots dictates and R. Kipling edits.)

To communicate at all, the animal has to have a human psychology (though a fascinating story can, of course, be written without – *Tarka the Otter* and *Salar the Salmon*, Henry Williamson, 1927, 1929, and 'B.B.'s fox story, *Wild Lone*, 1939, are such). This elevates the horse to a far higher status than it normally has, or had, so that kindness done to it brings emotions of memory and gratitude and reciprocal goodness. Cruelty is worse because it is cruelty to a fellow human who is powerless and cannot answer back or take revenge. Every event is magnified and given echoes, and feelings are aroused almost unfairly; or are they? The book had enormous influence for good in the treatment of horses and helped to abolish the bearing rein. It continues to be a bestseller a hundred years after it was written.

The factor that moves is that horses were, and are, victims used for pulling and carrying; and one of them is allowed to tell what being a victim feels like – this is special pleading. But there are no extraordinary tear-jerking or sentimental qualities in the narrative. The horse hero has good, gentle qualities – and in keeping with the period, a finer strain also: 'Ginger and I were not of the regular, tall, carriage horse breed: we had more of the racing blood in us.' The handsome, agreeable, sensitive nature of Black Beauty makes him interesting in human terms, and his downfall from carriage horse – sold with Ginger for three hundred pounds – to broken down hack – sold for five pounds and at a horse fair – is only just made bearable by rescue and happy ending.

Black Beauty's life embraces practically every event that can happen to a horse, and he experiences every kind of rider and driver, good and bad, from the coachman John Manly and the kindly and thoughtful cabdriver Jerry Barker, to the drunken Reuben Smith who ruins him by breaking his knees, and the extortioner Skinner who works his horses to death. Cabs and carriages exist no longer, but it is impossible to read about the horses' sufferings without being affected – no less so because a human voice is talking, Anna Sewell's, both in the person of the hero when told by his mother to 'do your work with a good will, lift up your feet when you trot, and never bite or kick, even in play,' and in the person of the kind lady who stops the insensitive carter and asks him to remove the bearing rein with gentle, persuasive fervour.

The book does give adults and children – who read it now and have done so ever since it was written – an insight, not exactly into how a horse feels,* but into what it would be like, if one could be

*Joseph Wenter's *Mannsrauschlin (Man's Delight)*, 1936, comes very near, in the Henry Williamson tradition, to conveying the experience of being a wild horse. No first person narrative will do.

**I HAD NO POWER TO MOVE, AND I THOUGHT NOW I WAS
GOING TO DIE.**

so transformed, to feel the bit, the blinkers, the bearing rein, the
good and foolish treatment, and to realise with the whole of one's
moral nature what was being done without being able to alter one's
lot. That Anna Sewell believed horses really had moral natures is
rather doubtful. Very little can be told of her life other than is

revealed in a few letters. A friend mentions a drive to the station during which Anna exhorted her horse to effort as one would a child: 'Now, thee shouldn't walk up this hill – don't thee see how it rains? Now thee must go a little faster – thee would be sorry for us to be late . . .' What she certainly did believe was that horses were put into the world for the use and service of man, and that as man does, or should do, God's will, so the vocation or animals was to do the will of man. Any human reading *Black Beauty* will be kinder to horses.

But one cannot help thinking about how the magic is worked. Humans look before and after, and pine for what is not, and Black Beauty experiences moral doubts: 'They were carrying young Gordon to the churchyard to bury him. He would never ride again. What they did with Rob Roy I never knew; but 'twas all for one little hare'; the pains of speechlessness: 'I held my face close to him, as that was all I could do to say goodbye, and then he was gone, and I have never seen him since;' and helpless regret, as at the climactic end of his pride and maturity he is left with broken knees and a dead rider: 'It was a calm, sweet April night . . . it made me think of the summer nights long ago, when I used to lie beside my mother in the green, pleasant meadow at Farmer Grey's.'

Unfair! Unfair, and yet the end justifies the means. This was the only book I have ever read right through, straight away, twice; but fond as I was – aged ten – I have not read it since and other books have been greater favourites and changed life more deeply. It made me look, on my way to school, more intelligently at the coal carts that plodded all day between the station and the gasworks, at the plaque on the wall that said for many years 'Please slacken bearing rein going up hill,' and I watched the carters putting on the metal brake shoes and wondered – as a horse – what it was like going downhill with a heavy load behind. But beyond these feelings was the one that if the horse were I, or anyone, and the story really about me, or people, then school was the breaking-in stable and many people were led or driven through life with a series of owners and made to run, walk or trot without being able to argue about it. The horse characters in *Black Beauty* are too human to be lightly dismissed or forgotten, and found immediate identification; Peggy, Captain, Lizzie, but more surely Ginger and Merrylegs. Aunt Merrylegs was the sturdy, self-confident one that nobody could argue with.

argue with. Aunt Ginger, pale, angular, auburn and clever, but
ruined by unlucky treatment in youth and difficulties and setbacks
since, had reared, refused and bitten her way through life until
'bearing it on and on until the end'. In a way this animal book
made one child love people more and understand them a little
better.

It was not until Ernest Thompson Seton in *Wild Animals I Have
Known* (1900) that animal dramas were written in which the creatures' physical lives were enough in their marvellous and detailed
authenticity to supply action without using human moral dilemmas.
Meanwhile, Jack London's *White Fang* (1905) and *The Call of the
Wild* (1903) have wolf heroes. *White Fang*, to me the most outstanding dog book of all, is an in-the-skin story with the dog as a
tragic hero with a background whose perfect authenticity one never
doubts. *White Fang* tells of a Canadian wolf's life from birth to old
age from the first chords of the overture ('Dark spruce forest
frowned on either side of the frozen waterway. The trees . . . seemed
to lean toward each other, black and ominous, in the fading light')
to the final, peaceful coda where wolf-turned-dog lies dreaming in
the sun with the puppies he has fathered. The life of the timber
wolf is described so that the human reader lives it, but without any
pretence that animal thinking is the same as human – only with the
insistence that they are like in quality, different in degree. The same
stimuli work on the wolf cub with the same results that would have
been produced in a human child, the differences being the rapid
ageing and learning processes of the animal, and the total lack of
questioning in his simple mind: 'The grey cub was not given to
thinking . . . yet his conclusions were as sharp and distinct as those
achieved by men. He had a method of accepting things . . . in reality
this was the art of classification . . . Thus, when he had bumped
his nose on the back wall a few times, he accepted that he would
not disappear into walls.'
This is the way every child learns, and every young animal who
has no power to ask why. But what gives the book a different sort
of drama, changing it from a brilliant animal story into a psychological study of great power, almost a case history, is the meticulous
detailing of the way in which circumstances mould character – in
this instance turning a natural young animal into an outcast and an

enemy of every creature that walked, ran, or flew. White Fang, like a human child, has parents, ancestry, cubhood and youth; forces work on him inevitably to alienate him from his own kind and turn him into the ferocious killer that he later becomes. He is only redeemed by the sharp intelligence that enables him to survive, which is, at the end, recognised by Weedon Scott, the human who loves and tames him. This classic study of the making of an outcast passes from loss of siblings and play to youthful servitude in the Indian camp, that schooltime where the puppy is singled out for bullying by Flashman Lip-lip because he is wolfish and different. This process accelerates his intelligence, develops his craft, cunning and aggression into games that are not games at all but vengeance and reprisals, until the puppy has grown to pack leader – by that time too solitary to have any relationship with his kind other than fighting them or ignoring them. White Fang is no Tom Brown. He changes before our eyes into a creature that knows no love, hates laughter and is only subdued by fear. Thence he changes again into the almost mindless fighting machine owned by Beauty Smith: 'to such an extent was he tormented that he hated blindly and without a spark of reason'.

The two pathetic interludes in which he tries and fails to persuade his mother – a similar prisoner in the Indian camp – to return to the forest make the story more bitter. Years later he meets her by accident and tries to approach her with the stirrings of memory, only to find that she had forgotten him and is another enemy. The book's happy ending is more or less believable, but the wonderful parabolic curve of the narrative is one long rush upwards to destruction and a short fall into domesticity. It is the first two-thirds of *White Fang* that stay inescapably in the mind, the turn of the screw being, as in all real animal stories, that the subject is in a way helpless and does not know what is happening, or how it is happening. But one cannot read this masterpiece without drawing human parallels.

Read at a very early age, this book makes a lasting impression, its stylistic faults and mixed metaphors passing unnoticed. It left in its wake some really resounding new adjectives such as ominous, indomitable, ignominious, belligerent, prodigious, ferocious and sanguinary, two nouns, Heredity and Environment, and perhaps made more of a change in consciousness than other, far greater books did – but Jack London is the Hardy of animal writers.

Ernest Thompson Seton, an outstanding artist and naturalist writing during the first thirty years of this century, is the pioneer 'nature' writer, with no first person narratives or identification other than the closest possible observation of what the animal is or does. There is no inhabiting of the animal's body and psyche in the mysterious way that Jack London and Henry Williamson manage and T. H. White suggests. Wild animals' lives are enough and many of these biographies end in sadness, stressing the inevitable meetings of hunters and hunted.

Tragedy, however 'natural', is sharpened by the animal heroes being more than usually beautiful, powerful, intelligent, or outstanding. Their human hunters have few virtues except persistence. Krag, the Kootenay Ram (*Lives of the Hunted*, 1902) is a perfect animal, full of delight in living, surviving fights for leadership of the herd – only to meet his human nemesis in Scotty, who stalks him for twelve weeks. This story, which has some of the inevitability of *Moby Dick* or *The Rime of the Ancient Mariner*, does not end with the kill, for Scotty is unable to lose the ghost of Krag, which is with him always. Even more tragic is Redruff, the Don Valley Partridge (*Wild Animals I Have Known*, 1900) where the development of the beautiful bird is paralleled by the appearance of Cuddy, the human hunter.

The lives of wild animals have drama written into them. There is no need to do more than chronicle their happenings without artificial padding – though much natural animal life has intervals, so charmingly described by E. B. White in *Charlotte's Web* where Wilberforce the pig spends long hours of eating, sleeping, thinking, scratching, and standing still. The Hon. J. W. Fortescue's *The Story of a Red-Deer*, 1897, written before *Wild Animals I have Known* but only just, takes another viewpoint that is unusual and has not, as far as I know, been repeated. It is one of those classics that blends observation with a discreet humanisation so that the animals have 'characters' and a carefully and gently humorous class structure. As nearly as possible one experiences what it is like to be a deer, with a life full of terror and pursuit, but also full of beauty and a certain kind of condescending pride. One does wonder that the story deals so sympathetically with hounds, hunting and the pheasant shoot but life-as-it-is has these things in it. As with Seton, hunter and hunted draw inexorably nearer, so the Red-Deer and the Tan Hound meet and part to meet again until the hound hunts his quarry to his death. But in between, the beautiful world of Exmoor is the background of the Red-Deer's youth and growing, a young aristocrat, son of his Lordship the Stag and Lady Tawny. The effect is of a gently moral tale of the nineties, with the deer perfectly placed at the top of the county hierarchy where everyone keeps to his place and recognises it. 'The Hind looked grave. "We are never unkind to the Trout," she said, "for they belong to the peat-stream, but you must never become familiar with them; Fallow-Deer, I believe, treat them as equals." ' And Fallow-Deer are not really to be spoken to because they are semi-tame and live in parks; they are bourgeois upstarts, corrupted by being fed in winter.

But such is the natural truth of the story that it does not seem comic for the Red-Deer to be taught to talk to Little Salmon but not to Little Trout. He is also taught obedience, politeness and courage, and his place in the order of things; no Red-Deer calf should know less. There is a rightness about the animals' social structure that is not only gently amusing but observedly correct. The animals that associate converse – the garrulous, deferential, broadly Devon Rabbit, the Pheasants and Blackcock, Badger and Vixen. Those that fear or prey upon each other are forever divided. Each animal's character is suggested in the delicate, slight human parody that underlines its actions and illuminates it: Aunt Yeld, the formidable spinster hind who imitates a stag's walk and bite; the foxes, rather rough, independent and uncivil, the badger 'a poor stupid old fellow, blundering on his way'; the pheasant conceited; a cat, foe to gamekeeper, poacher and animal, who comes to an inevitable bad end; the cockney ducks in the Park shouting rudely to the young deer 'Look out little 'un or your 'orns will drop off' (they were not 'true' animals and had been bought in Leadenhall Market); the garrulous old rabbit, a great grandmother whose reminiscences flow for ever.

None of this detracts from this wonderfully observed nature story. It seems that the immutable animal laws are made clear by the invoking of a human structure, as happens in *The Jungle Books*. Brief human appearances of riders and huntsmen are a subtle parallel to

9

the theme of animal birth, prime and death. The soldier going to the war and returning illustrates the virtues that Lady Tawny tries to instil into her son: 'If it should befall you that you must run for your life, as I fear may be only too likely, then keep up a brave heart and run on till you can run no more'; that no hind ever spoke to a calf does not make the grown stag's last run seem less courageous, or his end less noble.

Beside this apt and gently caricatured treatment can be placed that deservedly popular and much more commercially successful story, *Bambi*, Felix Salten, 1928. Felix Salten's deer, hares and pheasants take each other very seriously, however natural and unself-conscious their actions are. They talk about right and wrong, life and death.

> *'What was that?' asked Bambi excitedly.*
> *'Nothing,' his mother soothed him.*
> *'But,' trembled Banbi, 'but I saw it.'*
> *'Yes, yes,' said his mother. 'Don't be frightened. The ferret has killed a mouse.' But Bambi was dreadfully frightened. A vast, unknown horror clutched at his heart. It was long before he could speak again. Then he asked, 'Why did he kill the mouse?'*
> *'Because,' his mother hesitated. 'Let us walk faster,' she said.*

Bambi himself converses with other animals and insects: the butterfly pleases him, the grasshopper 'puts on a serious face', Bambi constantly learns from his mother by question and answer, the very leaves on the trees talk to each other, full of philosophic doubt about the nature of falling, the deer argue about Man and his third, or killing arm. While the story is accurate besides being sad and beautiful, to me the dialogue gives it an inner unreality that the Disney film brings out into the open. The wide-eyed human 'wrongness' of the fawns lingers on and one baulks at such descriptions of forest life as the death of a pheasant arousing 'the sympathies of a wide circle who tried to comfort his disconsolate widow'. Or again, in the hideously terrifying scene of killing with guns and beaters, a dying pheasant whispers, 'It's all over with me'.

But to be fair, the scene of Bambi's meeting with the old stag – a theme that appears and reappears through the book like a series of solemn chords – is enhanced by Disney's drawing, full of strange splendour. The dialogue between the two in the book, full of unvoiced thoughts, has an odd feeling of social ineptness, neither animal making contact with the other for, one feels, the foolish reason that they have not been introduced. And at a later moment the accusing speech of the Fox to the Dog ('You spy . . . you blackguard, you track us, you betray us, your own relations, me who am almost your brother') is as awkwardly unlikely as any animal dialogue ever written; it would only be valid in satire such as *Animal Farm*. However, as a poetic commentary on the shortness of animal lives, the narrative has haunting moments that mean, perhaps, more than the author intended. When Bambi's mate, Faline, old and tired, wanders away from him, his inability to recall the past or do or say anything other than watch her go is unbearably poignant. Pining for what is not is human, and to suggest not that the animal feels human grief but that it is quite unable to do so is the kind of truth that makes this story one of the great animal biographies.

The pitfalls of giving animals moralising voices, sad or happy thoughts, when you are trying to imitate nature rather than comment on human affairs, are many. René Guillot steps lightly over them in books that are less memorable than *White Fang* or *Bambi*, but solve all the problems very neatly; he gives his animals voiced thoughts in his naturalist's animal stories that are never obtrusive, never out of place. The leopards, elephants, cheetahs and others speak to each other in simple language that an animal might mean rather than use.

E. B. White has much the same success with farm animals in *Charlotte's Web*, 1952. Apart from Charlotte herself – the super spider who weaves magic messages into her web to attract attention, even including advertising slogans – the animals do what animals always do; eat, sleep, stand about, indulge in simple forms of play. The pig, Wilbur, is given just that enlargement of consciousness which can see into the past, a little, imagine the future, in part, and enjoy winning a prize at a fair because it brings praise. He is also afraid of dying. Otherwise, his thoughts flow in a natural, simple manner. He plans his day into a series of enjoyable intervals, starting with food, then sleep, then standing still, food again, sleep again, scratching and thinking. Compare with this the more human Hepzibah Hen who spring cleans and gives parties, and by excluding humans from her world has become one of them. Wilbur's conversation with the other animals is simple and non-moral.

'Imagine wanting a junky old rotten egg,' he says when Templeton the rat steals from the goose. Wilbur is surprised rather than censorious. An Alison Uttley rat might have been caused, quite gently, to repent, and a Beatrix Potter rat might have incurred some sort of punishment. Charlotte the spider, whose web, like that of Penelope, puts off Wilbur's natural fate indefinitely, is allowed 'feelings' towards the flies she traps: ' "Of course I don't really eat them. I drink them – I drink their blood. I love blood," said Charlotte, and her pleasant thin voice grew even thinner and more pleasant.' Spider thoughts could not be more natural or more blameless.

When you try to examine an animal from the inside out, transmigrating a human soul into an animal body is sometimes the best way, though it is not the only way. The method makes Paul Gallico's *Jennie* (1950) one of the best cat stories ever written, but by no means the best *animal* story. It is the old *Black Beauty* formula once more, a modified moral tale that is exciting and moving, involving the reader very deeply – the logical development of 'How would you feel if *you* were the cat and the cruel boy teased *you*?' That cat is not saying this to the reader, but the reader becomes the cat and says it to himself. Peter, the rich little boy with a cat-hating Nanny, becomes a cat and lives the life of a stray, finding a living here and there. He is befriended by Jennie, the disillusioned tabby, who has been loved by humans and abandoned by them and has since had to learn every trick by which such cats survive.

It is interesting to compare this book with – say – *The Adventures of Poor Puss*. There is the same conversation between two cats, with the older instructing the younger in the art of living, and at one point Jennie does indulge in a 'listen to my sad story', with 'I was born in Glasgow', and 'my earliest recollection', but this narrative is a short interpolation and the cats' lives are a series of the usual rather contrived vicissitudes given point because the boy in the catskin is learning. The 'real' cat is teaching him not only how to survive but how to harden his heart against humans. What emerges is twofold. First, there is the old moral lesson which early cat, dog and bird stories took so seriously – be kind to animals because they may have human feelings. Second, is a different kind of moral lesson in which a child is given a dream adventure in which he experiences a curiously adult love for someone else of his own kind. At the end he wakes and is a child again.

The weakness of this – and all such stories, from *Black Beauty* on, that are supposed to be about 'real animals' and given human voices – is that the whole thing becomes humanly tragic as if human prisoners in animal form were serving unbearable life sentences. The strength, in this case, is that Peter's sentence is not for ever (like that saddest prisoner of all, Stuart Little), and that within this framework a cat's life is observed with accuracy and wit and experienced by the boy with all the newness of a suddenly acquired skill. As the Darling children learn to fly, bumping round the nursery screaming with pleasure and eventually leaping through the window to freedom and the open air, so Peter the cat learns, starting with the washing of every part of his new body, and going on to bristle and threaten enemies, to pounce and kill, to eat new food and leap new heights he has never leaped before. He is at first bumbling and inept but becomes progressively more at home in the new role until at the end of the story life and honour depend on rat catching, escape techniques and a fight to the death. He dies as a cat, defending Jennie who has helped and taught him, to wake as a boy with the memory of his cat's life gone. The blending of boy-into-cat makes for humour and pathos and a time sense in which animals are supposed not to share. There is the boy's feeling of being doubly an outcast when as a cat he sees his old home. There are human parallels in the odd, outcast animals who inhabit the bombed ruin, the unlucky, orphaned, disinherited or merely weird and way-out, whom no one will own, accept, or want to know about. Peter's search for Jennie in the London streets is curiously like de Quincey's search for Ann. On the whole, the London background is less vivid than that of Tib, Tabby, Pompey, Grimalkin and Hopson. The really memorable parts of *Jennie* are those that describe with, one feels, uncanny accuracy how a cat washes, eats, stalks, evades, sleeps, purrs, expresses its feelings and lives; what a street looks like from below, what rain feels like on fur, what human feet 'eyeless and thus unable to see where they are going' look and feel like when one is ten inches from the ground. What, being a cat, one feels about dogs and children, and how cats are, when owned, prisoners of human convenience and when wanderers, outcasts who scavenge a living in town jungles. Jennie is, in her way, both human and heartless, and Peter, like the reader, experiences her life by dreaming true.

Like *The Wind in the Willows*, T. H. White's *The Sword in the Stone*, 1938, puzzled its original reviewers. 'Only the uncritical child,' said one, 'would find much in it to enjoy.' But the book David Garnett called 'One of the curious classics of English literature' was only doing, with Sir Thomas Malory, what *he* had done with the extraordinary mixture of myth and history he used to make the Matter of England. T. H. White's *Once and Future King* of which *The Sword in the Stone* is the first part, is full of humour and sadness, nonsense and lore, an individual mixture that is, according to taste, either wonderful or very unlikeable. The anachronistic delights – or barbarous misuses – of Merlyn's mistakes in time through living backwards pervade the whole education of the Wart, one day to be Arthur, Rex Quondam et Futurus. Malory's epic tells of the forming and final dissolution of the Round Table, and T. H. White causes the Wart to be educated to sympathetic understanding of the whole range of living things – growing into the wise, gentle, idealistic failure that he eventually and inevitably is. A tyrannical despot might have held the Round Table together. One whose sympathies are distributed with everyone and everything could never do so. The Wart learns through becoming. Through Merlyn's spells and the co-operation of Olympus, the Wart enters the lives of bird, fish, reptile and mammal, even those of trees and stones.

There are few better imaginative descriptions of what it might be like to be a bird, fish, or beast; and the Wart's simple, humble likeability is joined each time to what he becomes. One is made to feel that for proud, impatient, devious Kay, or anyone at the more unpleasant end of the human range, each change would have been a punishment. The idea is the same as Maeterlinck's or Lofting's – turn the diamond, learn the language, and the world of beasts is open to you. But in *The Sword in the Stone* the animals, birds and fish say not just what one would have expected, but just what one would have hoped. They are neither transformed humans nor curious circus performers, as Lofting's animals sometimes are – but their own secret selves made audible, speaking to the Wart and to us in human metaphor which turns the hawks in the mews into a military messroom, the snakes into dreamers of long, prehistoric dreams full of Latinate biology, the fish – or rather, the roach family – into hysterical hypochondriacs, the badger into a learned recluse and the hedgehog into a simple, old-fashioned, countrified soul who sings

old music-hall songs to placate an aggressor. The essence of each
animal and each tribe is made abundantly clear. While the Toad,
Rat and Mole are telling the reader more about aspects of human
nature, these animals are telling us about themselves. Here is Archimedes the Owl, and also the proud, nervous, philosophic *persona*
that is Athene's bird:

> *'Oh, what a lovely owl!' cried the Wart.*
>
> *But when he went up to it and held out his hand, the owl grew half as
> tall again, stood up as stiff as a poker, closed its eyes so that there was
> only the smallest slit to peep through as one is in the habit of doing when
> told to shut one's eyes at hide-and-seek, and said in a doubtful voice: 'There
> is no owl.'*
>
> *Then it shut its eyes entirely and looked the other way.*
>
> *'It's only a boy,' said Merlyn.*
>
> *'There is no boy,' said the owl hopefully, without turning round.*

The Wart learns to swim like a perch, what being a fish feels like,
what being underwater looks like with its upside-down spherical
horizon, colours and refractions, and sensations of suspension. As
a bird he learns to fly and to experience the owl's night vision as the
world seen as a photographer's negative. The hawks, kestrels and
ants, conforming to a rigid social pattern are the most humanlike
creatures. Running the gauntlet of the hawks in their mews, although it is like trying to join an exclusive club with terrifying,
unknown rules and initiation ceremonies, ends happily with the
singing of army songs. But the ant society has only terror in it, with
its anonymous, mindless patterns, worship of the leader, perpetual
radio reception of brainwashing messages and music. The ant adventure was one of those added to the original in T. H. White's
revision for the 1958 edition, where it replaced the battle of Robin
Hood and the Anthropophagi, human monstrosities, cannibals, so
worthy of death. The one Bestiary monster, The Questing Beast
herself, is an endearing animal mixture, amusing herself with
Questing because she cannot find a mate.

One does not have to imagine oneself inside an animal to capture
its essence; the complete identification managed by Henry Williamson in *Tarka the Otter* or *Salar the Salmon*, or the documentary
accuracy of Sir Percy Fitzpatrick's *Jock of the Bushveld*, 1907, are
marvellous achievements that need no human transformations.

Walter de la Mare enters the silver, secret, watery mystery of fish both by magic, and without it. *The Lord Fish* (1939) is a sorcerer who lives in a dark green and grey watery stone castle, set in the midst of an overgrown river in a forest where everything is cold and wet, maidens are turned into mermaids, rooms are narrow, cupboards made of stone, and the only way in is by diving under an arch. To be turned into a fish himself and be *caught* is the hero's fate; and in the Lord Fish's house 'full of suffling and sighing, the music and murmuration of water all day,' hung up with a row of others, John-turned-tench is tended and sprinkled by an ageless little girl with narrow face and grey-green hair, abruptly sloping shoulders and skinny hands and feet. 'Sprinkling, scouring and dipping she spoke to her charges in much the same way that a groom talks to horses.' It would be difficult to find anywhere a story that told more about the consciousness of fish, without apparently telling anything. The house, the river, the larder seem like a fish's dream of people, and John's transformation an intrusion into another world, as indeed it is.

PART THREE
Animal Edens

So fair a fancy few would weave
In these years! Yet, I feel,
If someone said on Christmas Eve,
'Come; see the oxen kneel

'In the lonely parton by yonder coomb
Our childhood used to know,'
I should go with him in the gloom,
Hoping it might be so.

'The Oxen', *Thomas Hardy*

14 Where there are No People

*Animal Land where there are No People is quite near, only you
can't see it. It is a kind of Garden Cage, with the North Pole and
the sea always roughling and wavy. In the summer they like to be
hotter and hotter, and in the winter colder and colder. They live by
the North Pole and in the leafy places near. It is always light
there, always day, they climb the poles and always play. That is
Animal Land.*

Animal Land Where there are No People, *Sybil Corbet*

As a child, one wanted to ask: Why are there no people? The
answer was self-supplied – they did not need any, they were better
off without them, they *were* the people. Sybil Corbet, the Daisy
Ashford of animal fantasy, makes this clear in her strange bestiary.
The creatures exist in a carefully balanced world that needs no
humans to help to run it. Each animal is as emotionally different
from the next as a human is and none, with a very few exceptions,
is a predator or victim (apart from the usual expendable fish and
birds); they seem to have moral natures which enable them to be
consciously happy and good in a way that humans are always trying,
and failing, to achieve.

Animal fantasies that banish people usually have this happy,
idyllic quality that human intrusion would quite spoil. They exist
in worlds that are better, simpler, truer, more innocent than the
human one. One longs to enter such places, but by their very
nature, one never can. The Edenlike world can be suggested in
various ways. It may be a place that is, as in mouse stories, existing
all the time just out of sight or reach or notice. It may be a place that
reverses the usual order of importance so that humans are at the
bottom of the scale and animals at the top, so that though men may
be present, they are hardly noticeable. Lastly, it may make its
animals so human that they take over all the better human charac-

teristics, only adding animal strangeness and animal innocence, as to Sybil Corbet's beasts.

A self-contained hierarchy of the first kind that dispenses with humans but still acknowledges that they are there, up above, is Olwen Bowen's farmyard comedy of *Hepzibah Hen*. This saga of several books, and a Children's Hour favourite from 1926 is the antithesis of *Animal Farm*. The 'farm folk' are obviously running the farm very successfully by themselves, with brief, off-stage help from the farmer and his wife. The animals' names fit them rather arbitrarily like comic hats – Dorcas Donkey, Alphonso Ass, Gwendolyn Goose, Gertie Grunter, Chirabelle Chicken and many others. The whole thing has a brisk, no-nonsense, rather feminine humour. The gossiping hens make sly, witty remarks about everyone else, and like a real – but ideal – farmyard there is much amusing surface and slapstick activity with no depth at all and no hints that there is any kind of world outside the farm. The animals live together like a girls' school of mixed adults. Their preoccupations are those of children playing at being grown up in a small community of suburban housewives, all the women on Christian name terms. What shall I do to make my feathers grow? says Hepzibah, rather like Chicken-Licken in the old Beacon Reader. All the other animals give advice like a series of answers to correspondents. Chirabelle too is concerned about fashion and appearance, as are all the female characters: 'My beak won't polish really well, and my tail won't curl, and Hepzibah won't let me use machine oil to make my feathers shine' . . . 'She thought she would like to be shingled like Sheila Sheep,' said Gertie.

There is no family life here, but a selection of free individuals in lives full of incident. Cuthbert Cockerel is no one's father. Chirabelle and Hepzibah seldom draw any of their comedy from being mother and daughter; everything is bright and 'good'. There is much talk of 'dinner' but no one dies, or disappears. Easter Eggs are 'eaten', Reginald Rat's activities are merely 'annoying' in an anti-social sort of way, Shirley Sheepdog has a hockey-mistress manner, brusque and jokey and 'knowing' about the farmer.

One should add that there *are* a few hints of what a farm is really for, but they seem to relate to a kind of social code – one does not mention the word 'Christmas' to a turkey, or 'Pluck' to a hen. But Hepzibah's bright world is concerned with comic social details such as what to serve for tea when donkeys are coming ('Carrots and thistles, thistles and carrots, I haven't got any of either') or those female adult preoccupations with things like Dirt and Damp which sometimes clouded one's youth ('It's so wet underfoot now that it *has* stopped raining, and I really *did* want to go to the Sewing Party this afternoon').

This was not, perhaps, conscious social satire, but to children it brought amused recognition and a great deal of pleasure. Perhaps so much of the stories consisted of conversation, they broadcast particularly well, and as a child I found Hepzibah uproarious. It is interesting to compare this farmyard with that in E. B. White's *Charlotte's Web* which has almost the same cast. The American farm is far more 'real', Olwen Bowen's more unlikely, more idyllic, yet more human. Her illustrator, L. R. Brightwell, added pictures with clear colours and outlines, pleasing in the Johnny Crow style, though not as delicate as those of Leslie Brooke. The animals are neither dressed, nor is their anatomy altered or humanised, though their features are twisted a little to convey human emotions; their antics are human without any suggestion of cartoon.

Olwen Bowen's *Taddy Tadpole and the Pond Folk* (1933) is interesting in that she attempted to apply the same method to the world of the Water Babies – which proved resistant. Pond Folk are not quite as believable as Farm Folk, partly because one cannot, as a rule, observe them; parties, gossip and adventures, tadpoles doing exercises to make their legs grow, go ill with the inexorable successions of predators and prey that go on in reality below the surface. But comedy of a rather black kind does not always go amiss. 'I'm sick of this old Pond. Nothing ever happens,' says the Dragonfly's Baby. Mrs Gatty would have given it more formal words, and preached a lesson on that favourite Victorian phenomenon: metamorphosis. In Olwen Bowen's story the larva is drunk by a cow in the next minute. Here, Brightwell's illustrations have a beauty and accuracy that balances some of the slightly unfortunate humanisation. *The Water Babies* is hard to forget. Perhaps pond life is, in reality, more Victorian than one had ever considered it to be.

Elizabeth Beresford's *Wombles*, 1968, are a modern example of the same kind of almost-Eden existence. These bearlike creatures live happily, just out of sight, independent from the human world and at times seriously incommoded by it, yet joining it for their 'work' which is tidying-up the litter that humans leave and making use of it for their own purposes. Their social life is well organised and fairly complicated, carried on underground. Wombles have not the sad poetry of Moomins; they are more like almost-human Teddy bears living in burrows. They are Hobbitlike, with Hobbits' useful way of not being seen unless they wish to be, which happens more often than one might think. They can dress like humans, and sometimes be mistaken for them. They can 'pass' as humans when they wish – i.e. making journeys on the Underground (a natural form of transport for a Womble) or pretending to be Council workmen in order to dig holes in the road (for a new burrow). They can go into human shops, use gadgets like binoculars or cameras, go to garages, use telephone kiosks, all without arousing undue attention. One of the oldest and most influential is given, at one point, an audience with the Queen (in order to gain permission to dig under Hyde Park).

In appearance they are round and furry, with 'paws' (which do not incommode them, as Paddington's paws or Larry's hoofs do). Their chief attribute is tidiness, and the uses they make of what others leave behind. Their names are geographical: Orinoco, Bulgaria, Tomsk, Tobermory. They are virtually sexless (like Hobbits) apart from the Auntlike females Adelaide and Madame Cholet. They are vegetarian, peaceful, cosy, in a way that Hobbits are cosy, with their family history, firesides and armchairs and no school at all for children apart from Womblegarten.

Is the idea better than its execution? The most satisfying thing about the Wombles – whose adventures are amusing rather than poetic, moving, or extraordinary – is that they seem to be a race that has been 'left out of the lists' like Hobbits, as they appeared to Treebeard the Ent. They have clearly been around almost since the world began, unnoticed or mistaken for something else. Great Uncle Bulgaria discovers Early Womble cave drawings under London: 'Look at that small Womble there with his paws full of bits and pieces – why, they must have been tidying up this part of London before there *was* any London.' This seems to make them believable, probable and the sort of race that *ought* to be; they are attractive, do no harm, and like ourselves are menaced by progress. Like us, they need space to move and are getting less and less of it, but unlike us, they have a remarkable capacity for having their cake and eating it. ' "Look at that," Great Uncle Bulgaria waved a paw over the maps of Surrey, Sussex and Kent. "All being turned into houses and roads and estates and goodness knows what else. By the year two thousand there won't be any fields left, but I shall be dead and gone by then, so it won't worry me." '

But Wombles live, apparently, for ever, so Great Uncle Bulgaria might well be about in two thousand giving TV interviews on ecology. Wombles fill a deep human need to feel free yet protected, *with* human society yet sufficiently against it to be constantly on the move away from it – to have everything both ways, which is what most fantasy is about. A similar story about human characters would have to make them childish, or 'different' like H. E. Bates's Larkins, or actually children. One of my own children invented a very similar fiction about a race of burrowers who were free in a subterranean world and could come up where they chose, irrespective of gates, boundaries and land ownership. But, like the Wombles, too much human intervention menaced them. The Wombles are idyllically successful. When their burrow on Wimbledon Common caves in after the passage of the 'most enormous lorry ever seen', they come up in Hyde Park, reclaiming an old burrow that is already furnished with Sheraton, Chippendale, sedan chair, a seventeenth-century clock, two Ming vases and early Rockingham – besides cave drawings. The thought is very agreeable. One could do worse than be a Womble: perhaps they will outlast humans, and why not?

Upside-down Edens depend on the assumption not that animals can manage without people but that the animals are more important than people and can keep them in their place – as attendants on and ministrators to – well, usually dogs and cats. It is not often outside satire that cattle, birds, bears or fish have the upper hand. It is with human pets that the natural order is reversed and the partial truth of this is enough to make one more uneasy about the famous Cat or Dog worlds of *Orlando* and *One Hundred and One Dalmatians* than one is about *Babar*.

Dodie Smith's *One Hundred and One Dalmatians* (1956) has no compromises about the ideal world; it is given over to Dog Power. The joke, if joke it is, starts with the first line: 'There lived in London a young married couple of Dalmatian dogs – who were lucky enough to own a young married couple of humans – who were gentle, obedient and unusually intelligent – almost canine at times. They understood quite a number of barks.' Swift says the same thing without meaning to be funny. The two Dalmatians, Pongo and Missis, are served and supplied by their doting Mr and Mrs Dearly and the Splendid Vet. With their fifteen puppies they have nothing left to ask for in this life – until the puppies are stolen by a wicked (human) sorceress. Without human aid – what good are humans anyway? – the devoted dog parents manage to rescue their children from a manor-house prison and with some eighty others, similarly captured, find their way home and persuade Mr and Mrs Dearly to adopt them all and move to the country. Seldom has Dog Power been more effectively deployed, especially as the villains are routed at the same time. All the dogs are good, virtuous and beautiful, but they all recognise that humans can be misguided, criminal and stupid, and allowances have to be made. Making the world safe for Dalmatians is the unvoiced ambition behind these proceedings.

As in *Black Beauty*, the animals talk to and understand each other. They talk to and understand humans, but the stupid humans do not reciprocate. It is a marvel that the dogs put up with them and rather uncharitable to suggest that perhaps they need the shelter, warmth and food that humans provide. 'Humans seldom manage to recognise more than half a dozen barks, if that. And barks are only a small part of the dog language.' Clearly, dogs are the more intelligent breed and do, as is suggested by this story, secretly run things by manipulation rather than overt force. After all, the best humans are very likeable. Even a rather sadistic small child is excused because he has not, hitherto, known enough dogs. And humans can be generous. The puppies in captivity have become besotted with television, which they have not seen before. 'Can we have it when we get home?' one of them asks. 'Indeed you shall, my darling,' says Missis. 'Somehow, somehow, the Dearlys must be made to buy a set.' The triumphal journey by coach to the house in the country, the route lined by interested dogs, is rather noisy: but 'the Dearlys didn't mind. They thought happy barking was a pleasant noise.' The fable is full of wit and fun, and some sentiment, but as an Eden story it is too thought provoking for real enjoyment.

Orlando's world – (*Orlando the Marmalade Cat*, Kathleen Hale, 1938, and many sequels) is far more visual, with its bold, beautiful colour lithography, drawings full of witty detail and text full of equal amusement, but the theme is the same. Cats are the dominant

species and the rest of the world owes them homage and respect:
'After dinner they went to the skating rink where the orchestra
recognised Orlando and played "God Save our Gracious Cat".'
Partially for cats makes the text, with its witty parallels and outrageous puns, more acceptable than that which describes the dogs'
world. Humans as lesser creatures are hardly present and therefore
the assumption of the cat's superiority is more implicit, less
laboured. The stylish pictures, with their transformation of everyday scenes to the cat's view, are disarming. The London streets are
changed so that buses and cars look like cats; the advertisements
show the humans keeping up with the cats, with the Joneses nowhere; tiles are paraded by cat pedestrians, the humans foreshort-
ened midgets below. Humans tend, when they appear, to wait on
cats, to sell them things in shops, to defer to their opinions, to run
cat shows for the cats' amusement and be invited to the cats' parties
or invited into their houses as a special treat. But there is no question
of a reversal of ownership. There is evidence in an early book of
someone called 'Master' whose function and privilege it is to provide for Orlando and his family, and who takes no action at all when
'Grace combed up Master's oldest blankets into nice fluffy new ones
for invalid cats'.

Orlando is, like Pongo, virtuous and beautiful, resourceful and
dignified, and the stories concern his idyllic domestic bliss as much
as his adventures. 'Orlando was like my husband,' Kathleen Hale
has said, 'absolutely splendid and reliable. And Grace was the sort of
female that I secretly wanted to be.' Their happiness is only occasionally ruffled ('They had a slight misunderstanding over the
largest piece of fish . . . "Excuse me," said Orlando. "Forgive me,"
said Grace, "my nerves are on edge." ') Orlando is always taking
Grace out, buying her clothes and other gifts. They are devoted to
the kittens who in turn devise surprises and entertainments for their
parents. Family life is cushioned and perfect. The kittens are sometimes naughty, Grace sometimes feels middle-aged, but never for
long; Orlando cheers and comforts her, recalling the past or telling
her that she is beautiful or giving her a fur coat.

The Orlando books are holidays from life as it is, giving another
species a chance of being dominant without suggesting that they
are out to manipulate humans by being more human than they. The
cats are always catlike, never really humanised, however much they

enjoy civilised living. Dining out, they sit on their chairs as cats do, not as those cat-headed people in *The Poll Parrot Picture Book* who all have their feet in shoes, on the floor. Orlando, kissing Grace, gives her an eye-closing lick and greets her with the 'half-purr, half-mew' that cats use to each other but very rarely to humans; and although Grace has her apron, fur coat, mouse tippet and cornflower hat, Orlando wears, and needs to wear, nothing.

The ballet 'Orlando's Silver Wedding', performed in the open air theatre at Battersea Pleasure Gardens in 1951 was a delight to eye and ear and seemed like an inverted human tribute to cats as the Beatrix Potter film appeared to be more a human celebration of frogs, mice and squirrels than a tribute to the artistry of the author. Feline Harold Turner and Sally Gilmore (whose 'Lady into Fox' must have suggested this casting) brought Orlando and Grace alive in dance and mime, while operatic voices sang the words to Arthur Benjamin's music. One expected to see Orlando himself among the audience rather than on the stage.

If you turn the world into Elephant Land rather than Dog Land or Cat Land, there has to be some sort of human compromise if anything is to take place outside the Jungle. Elephants are not pets. They are large and noble or menacing, strange and undomestic, and like dragons they have to be tamed and reduced – which explains the childlike Babar, adopted baby and 'friend' of that useful character, the Old Lady, who plays Mr Brownlow to his Oliver Twist. Babar exists in a perpetual, infantile middle age. The simple colourful illustrations of the de Brunhoffs, father and son, make the appeal of this device quite clear; Babar does what most small children would like to do – joins in the adult world on a child's terms, and gets away with it. There is no one to tell him not to. He can wear grown-up clothes, ride up and down in the lift, go fishing, drive a car, marry Celeste and become King of the Jungle all because his real self is hidden behind an animal hide and he is neither child nor adult but a bit of both – in that ageless state that is the speciality of large, rounded, slightly cumbersome or 'strange' animals like elephants, sheep, crocodiles, hippopotami or bears.*

*Mary Tourtel's Mrs Rhino is a perfect old lady, slightly stooped, dressed in clothes that were fashionable just before the First World War, and a hat of even earlier date usually seen in accurate productions of *Charley's Aunt*. Beatrix Potter's sheep are motherly and slightly stupid. Paddington lives in a permanent and delightful age-ambiguity that helps him to get away with anything. Albert is not only solid but worthy and will probably end up an alderman.

Babar is not particularly wrinkled and wise. He is drawn with a stubbiness, a simple, large-eared, dot-eyed, triangular face that might be child or old man and is probably midway between the two. When he marries Celeste and has children they are the same, exactly like their parents in miniature – tiny, tuskless adults.

Babar has the best of everything while remaining apparently uncorrupted. He is a child-become-Olympian with Olympian power and a child's tastes which is, perhaps, as near paradise as it is possible to go. He visits Paris, meets and is adopted by, his rich Old Lady who hands over her purse without question – it is all like one of those dreams that are a list of things that one would like to happen, as long as one is in control of the dream. In dreams, as in life, catastrophe usually sets in, but as Babar stories are written for very young children, all is calm. Or, if Babar by mischance does get involved in a shipwreck, a circus, or a fight, it is of the play sort, unreal and harmless.

As in the *Paddington* books where Paddington needs the Browns before he can exist, Babar needs his patroness – but he eventually graduates to Elephant Land, where she is merely a useful guest. There, King Babar has a city and a palace, and the court sculptor carves a portrait statue not out of a block of stone, but from a whole mountainside – it is vast, triangular, stubby and monumental like its subject. But King Babar retains the common touch and, a bicycling monarch, is always ready to mix with his subjects. People are neither necessary nor admitted to this playworld where everyone is a concealed child and their only human friend is not a bothersome parent but a benign Granny.

Walter de la Mare's Three Royal Monkeys (*The Three Mulla-Mulgars*, 1910) is the old, never failing quest story of a journey towards a far off paradise transposed into animal terms. It has likenesses with the prototype quest stories, *The Pilgrim's Progress*, *The Odyssey*, *King Solomon's Mines*,* *Through The Looking Glass*, *The Water Babies*, *Treasure Island*.

The three monkeys, princes of Tishnar, set out to find the country of their birthright helped by the wonderstone, an emblem given

---

*This seminal book left traces in Tolkien, C. S. Lewis, and E. Nesbit: The Silent Ones and The Hall of the Dead have amplified echoes in *The Uggly Wugglies*, *The City of Charn*, *Rath Dinen*, *Gondor* and *The Argonath*.

to them by their mother. The elements of the story are quite familiar
– the secret royalty of the characters, the youngest son, Nod, being
the bearer of the stone and hero of the story, the directions given
by a dying parent or old person, the map or talisman and the gradual
stages of the journey, often following in the steps of someone that
has gone before, in which the hero is slowly translated into a
different person from the one that set out. But the difference here
is deeper than the difference between monkeys and men. Walter
de la Mare sees the monkeys as a kind of man: a special, poetic,
rare race like men and yet unlike, gentle, delicate, full of courage,
near to natural things and finer than men and more sensitive. The
monkeys have hopes and fears, poetry and memory; they meditate
on their forbears, childhood, nameless terrors and wonders, the
beauty and strangeness of other animals, the industry of insects.
Beside them Andy Battle, the one man in the story, is a vast, crude,
coarse, blundering giant.

In a way, the three monkeys are like man – shadows, animal
children with men's intelligence and children's grace, beauty and
innocence; in another, they are farther away, across a deeper gulf
than the humanisations of such authors as Kenneth Grahame or
Hugh Lofting. Walter de la Mare's fondness for monkeys – which
he sees as grave, lovely, pathetic, helpless miniature humans yet the
most intelligent and 'different' of animals – is even more evident in
The Old Lion (1910). That sad, gentle story examines the relationship
between monkey and sailor even more closely than that between
Nod and Andy Battle. Jasper, the monkey bought by John Bumps,
second mate of the Old Lion, had 'a neat pretty head, wonderfully
slender hands and long thumbs and . . . (when it) turned its solemn
hazel eyes on Mr Bumps he felt acutely homesick . . . and the tiny
liquid syllables which issued from the small mouth were a message
from friend to friend.'

Jasper learns English which he pronounces with a strange,
delightful hiss. Stolen from John Bumps, he is bought by an animal
trainer and made to act on the stage in human clothes. He makes a
fortune for himself and his trainer though the tiny dignity with
which he speaks and performs frightens as much as it entertains
the people who flock to see him – among them, at last, John Bumps.
Man and monkey are reunited, only to part; the sailor carries out
Jasper's one wish, to go back to Africa. At last Jasper, his finery

and fortune, are left on the river bank of his home. Jasper returns to his people and the money chests are left untouched, the old sailor desolate. It is difficult to communicate the flavour of this sad, moving story with its message that animal and man can meet only rarely, and only for a time; their final destinies cannot be shared.

In its way *The Three Mulla-Mulgars* is less haunting and less disturbing because the monkeys' paradise is their own. It is perhaps easier in creating an idyllic world to create its inhabitants, too, according to one's own rules. A Moomin, Clanger or Hobbit can live in a happier world than an almost human ape, if on a rather lower level. The agreeable rotundity of these creatures – and most of Sybil Corbet's too – is a clue to their predominantly 'cosy' nature, which need not necessarily exclude poetry of a kind. Tove Jansson's Moomins (*Finn Family Moomintroll*, Finland, 1946, and many more) live in a strange, original, 'removed' world, apparently much pleasanter than the real one but not without its own perils. This happy, eventful, half-supernatural society of small animals and eccentric, ghostlike creatures exists in a place where myths come true. The odd things that happen are a mixture of enchantment and cosmic disaster, and with so much going on in the way of weather – storms, snow, floods, comets, droughts and earthquakes – it is perhaps appropriate that the few human supernumeraries are a group of detached scientists in a remote observatory.

Human society has, happily, not reached Moomin valley. Tove Jansson has not cast animals into human moulds, but has invented new types. The Moomin family themselves – father, mother and son, rotund hippopotami – live in a house as round as themselves and have a gentle, old-fashioned, Victorian family life with father writing his memoirs, mother engaged in Mrs Beeton cookery and their son old enough to go out and have adventures, yet young enough to fall into his mother's embrace when things get too much for him. Inside the Moomin house, snug and round as a womb, nothing goes wrong, even when it gets snowed up or magic flowers sprout and turn it into a jungle. Outside, the weather may roar, magicians cast spells, monsters lurk in caves or in the sea, chasms open, comets fall and the hideous evil Groke stare out of the darkness; but the extraordinary atmosphere of love, tolerance and humour radiating from this delightful family takes away the sting. There is no suggestion that the ups and downs and adventures are in any way harmless. They are real enough, and strange enough for the world to seem full of fear and sometimes of evil, but warmth from within and the certainty of love is enough for the Moomins, totally at home in this haunted, precarious and very beautiful world. Their warmth attracts other creatures to it like moths. Some of them are strange and remarkable, some apparently quite normal to the Moomins though not to us, and they take part in various adventures and remain in Moomin valley, happily attached to the family whose hospitality is perpetual and unquestioning. Some of these creatures are adult human parodies: the Muskrat who lies about in a hammock philosophising on the uselessness of everything; the Hemulen, merely one of a race, who is sadly oblivious to everything except botany, trudging through the tropical undergrowth in a long nightdress with a magnifying glass and a vasculum (Hemulens as a race are creatures of long, slow ideas, self-absorbed, melancholy and give to collecting); Thingummy and Bob with their suitcase, talking to each other in Spoonerisms, Sniff, Moomin's friend; Snuffkin and the Snorks, introduced as species ('They saw a Snuffkin,' 'Those Snorks I saw a month ago'); and beyond all the strange Hattifatteners, curious ghostly little white Jumblies who can neither speak nor hear, and only see dimly, forever looking for something (nobody knows what) semi-electric and worshipping a barometer in a lonely glade.

But although this odd, mixed society is full of beauty, poetry and vivid nonsense, it is not one which I feel I would like to join. It gets on perfectly well without humans anyway, and there is an undertone of terror and melancholy which not even Moomin-mamma can dispel. Tove Jansson's illustrations have this same innocent but strange and melancholy quality. Perhaps the following passage from her autobiography (*A Sculptor's Daughter*, 1969) gives a clue to her imaginative qualities:

A great big black creature was creeping towards me. I got cautious and stood still. The creature was shapeless. It was one of those creatures that can spread itself out and creep under the furniture, or turn into a black fog that gets thicker and thicker until it is quite sticky and gets all round you and fastens itself to you.

I let the creature get a little closer and put its hand out. The hand crept along the floor and then was pulled back suddenly. The creature

Comfortable rotund, compare with pages 108 and 109

came even closer . . . occasionally its shape changed just slightly and its
black tummy swept over the concrete floor. It was getting dark in the
studio. I knew that it was me who had let the creature out and I couldn't
capture it and lock it up again . . . anyone can let Danger out but the
really clever thing is finding somewhere for it to go afterwards.

A child, hidden under a black tulle skirt, creeps towards its image
in a mirror. The transforming imagination invents myths and reinforces them with logic. Perhaps finding somewhere for Danger to
go needed Moominland with its seas, forests and mountains and a
pair of old-fashioned parents to guard the animal children – who
are non-human and so always good – from the cold and the dark.

Hobbits have cousinship with Moomins – they share the same
pre-industrial idyll, guarded against surrounding evil. They are
animal pretenders; by all the rules they should be a race of mice or
bears, but they succeed in being a very human bear-derivative,
rather like the genus Womble, and a new kind of human. As in
Moominland, the industrial revolution has not reached Middle
Earth, which partly accounts for the sad, hypnotic charm of all that
goes on there. (*The Hobbit*, 1937, *The Lord of the Rings*, 1954, J. R. R.

Tolkien). Middle Earth is somewhere in the past, and the wicked genius Sauron is doing his best – and in *The Lord of The Rings* almost succeeding – in advancing history with a rush and bringing the industrial revolution to pass. Mordor and Isengard are full of factories and satanic mills. The lure of the *Ring* saga is that Sauron is defeated and the whole horrid onslaught of iron and steel and wheels and machines and slavery and industrial pollution that we have learned to regret, is overthrown, repulsed, and somehow put off, so that everyone can live happy, pastoral lives with lots of presents, celebrations, food and drink in beautiful surroundings which still are, of themselves, passing away so that nostalgic regret is underlying every statement. This is a perfect recipe for a certain kind of literary enjoyment and it is interesting to see how it is done. This kind of society must always be in competition with the world as we know it, and the various ways of dealing with this aspect of story telling show the Eden principle in action. You can outlaw humans by making cats or dogs or monkeys important. You can make the fact of competition interesting by giving mice human characteristics and showing them in retreat or hiding, or by inventing a bear-like, underground race – Wombles – in similar retreat. You can place a human-rejecting race on a distant planet and call them Clangers, or invent a new, pre-industrial race and put them into the past. Hobbits have all these characteristics. Human but bearlike, they are 'Diminutive Cheeryble Brothers with a dash of Winnie the Pooh', as one of the first reviews of *The Fellowship of the Ring* said. They are small, rotund, brown-skinned, furry-footed and woolly-headed, divided into 'breeds' of Harfoot, Stoor and Fallohide. They do not build; they live in burrows and caves and holes and tunnels and usually dislike water. They 'do not understand or like machines more complicated than a forge-bellows, a water mill or a hand loom'. Men, if they have not seen one before, stare at them as if they could not quite believe their eyes.

Hobbits – even the oldest of them, Bilbo Baggins himself – have that toy-bear quality of permanent middle age with childlike tastes, simple, unimaginative common sense and delight in food. When you meet a thin one – Gollum – he is evil, corrupted and wrong. To make heroes out of these creatures is to satisfy human desire for the simple, kindly, ordinary and rather unimaginative younger son to succeed and win not the Princess – for the animal kingdom is always in this context sexless – but the kingdom itself. Everyone can then go home and live happily ever after without any of that unnecessary stuff about love and weddings. That this ideal is realised in a dwarf-bear-person puts it unattainably outside human expectation, not only in the pre-industrial past but in a never never country peopled by a mixture of races from whom, it is suggested, some of the fallen humans we have since become may be descended.

One almost wishes it could be true. Hobbits are much pleasanter than historical reality. Let me add that when I read *The Hobbit* as a child I so fell under its hypnotic enchantment that I decided it must have been written specially for me. *The Lord of The Rings* reinforced this view. The almost unbelievable nostalgia induced for a time and place that one could never visit still held, even when one separated and analysed the ingredients and decided that the Argonath came out of *King Solomon's Mines*, the Mines of Moria out of George Macdonald, Smaug out of the *Volsungasaga*, and that Minas Morgul was a radar scanner put to interesting use.*

As Hobbits and Moomins are pre-industrial. so Oliver Postgate's *Clangers*, 1969, are post. Mild and gentle, they and their pleasing world cannot compete with Man. Ther have to be literally beyond earth's orbit, removed, on a planet of their own. If they had powerful telescopes – which they have not – one feels they might observe what was happening on earth, and recoil from it. The delightful, animated films which describe their life show a race living in a metallic world, a small round planet that is, in many ways, the opposite of earth, more interesting on the inside than the outside,

---

*As in *Le Morte d'Arthur*, the ingredients count less than what is made out of them. The spell works, even if people like M. R. James or John Fowles tell you exactly *how* it works. Two examples of Professor Tolkien's likely sources illustrate this point. The incident of Sam and the Watchers in the Orc Tower (*The Return of the King*) occurs first in 'Jack the Giant Killer' where Jack in a cap of Darkness passes between gates guarded by griffin heads which cause an intolerable trumpet blast, making the castle foundations tremble. Sam, too, is invisible; he is wearing the Ring. As he passes the Watchers there is a clanging bell and the crashing of the gate arch. But perhaps the most striking parallel will appear to anyone who reads H. G. Wells's 'The Crystal Egg' in which it is obvious that Wells thought of the Palantir, or seeing stones, first. A glass ball in an antique shop is shown 'to be in some physical but at present quite inexplicable way en rapport' with others that exist on Mars. Whoever looks into the ball can see, and be seen by, 'the multitude of soaring forms' or archaic, bird-like creatures flying round their turrets, resolving into a single eye on the other side of the crystal. Pippin's experience with the Palantir is the same. Mr Cave, the antiquary, dies with the Crystal Egg clasped in his hands; in *The Return of the King*, the owner of the Palantir has the same fate. But nothing can make Tolkien and Wells alike; Pippin's vision, however much it resembles Mr Cave's, means something entirely different. Magic lies in the method or rearrangement of material, sources are bones, lifeless by themselves.

rich in ore that has obviously been used not for work, but for play. The little, snouted, porcine creatures that inhabit it have used metal for clothes and adornment, for mugs and plates and a simple flying boat that rises, not by rockets or machinery, but on an ascending musical scale.

The Clangers, with their typically close and happy family life, have voices and thoughts, but no words. Their whistling 'speech' conveys these thoughts without any articulation, and the other odd creatures who live with them – the gurgling dragon and cheeping frogs – express themselves in a similar wordless way. The human intrusions that sometimes appear in the shape of rockets or pieces of space rubble are treated as rather annoying litter. Human astronauts land, stump about looking foolish and clumsy, plant a flag and go away; the Clangers continue as before. Human artefacts and mechanisms are always rejected. A television set seems crude and unnecessary, a machine for making plastic gadgets is a disaster. They are returned into space with polite contempt. A final and wonderful use of the stuff of machinery (which is, to a Clanger, a mis-use of metal) is to turn it into a meccano hen with a nest of nuts and bolts. This creature is beautiful, useful, strange, humorous and alive like the Clangers themselves.

This tiny, closed, musical society is totally, blissfully happy and the effect is to make one hope that no humans will ever join it.

The Log of the Ark, Kenneth Walker and Geoffrey Boumphrey, 1923, is the only attempt outside the work of C. S. Lewis to deal with an Animal Fall. The retreat from Eden involved animals as well as people, and the return of the Golden Age (or assumption in the previous stories that the Golden Age is able to carry on by itself outside the human sphere) should bring with it friendship and reconciliation between animals and men, predators and hunted. Meanwhile, we have to manage as well as we can. For animal societies to be truly happy they must be placed beyond human reach in far-off valleys, distant planets, or mirror-country where roles are reversed – or, as in this charming and inspired pre-Dolittle story, before the Flood. The world before the Flood was, according to its authors, a happy, dry, well-populated place full of talking beasts, many of whom have since become extinct, such as Clidders, Wumpetty-Dumps, Luminous Puffins, Cleets and Jigger-dees. All these animals are talkative, friendly and helpful until the Flood comes. Then the differences begin to show. The monkey, the most intelligent of the beasts, is the one to notice the building of the ark, and to get the idea of boarding it. In the catastrophe and rush to embark it is the odd and bizarre animals that are overwhelmed. All the others are taken in, even mythical beasts and uneducated ones that don't know their own names and are just called Seventy-sevens.

Once on board, the animals behave like joyful children on a cruise liner, from the Hippo full of jokes, to the Sloth who takes so long to say anything at all that no one listens to it. All the animals have baths and porridge and seats with their names on, keep their own cabins tidy, and arrange a concert. But, though this is still a kind of Eden, the animals have brought their own Satan with them: in all their doings they are trailed by 'the loathly Scub' who lurks in dark corners, spreads lies and despondency and becomes the first animal murderer. He can never be lost or shaken off. The animals change. Was it the diet of porridge and treacle? Noah wonders. The change is psychological rather than physical. The animals develop philosophic doubts about the end of the water and the edge of the world and the Seventy-sevens are lost overboard with the dreadful requiem; there will be no more Seventy-sevens, we can never grow new ones.

At last the land appears, and with great excitement the animals go down the gang plank, the Sloth on the under side, to animal jokes and laughter; but hunters and hunted are defined and divided. If the animals are not conscious of good and evil, as men are, they are conscious of fear and will never live with each other or with men without fear again. ' "They're changed," said Japhet, "and I don't think it will ever be the same again." "I don't know what to think," said Noah.'

15 Fallen and Redeemed: Animals in the novels of C. S. Lewis

My first stories were written and illustrated with enormous satisfaction: they were an attempt to combine my two chief literary pleasures – dressed animals and knights in armour.

Surprised by Joy, *C. S. Lewis*

Invented Edens have never been equally shared between animals and men until the decline of religious belief and man's displacement as the centre of the universe. It is ironic that the most memorable of such places is Narnia, a land that is under the power of Aslan, the Christian Lion. C. S. Lewis only manages this pleasing arrangement by putting the action outside the earth and into a parallel world (*The Lion, the Witch and the Wardrobe*) or on Mars, where animal and human sharing is even more marked, in *Out of the Silent Planet*. Mars, or Malacandra, reduces the humans to animal status; Narnia raises the animals to human heights by turning them into Talking Beasts.

The animal strain is present in all the *Narnia* books, and in the science-fiction trilogy. It shows itself in two ways: the homely (the dressed mice in Snug Town) and the heroic (the knights in armour) combine not only in C. S. Lewis's unpublished juvenilia, the stories of Animal-Land or Boxen, but in his children's stories, culminating in Aslan himself and the courtly mouse Reepicheep.

Mouse Town is not everyone's idea of heaven, but it is significant that an imagination whose first promptings of beauty (we are told) came from the illustrations to *Squirrel Nutkin* should indulge in 'dressed animals' and perhaps, wanting to write grown-up novels or histories that were not allowed to get interesting on the first page but only on the second, should change this into the country of Boxen, the name given to the invented place 'Animal-Land' that adjoined India. It was the way that this imagination wanted to go; it is no coincidence that among the children's stories he most quotes from and must have most enjoyed, *The Wind in the Willows* is prominent.

The animals in Boxen are there because they have to be, but as animals they are rather an arbitrary assortment – a bull, an owl, horse, sheep or cat, ruled over by a frog (Lord John Big). It seems to have been as natural for C. S. Lewis to write about animals as it was to write religious allegory. The *Narnia* books and the science-fiction trilogy combine the two and it is interesting to see how in both series, ideal worlds are shown to be populated first by animals, later by humans, who tend to bring evil, conflict and doubt. In every case the animals exist as themselves, never as counterfeit men, always 'good' and uncorrupted. From Boxen – which, in its way, must have been rather like *Reynard the Fox* – we have moved to worlds containing rational, talking creatures in animal form, equal to men but quite different from them.

But in the first two novels of his science-fiction trilogy – *Out of the Silent Planet* (1938) and *Perelandra* (1943) – Lewis describes worlds of astonishing beauty with virtually no human populations at all, but very definite animal ones, with fur, feathers and scales. Earth is made to appear dull by comparison, its inhabitants dark, flattened and bulging to a Martian eye. In much science fiction other planets are alien and terrifying; to describe them otherwise is as untraditional as writing successful children's stories full of explicit religious allegory (of which there is far more in Narnia than in the work of George Macdonald).

Ransome's arrival on Mars in *Out of the Silent Planet* is marked by terror. He is a reluctant, kidnapped traveller and when he overhears that he is to be given to creatures called Sorns, he immediately thinks of horrors – perhaps of the two things that most frightened the author as a child – insects and ghosts.

'Wait till he sees a Sorn,' say the villains Weston and Devine; and Sorns are bird-ghosts of giant height, disturbingly almost human. Ransome's one thought on seeing one is to escape. He runs through, and hides in, the beautifully coloured and strangely elongated country, until he meets more living things, a herd of tall, pale, furry giraffe-kangaroos who are eating the tops of trees.

Reassured with the idea that the planet has animals on it as well as ghosts, he is still unprepared for his first meeting with yet another inhabitant: a gleaming black creature six or seven feet high, 'something like a penguin, something like an otter, something like a seal, something like a giant stoat'. He is rooted to the ground with fear, until, in one of the great passages of this book and the key to the *Narnia* stories, the creature opens its mouth and begins to make noises. Ransome – a scholar and a philologist – at once realises, in spite of his terror, that it is talking. That animals could be rational had not occurred to him, and as it did, it overturned the world: animal and human had no more meaning.

This, one feels, is how C. S. Lewis wanted things to be, for he had created a world in which it was so. Hross and man confront each other with a kind of balletic advance and retreat, each afraid, yet each attracted – it was 'foolish, frightening, ecstatic and unbearable all in one moment'. Later, when they have learned each other's names, Ransome and Hyoi sit on a river bank eating a kind of Martian vegetable, Ransome is struck with fear because the creature is not a man, but is seven feet high, covered in hair and whiskered like a cat. But it is when he can make the change and consider it as an animal that he can love it 'as though Paradise had never been lost and earliest dreams were true', for it has the charm of speech and reason. Here is the romantic Eden before the fall, glimpsed in John's Island in *The Pilgrim's Regress*, 1933, where man and animal are not only equal, but friends. In more mundane fashion, it is the old story of the child who longed for his dog, or his Teddy bear to speak, and as a man, made up stories in which they did. It is Animal-Land and Paradise combined. All the science-fiction stories and the whole of the *Narnia* cycle are played on this note. In *Out of the Silent Planet* there is Eden, in *Perelandra* the reader witnesses the story of the fall, in *That Hideous Strength*, the fall has already happened. But in all three there is the reminder that the fall of man brought the fall, or fate, or exploitation of animals with it.

Out of the Silent Planet has other interesting ideas concerning Mars – or Malacandra, in Martian language – as an idealised Animal-Land. Ransome comes to realise that this is a planet with no countries, only three different races. Manlike, he tries to rationalise their society (late Stone Age?) and to wonder which of the three species – the Hrossa, the ghostly birdlike Sorns, or the reptilian Pfifltriggi –

is the dominant one. He finds out that they are equal but different in nature, one poetic, one philosophical and one physically creative, and that the same God that made them made men too. He hears of an earlier race which has died out, for none are intended to live for ever.

In one sense in this book there are man-bird, man-seal and man-toad, yet in another the men in the story are made to feel small, insignificant, ugly and at the end, for all their space ships, foolish.

At the very end comes animal vengeance which C. S. Lewis uses and re-uses to remind us that since the fall animal creation has been consistently killed, enslaved and abused. In this novel it is comic vengeance taken on one of the men, the wicked scientist Weston who is here the villain, later to become the arch villain of Perelandra. He is removed to have his head bathed in cold water, 'to cool him off'.

This is a joke to the Hrossa and Pfifltriggi but to Weston, whose plans would have prostituted and exploited both animals and humans, it is a real revenge. From first to last he has never realised the Malacandrian's nobility, but takes them to be animals or creatures of a low order: he can never regard the non-human as equal.

We dipped his head in the cold water seven times (says a hross). The seventh time something fell off it. We had thought it was the top of his head but now we saw it was a covering made of the skin of some creature . . . then we dipped it seven times more. The creature talked a lot between the dips and most between the second seven, but we could not understand it.

The ignominy was cruelty to Weston, who was expecting torture and a martyr's death. A very similar incident happens in the *Narnia* story at the end of *The Magician's Nephew* where the Wicked Uncle, another Weston figure (but even worse because he is a magician as well as a scientist), is dealt with by the Narnian Talking Beasts of whom he is naturally terrified and whose language he does not understand. The Beasts' intention is kind but the result is nightmare, quite unbearable if it was not comic. They think he is a tree and try to plant him, the wrong way up.

The animals' revenge in *That Hideous Strength* is nightmare come true, brought about, significantly, by confusion of language and man's reduction to the level of the animals he has been exploiting.

Once again the animals are not guilty – they are doing nothing except obeying instinct.

In both the Edens of Mars and Venus the evil comes from without in the shape of a man, and animal characters, rational or otherwise, are shown to be guiltless and uncorrupted. They do not even understand evil; it is so rare among them that it has to be explained in terms of something of almost legendary rarity, strange and unfortunate.

The classical and northern elements which always combined in Lewis's work – making the inhabitants of Narnia a combination of Chiron and Squirrel Nutkin – reappear in Perelandra, the Venus of the trilogy, a planet as warm and fluid as Malacandra was hard and cold. Ransome speculates among other things on whether situations and creatures regarded as legendary on one planet become real on another: an idea which appealed greatly to Lewis and which he used in Narnia and in the science-fiction short story 'Forms of Things Unknown'. On Malacandra Ransome is shown comparing the Sorn Augray with the Cyclops of Ulysses, and throughout the *Narnia* books there are an astonishing and not always happily mixed number of creatures from different legends – the ones that appealed to the author most – inhabiting a created world that is obviously England only better.

In *Perelandra* the legend is that of the temptation of Eve, which Ransome is allowed to witness in the hope that he will be able to prevent it. But the tempter is not an animal, not even the most unpopular one of all, whose only apologist has been Rudyard Kipling; it is the wicked Weston again, the power-mad humanist, a type Lewis regarded as the worst in existence and who is later taken over by the forces of evil becoming, like them, unkillable and all but invincible.

The animals in this novel do not speak and are all in a state of nature in an Eden which, allowing for differences of climate and ecology, is rather like that of the Bible. Eve is shown at the summit of creation, 'The Lady' whom the animals know and love and obey. The devil in the form of Weston tries to bring about her downfall by argument and persuasion, leading up to the great temptation – the invitation to walk on the fixed land, the forbidden place. The interesting idea is advanced that God put it there in order to be able to say No; it would have been equally interesting if C. S. Lewis had suggested that Adam was the one vulnerable to temptation (but in the last novel of the trilogy a man *is* tempted, by the offer of power: Eve in Perelandra is tempted through latent feminine vanity).

The Perelandrian animals are beautiful, mythical and heraldic: a tame, winged dragon, flying frogs, rideable dolphins and a creature called the Singing Beast which suggests an okapi but which is described as being like a dog with the legs of a camel, the neck and head of a horse, but vast in size. It is a cuckoo beast, suckled and reared by a mother of another kind. Lewis shows it existing with such strange, hidden, sad joy, beauty and shyness that words other than his own reduce it to a cartoon anomaly.*

The animals in *That Hideous Strength* are earthly ones, non-rational, but important enough to be heroes or victims, in the former sense pets (of a kind), in the latter, inhabitants of a zoo. C. S. Lewis's insect fear, exorcised by a harmless monster in *Perelandra*, also suggested 'either machines that have come to life, or life degenerating into mechanism', and dominance of the female and the collective. *That Hideous Strength* shows just such a process beginning to take hold when the mysterious Ministry, the National Institute of Co-ordinated Experiments with its ambiguous initials, takes root and gains power by infiltration and persuasion as a prelude to inevitable force. One of its principal officers is the sadistic lesbian Miss Hardcastle.

A subsidiary interest of this devilish symposium is animal experiment and a large zoo is kept for this purpose. The opposing side, who live in a place called The Manor, St Annes, an almost enchanted country house, have animals as pets including a vast bear called Mr Bultitude who has escaped from a circus and whose delight it is to sit in the bathroom on cold days. It is Eden again; all the pets seem

---

*It seems to be extremely difficult to make up a convincing new animal. The best most science-fiction writers and others do is to add up pieces of old ones, as in the game of head, body and legs. The animals of heraldry, legend and the Bestiaries are formed in this fashion, so that in theory one could draw quite an accurate picture of the Questing Beast from the list of parts given. Usually in science fiction a new animal is a new monster put together from the parts of insects, plants, fish, etc. that most terrify and repel, i.e. John Wyndham's Triffids when analysed, come apart as Venus Fly Trap pineapple rattlesnakes. But one of this author's most telling pieces of black humour occurs in *The Chrysalids* when, after atomic pollution animal and human deviants are hunted down with fanatical religious fervour, one of the characters meets and recoils from a creature 'as obvious a deviant as ever I saw'. It is, equally obviously to the reader, a hyena, one of the few creatures that looks, in reality, as if it had been put together from spare parts like Frankenstein's monster.

to have arrived by their own free will and to lead lives of equality with the humans, unencumbered by leads, fences or locked doors, in harmony with man and each other. The opposition torture their animals in cages.

The 'good' humans are an odd collection of the simple and the intelligent. Perhaps one is justified in peopling Eden, or even Heaven, with the characters one has most loved and admired (in *The Great Divorce* George Macdonald is Heaven's interpreter and guide) and Hell with those for whom one feels the most horror – scientists, experimenters, those whom sheer logic has rendered inhuman, the power-mad manipulators, the merely vain. In a scene of orgiastic horror during after-dinner speeches at a banquet, the humans lose the power of language and with it their ascendancy, and the beasts from the laboratories attack and destroy them. The 'good' bear Mr Bultitude annihilates the evil 'head' of the Institute by eating it, prompted by simple hunger. The animals are neither good nor bad; they are themselves, simple and amoral, creatures with whom the planet is unequally shared, neither agents of witchcraft nor of heaven. Though at the end a few of them appear to speak in the manner of Balaam's Ass, they are not rationally intelligent; but in the war between good and evil they have a large part to play. At the end, when the occupants of the Manor are revealed to each other in beauty that has always, in mundane life, been hidden, the mating of the animals in the garden is part of the joy of revealed love.

It would appear to have been as difficult for C. S. Lewis to avoid religious allegory, as it was to avoid the prominent role that animals, usually intelligent and often humanised, play in it. It is, of course quite in order to write heroic romance dealing with the struggle between good and evil without any religious theme. *The Hobbit* is such a book. When *The Lord of the Rings* first appeared one critic found its lack of religious feeling remarkable enough for comment – as remarkable as its lack of women. But aim at the distant hills and you find yourself going in at the front door, as Alice did. Whatever kind of story Lewis thought he was going to write, religious allegory appeared. This is illustrated yet again in the recorded conversation between Lewis, Kingsley Amis and Brian Aldiss (*Unreal Estates: Of Other Worlds*, 1966) when Lewis remarks, 'The starting point of my second novel, *Perelandra*, was my mental picture of the floating islands. The whole of the rest of my labours in a sense consisted of building up a world in which floating islands could exist. And then, of course, the story about an averted fall developed.' To which Aldiss replied, 'I am surprised you put it this way round. I would have thought that you constructed *Perelandra* for the didactic purpose,' which shows how wrong one can be.

In a sense, Narnia is Malacandra and Perelandra over again; in another, it is Mouse Town and Knights-in-armour; but it is a long, long way from Animal-Land.

In the beginning of *The Lion, the Witch and the Wardrobe*, Lucy, exploring, enjoying the feel of the fur coats, discovers with a beautiful tactile pun that they are turning into pine and spruce and the mothballs into snow. Lewis uses the device of the Parallel World, a favourite in Fantasy literature. It is a world not reached by space ships but by magic (Lewis quickly abandoned the space ship as a device for travel). Lewis Carroll does this too, and so does E. Nesbit who has exactly the same opening of a cupboard or wardrobe door in a story called 'The Aunt and Amabel'; it is used by contemporary writers such as Alan Garner. C. S. Lewis makes Narnia an ideal world in which the oreads and enchanters mingle with dwarves and talking mice. Few writers have given a magic place such definition, such solid geography and such a gallery of characters. From the mind of a writer so stocked with images of the classical and 'northern' kind, so coloured by Christianity, the first elements of the story appear; the faun, the ice-queen and the golden lion. The result is a wonderful and at times uneasy mixture of ingredients, like a rich but indigestible Christmas cake. Critics of Narnia have tumbled out the words *rich* and *strange*, thought for a bit, and then come up with *strange* and *rich* again, as if almost at a loss; indeed, it has some affinities with Prospero's island. This ideal land has, for the sake of adventure and dramatic conflict, to have evil in it, and it is presented as an unredeemed country, waiting for Aslan's death and resurrection.

As the books progress, one can see the creative imagination at work. At first, the classic strain – the fauns, dryads, centaurs and others – is far stronger. It blends with the Northern European element, the witches, giants, dwarves and earthmen, and the inevitable Talking Beasts, ruled over by Christ the Lion, Aslan, son of

the Emperor over the sea. Perhaps the uneasiness that adults feel
is not shared by children, who do not notice that the child Edmund
is made to play the part of Judas, being led astray by such ordinary
means as sherbet and Turkish Delight (evil confections from *The
Arabian Nights* that Lewis disliked as a child); or that Susan and
Lucy are like the two Marys at the tomb on the morning of Easter
Day.

The Talking Beasts come, in the end, to dominate the whole
narrative, resulting in the wonderful animal characters of Reepicheep, Bree and Puddleglum. Aslan is shown creating and dissolv-
ing the world, and at the very end it is animal nature that brings
about its destruction. The cycle has returned to its beginning, in
Animal-Land, and Mouse Town. The animals have become human
enough to have heroes and villains, tragedy and triumph, but C. S.
Lewis never quite returns to his original. There is never any confusion as to *which* order his creatures belong to: they are always
themselves.

But in the first book, this element is muted, the classical and
religious elements are strong. It is interesting to note that in all the
Narnia stories the classical characters are invariably 'goodies'.
There is never an evil dryad, faun or centaur; creatures like hydras,
gorgons, chimeras or harpies have not found their way into Narnia.
But when one comes to the 'Northern' animals, Lewis seems more
at home and characters are more flexible. The White Queen is a
snow queen rather than a Circe, some dwarves are good and some
corrupt, there are good and bad giants (but no clever ones) and
even a pleasantly childlike and enthusiastic lion. The really bad
characters are all from the Northern kind – wolves, fungi, ogres,
ghosts and werewolves. Northern and classical do not emulsify
with smoothness. Perhaps it is inevitable that they find themselves
in opposing armies.

The only non-human characters to be given any depth in this
first story – which is full of ideas, images, descriptions and incident
without much character interest apart from the reform and repentance of Edmund the traitor – are the beavers, and Mr Tumnus the
faun. They are all essentially homely, and the faun, a highly intelligent person, is Northernised. He lives in a cave and serves tea. The
cave has a carpet, chairs, table and dresser, and bookshelves with
such titles as *The Life and Letters of Silenus, Men, Monks and Game-*

keepers: a study in popular legend. If a faun could be found living in an English wood, his home would certainly be like this. The beavers are even more literally Northernised: they live in a log cabin with snowshoes, rocking chair, stove, sewing machine and fishing tackle. They are completely humanised (apart from Mr Beaver's fishing by paw). Mrs Beaver, when at last they leave the lodge in haste, wants to bring her sewing machine. 'I can't abide the thought of that witch fiddling with it and breaking it,' she says. On the journey the beavers walk on two legs and hand round spirits in a flask. There is even the odd adjective 'wrinkled' applied to one of Mrs Beaver's paws, indicating age and slight animal-person confusion.*

The later animals that join in the battle with Peter to help win him his kingdom are all of the fairy-tale, heraldic or mythical kind: bears, leopards, stags, lions, horses, nothing either odd or ordinary and nothing comic, no elephants, giraffes, cats or monkeys (these appear in later books). It is clear that the animal strain is not the strongest, or even among the strongest strains, of this story which is concerned with human sin and redemption in an invented world. The animals are always present, they talk and fight and everything ends with a mixture of thrones and sand-between-the-toes, the four children living happily ever after into a courtly middle age before they find their way out through the wardrobe into the world again. Everything is harmony, animal, myth, classical and northern are all united as is suggested by the little party in the wood that is the sign of the end of the witch's rule: squirrels, fox, dwarves and fauns all having Christmas dinner together. Father Christmas and Silenus should surely have joined them.

In the second and less successful book *Prince Caspian*, the animal element is stronger – as with each succeeding instalment. The Prince's lost kingdom consists almost entirely of Talking Beasts who are exiled or in hiding, and who later make up the rebel army with a number of dryads, fauns, dwarves, centaurs (why is it that Northern myth does not supply any heroic or delightful animal-human creatures?). Here we see the Narnian creatures beginning to form themselves into a workable population. The 'small' animals

---

*This same adjective is used in *The Wind and the Willows* when Toad, disguised as a washer-woman, has been soaping the clothes on the barge for a long time and to no purpose (an unconvincing episode; clothes-washing is not difficult). He begins to get worried because his 'paws' are becoming wrinkled, not with age, but with water-soaking; odd, in a Toad, but it isn't a Toad – it's the irresponsible, car-stealing, jail-breaking man.

are larger than life and the 'large' ones smaller; and as in Malacandra, the racial mixture is slightly comic.

The book is most notable for the introduction or C. S. Lewis's best animal character, significantly, a mouse. But Reepicheep is not part of Snug Town, a place that the faun Mr Tumnus belongs to, but of the Knights-in-Armour and Courtly Mice mentioned in *Surprised by Joy*. He is described as 'gay and martial', makes grand gestures and talks like a mixture of Sir Thomas Malory and an old-fashioned general: he wears a rapier and twirls his long whiskers as if they were moustaches:

'*There are twelve of us, Sire,*' *he said with a dashing and graceful bow,* '*and I place all the resources of my people unreservedly at your Majesty's disposal.*' *Caspian tried hard* (*and successfully*) *not to laugh.*

The joke, even though Reepicheep is described as over a foot high, is his smallness – always the joke with Mouse characters in stories displaying them as bustling housewives in doll's houses, or triumphing over impossible odds (*The Rescuers*). Reepicheep starts off as part of this tradition, the joke being made even more pointed by the largeness of his heart, the size of his courage and self-esteem and Caspian's and Peter's tact and politeness in dealing with him.

At the end of the book, Reepicheep actually answers Aslan back –
a thing that no other animal, creature or human dares to do, in any
of the *Narnia* stories. Aslan is rather like a schoolmaster with an
outsize but invisible cane. He tells the Mouse that he should think
a little less of honour and glory, and the Mouse reminds him that
'a very small size has been bestowed on us Mice' and that they cannot help guarding their dignity above all. It is a courageous and
prompt answer and Aslan is won by it.

This is a very long way from the tiny Aesop creatures who,
mouse-sized and dumb, gnawed away the ropes that bound Aslan
in *The Lion, the Witch and the Wardrobe*. The third and best of the
Narnia books, *The Voyage of the Dawn Treader*, has Reepicheep the
mouse as its central, tragic hero; and this, in a fairy tale involving
humans, is unique. At last, animal creation has taken human status
and intelligence; we are back with the Hrossa and Sorns again. The
status of the Mouse is the same as that of the courtly members of
the crew (he is a Knight of the Order of the Lion) and the story
concerns, among other things, his quest for the end of the world
culminating in his strange and poetic death which has true heroic
sadness. But there is a difference between Reepicheep and the
humans – he is not quite a human in disguise. He is in some ways
better and braver (in the adventure of The Dark Island and the
Magician) and more level headed (with the Sea Serpent). He gains
and loses by being a mouse and not a man, and the differences are
explicit. He does not feel the shudders of horror that the others
feel in the Dark Island; he has no dreams and cannot understand
human fear of nightmare; he feels no exhaustion in the tropics and
can stay awake to guard the water supply (or else is able to subdue
the flesh more easily than the humans).

It is odd, perhaps, that *The Voyage of the Dawn Treader*, the most
satisfying of the *Narnia* books, is the one with the least of Aslan
in it and the fewest Talking Beasts. Religious allegory is unobtrusive
and there is a strong Arthurian odour. Part of the interest, especially at the beginning, is the improvement and recemption of Eustace,
the ordinary boy. We first see Reepicheep through his eyes.

*Something very curious indeed had come out of the cabin in the poop and
was slowly approaching them . . . it was a Mouse on its hind legs and
stood about two feet high. A thin band of gold passed round its head*

under one ear and over the other and in this was stuck a long crimson
feather. (As the Mouse's fur was very dark, almost black, the effect was
bold and striking.) Its left paw rested on the hilt of a sword very nearly as
long as its tail. Its balance, as it paced gravely along the swaying deck,
was perfect, its manners courtly.

This personage is unstrokeable, uncuddleable. Indeed Reepicheep
and Talking Beasts in general inspire a certain amount of awe; the
only people who do not feel it and do not like the situation are the
strangers or evil humans or those who have got into Narnia by
some sort of mistake, such as the Telmarines, who, when given the
chance to stay in Narnia, decline.

'Live here, with a lot of blooming performing animals! No fear,' they
said. 'And ghosts too,' some added with a shudder. 'Thats what those
Dryads really are' . . . *'I don't trust 'em,' they said. 'Not that awful*
Lion and all.'

This is Uncle Andrew's reaction in *The Magician's Nephew*; it is
also that of Professor Weston in *Out of the Silent Planet*. 'Ugh, take
it away,' says Eustace when, brought unwillingly and by mistake
into Narnia, he sees Reepicheep. 'I hate mice. And I never could
bear performing animals. They're silly and vulgar and – sentimental.' One feels a certain sympathy for him, though this is far
from the author's intention. Reepicheep immediately has cause for
single combat with Eustace; and one can hardly blame Eustace for
disliking this adventure into which he has been pulled. It promises
to be uncomfortable, messy, dangerous, and starts by making him
seasick and is going to be full or characters and situations he has
never met and would not have chosen (this is blamed on the wrong
school – a potent Progressive source of corruption, responsible for
the treachery of Edmund – and the wrong books, or rather, lack of
the right ones). Eustace does the only things he knows; complains
and threatens, tries to contact the British consul, tries to maintain
his identity by talking about liners and aeroplanes, and in the end
keeps an aggrieved diary. In short, he behaves in typical Professor
Weston fashion. The first half of the book has considerable pace and
fascination through the conflict between Eustace and his surroundings.

Of course Eustace cannot win; Heaven is larger than the world.

He must learn to like Heaven, or Eden, with its Equality for Animals, or go away. There is an exactly similar situation in *The Great Divorce* where the visitors from Hell neither recognise nor like Heaven. The scene is set for the Animal Revenge, which here is two-pronged. Eustace tries to humiliate Reepicheep – it was meant as a joke, he says afterwards, but the Mouse has no sense of humour and again offers single combat. 'I'm a pacifist,' says Eustace, but the Mouse has never heard of them and Eustace is beaten with the flat of his sword. As he has never experienced corporal punishment at the Progressive school, the sensation is new. His subsequent dragon adventure – being changed not only into an animal but into the ugliest, most feared and hated creature in the world, with a boy's consciousness but carnivorous and cannibalistic instincts, to say nothing of a painful iron band immovably stuck on his foreleg – is a punishment almost too terrible to contemplate; far beyond any-thing meted out to Weston or Uncle Andrew. But as this is a chil-dren's story Eustace emerges at last, a sadder and a wiser boy. He has been made to fit into Narnia, like a bulgy Lost Boy into his tree (Peter did something to him and it was all right).

The Mouse throughout behaves with gallantry and courage so great as to be almost foolhardy, but never comic; always as immune from human envy, fear and greed as if he were lacking in some faculty. The end of the book becomes more and more like the quest for the Grail as they reach Ramandu's Isle with its holy relic, and the Utter East, where prophecy has told the Mouse that he will meet his heart's desire. And so dies Reepicheep, launching himself over the world's edge in his tiny coracle, heroic, courteous, tiny, humourless and unforgettable, nonhuman, lesser and greater and completely other.

The only other characters to compare with Reepicheep in stature are Puddleglum the Marsh Wiggle and Bree the horse. Puddleglum, in 'The Silver Chair', is hardly animal; he is a humanised Pfifltrigg, animal in his webbed feet and fingers with serious saurian views of life. It is made quite clear that Wiggles are a separate species in the Narnian world. Puddleglum is something between Mark Tapley and a frog. His arms and legs are very long – long enough to frighten the Giant Queen; Pauline Baynes' illustration shows Puddleglum on the floor before the Giant's feet in a half-collapsed position, rather as if a small human grasshopper or locust was poised for a spring, its knees higher than its ears. Puddleglum's hair is green-grey and flat like reeds, and he smokes strange, heavy tobacco that trickles out of his pipe like foggy water.

He – always 'he' and not 'It' as Reepicheep is described – appears to hope for disaster and to thrive on it, to court it by mentioning the worst before it can possibly happen. In reality he is well pre-pared, sensible and the best companion Eustace and Jill could have chosen for their adventure (or have had chosen for them by Aslan, who, though absent, influences the happenings in this story, Will-of-God fashion). Puddleglum is slow, sure, steady and has the reptilian virtues of being cold blooded and reliable. One would imagine that in winter he might hibernate, but on the contrary, he leads the children through storms and snows to the wild lands of the North, his only weakness being drink, his greatest strength his clear-sighted, unemotional pessimism – always ready to doubt a honeyed voice or a deceitfully fair face. He is not taken in by the Lady, the wicked queen who is an enchantress and a shape-changer. (Beware! Aslan has warned elsewhere against half-and-halfers. It appears that the author only admits the fixed and finished off cate-gories into the animal Eden; there is no evolution and certainly no blurring. It is all like Genesis.)

Puddleglum remembers Aslan's rules when the children have for-gotten them, is unexpectedly brave and – another animal virtue similar to that of the heroic Mouse – toughly immune when the witch tries to drug and hypnotise the party into forgetfulness and make them believe that the counterfeit, underground world is the real one. Puddleglum has a heroic last stand in which he uses his cold webbed feet to stamp out the Lady's fire, and asserts his belief in the sun and his determination to spend his life, however short, in looking for it.

As a character he is vivid and unique and earns the children's love and gratitude. As a species he is lacking, as he is the only one of his kind we are allowed to see; Wiggles are said to be solitary. He is the most manlike of Narnian creatures, perhaps only a canny, careful East Anglian after all.

If Reepicheep is the most memorable mouse ever created, Bree is one of the most interesting horses. 'The Horse and his Boy' has the amusing situation of animal creation being not merely equal or different from human but, in its own rather snobbish opinion, better. Aslan, after all, created the animals in his image, and humans were an afterthought, a transplant, as is shown in 'The Magician's Nephew'. 'The Horse and his Boy' takes place outside Narnia and had the most purely human excitements about it – battle, treachery and fugitives – but in many ways it is the least characteristic of the *Narnia* books and bears about the same relation to the others as *A Tale of Two Cities* to the rest of Dickens. It concerns the adventures of a Narnian Talking Horse (trained by mistake as a warhorse of Calormen), a Boy who is from Archenland and does not know it, and their struggles to find their way home.

Calormen, the Eastern land on the borders of Archenland and Narnia, is neutral, but inclined to burst into enmity and conquest. Its inhabitants are practical, money-minded, devious and reflect the sad fact that the author as a child could not stand *The Arabian Nights*; his allegiance appears to have gone as far south as Greece and no further (the strongly Eastern flavour of Christianity has been absorbed into Europe for so long that it has almost lost its original tang).

The adventures are exciting and dangerous and of the two main rational characters the Horse is much the stronger. It is older than the Boy Shasta, wiser, better educated, capable of leading him out of danger and saving both from slavery. Some of the strange amusement of the story comes from the un-Narnian situation of the Horse's having to be ridden if the two are to get anywhere, partly for speed and partly for disguise. (One does not suppose that Narnians rode Talking Horses, except by invitation, as Jill and Eustace were invited to ride Centaurs in 'The Silver Chair'; a ride with learned conversation as an awe-inspiring accompaniment.)

The Horse teaches the Boy to ride; later they are joined by a Girl and a Mare, similarly running away. They make a perfect quartet, and the situation is an appealing one. But 'The Horse and his Boy' is the least magic, the least poetic of the *Narnia* books, and Aslan has a sterner, redemptive effect on all four main characters except perhaps for Hwin the Mare, who is, unusually for C. S. Lewis, a female of great charm and courage. (The human heroine, Aravis, is described as rather a tomboy: 'interested in bows and arrows and horses and dogs and swimming'.)

The names of the horses have interest. It is always difficult to name a humanised animal according to the sound it makes. Only

Swift has ever attempted this with the horse, with a result that is as unspellable as it is unpronounceable. The easier way is to name the animal by what it does, or what it looks like: Goldenshoes, Truffle-hunter. Occasionally comes a really inspired name like Mrs Tiggi-winkle or a beautiful foreign one such as Shere Khan. Bree and Hwin are pronounceable, accurate ideas of what a horse sounds like, having clear sexual indications. Lewis's names have not the inspiration of some of those in the *Ring* saga, such as Meriadoc Brandybuck or Belladonna Took, but he is writing with careful simplicity while Tolkien is writing as the historian of a distant – if imaginary – period which children may enjoy but which is not presented for their entertainment. Thus the capital of Calormen, Tash-baan, is a noise of cymbal and gong, while the names Gondor, Lothlorien have a flavour of another language – as the author intended.

Bree's greatest weakness is his personal pride. Part of the comedy of his character is that a dignified creature or person, when he loses his dignity, can be very funny indeed. Bree persists in talking to Hwin, rather than her girl rider. He worries about whether he looks funny when rolling and wonders if rolling 'isn't done' in Narnia – he is a very socially conscious horse. He is patronising to Shasta and thinks humans are 'funny little creatures' and quarrelsome. He objects to having to disguise himself as a working, dumb horse and is awkward and difficult about it. He loses his pride at last by becoming too intellectual. He is caught out trying to explain rather pompously to Aravis and Hwin why Aslan is not a real lion (or why religion is just a myth). One feels that it would be a bit unfair to humanists if God should come and tap them on the shoulder; one of the facts of life in the last few centuries is that God does not seem to have had much of a hand in it. But in Narnia things are different, and when Bree finds that Aslan is true, he feels almost as unpleasant as Edmund and Eustace did. By the end of the book he has not quite recovered and is still worried about rolling, a subject on which Hwin is quite at her ease.

In comparison with Bree, the horse Fledge in 'The Magician's Nephew' is a simple creature. He starts life as Strawberry the cab-horse and is the only animal of note in this, the sixth book of the series, which concerns the founding of Narnia and creation, by Aslan, of all the animals.

'The Magician's Nephew' is the most obvious blending of parts. It has a great number of possible sources which have been used and transformed and made new; there is the Bastable world of Digory and Polly, the similarly E. Nesbit magic rings which transport when touched, the Rider Haggard city of Charn with its Hall of Effigies, the Arthurian Deplorable Word, the Siege Perilous warning on the magic bell and the Dolorous Stroke effect when it is rung in anger by Digory. There is the morbid Victorian Theme of Digory's dying mother, who is cured with a magic apple which, in this story, is as if one of Iduna's could have been grafted on to the tree in the garden of the Hesperides.

The greatest theme is the creation of Narnia by Aslan out of Nothing. It grows gradually from stars to mountains and rivers, grass and trees and last of all the animals, its natural and uncorrupted inhabitants, who rise out of the earth as if they were made from it. The group of human onlookers are intruders, by a magic mistake.

From the animals, Aslan chooses certain pairs to touch and breathe on. They become Talking Beasts, and Narnia is founded at last with creatures whose first act is to do the most human thing of all – 'they began making various queer noises which . . . no one has ever heard in our world' – and animal laughter is heard, perhaps for the first time ever. The animals observe the people present but do not recognise them, thinking they are vegetables (a legitimate mistake; Narnian Talking Beasts are never dressed, and Aslan has already created walking trees).

Strawberry the cabhorse, who has been given speech with the others and later becomes Fledge the hippogriff, is no ordinary horse. The cabman has already mentioned that his sire was a cavalry charger (the old warhorse, Captain, of *Black Beauty*?). But he is grateful to the cabman who has treated him kindly. Even with wings and a changed status – he has thrown off his earthly slavery and become free – he is both proud and humble, recognising that the cabman who put him in harness had no choice, being just as much a slave as he. Of course the cabman and his wife are the same and have simple, animal souls. Aslan at once transforms them into the King and Queen of Narnia, the Adam and Eve from whom all humans spring.

The story explains and in part contradicts the others; the author is filling the gaps and providing causes for effects which were there because they were there, like the tree of knowledge.*

The animals' revenge on Uncle Andrew, already mentioned, is a milder version of what happens in two earlier science-fiction novels. The scientist Weston is punished, not through malice, but because the Malacandrian creatures are trying, in a fairly simple way, to do what they think best. Neither man nor creature really understands what the other is trying to do or say. The animals in the banquet scene in *That Hideous Strength* are not rational. The humans have brought about their own downfall. There is an interesting parallel in 'The Terror', a short story by Arthur Machen, in which domestic and farm animals begin to murder humans in revenge for the human exploitation which they cannot escape. But Machen did not suggest that the animals were conscious killers, only that man's murderous instincts had turned against himself.

It is quite natural that the newly created Talking Beasts, who have mistaken the children for cabbages, mistake Uncle Andrew for a kind of tree. When they discover he is Animal, they make a cage and try to feed him; it is the scientist-magician's logical fate – in a land where animals are his equals – the tables are turned at the Zoo. The joke is that the animals are no *more* sensible than humans usually are, and shower Uncle Andrew with their favourite food, much as Tigger was given everything except Extract of Malt. Uncle Andrew has everything except the brandy he wants. He is terrified of Aslan, and hears only roars, squeaks and growls as the Beasts try to speak to him.

In the final *Narnian* story, 'The Last Battle', the fall of Narnia is brought about by animal means and not human. The only delinquent Talking Beasts occur here – the Ape, Shift, and the Cat.

Shift, who is lazy, artful, ambitious and greedy, starts by exploiting the gentle donkey Puzzle and goes on to exploit all the other Talking Beasts by working on their simple, loyal credulity. In a way, he is a Beast descending into Humanity, for this is what

*It is interesting to speculate on sources again; i.e. on its first day of creation the fertile soil of Narnia grew a lamp post from a piece of iron, gold and silver trees from loose change and a toffee tree from a sweet. It all sounds rather like the fertile valley at the end of David Lindsay's 'Voyage to Arcturus', much admired by Lewis, where any seed or branch or leaf that dropped sprouted and grew visibly.

humans do. Shift even ends by dressing like a human. The Ape's aim is to sell Narnia to Calormen. Only the Cat sees through the Ape's trickery and connives at it, and is punished in the inevitable way by losing its faculty of speech, becoming witless and wild. Cats are often heroic or treacherous in folklore or fairy tale, seldom neutral. This cat is very cool and logical. It is the dogs which are preferred, as in Maeterlinck, they are all heart and rather mindless affection. They join eagerly in Prince Tirian's last stand and are among the first to enter heaven. It seems that the good characters are to be defeated, and the harshly neutral dwarves (ambiguous characters, sometimes out of Snug Town, sometimes very much not so) and the wicked *Arabian Nights* people out of Calormen, are going to win; but Aslan defeats them by putting an end to Narnia, Calormen and all.

It is difficult to be neutral about Aslan, as character or animal or symbol. He is always *there*, the instrument of the author's ideas, and it seems at times as if he *is* the author, who is rather enjoying himself. Aslan is the eternal Big Brother, the irrefutable and ultimate authority, the person who not only upholds the rules but also seems to have made them. To disobey is unthinkable and always brings disaster, sometimes swiftly as happens to Aravis when she is attacked and scored by ten claws in retribution for ten strokes given to a serving maid she has tricked. Sometimes the retribution is horribly and inevitably slow: the sad death scene of Caspian at the end of 'The Silver Chair' springs partly from the unpleasant tempers and disobedience of Jill Pole and Eustace Scrubb at the beginning. Indeed the book is notable for the set of instructions or commandments given by Aslan which must always be followed even when not understood.

Aslan cannot ever be ignored. The rather worldly and un-Narnian Susan, present in the first two stories, is banished from the rest. Aslan cannot be laughed at. Edmund has a feeble try in *The Lion, the Witch and the Wardrobe* and soon feels sorry for it. It is impossible to look Aslan in the eyes and tell a lie or make an excuse: even his name has a shaking, unpleasant effect on wrongdoers, as it cheers the good characters and fills them with hope. His very presence in the Earth world (back view only) is enough to unmake a whole Progressive school. The religious tones are explicit: if Talking Beasts disobey, they lose their speech. A 'lapsed bear' is mentioned. It has to be hunted, fought and killed; the fate of the wicked cat is similar.

Aslan made Narnia, and when all the nasty people of Eastern fairy tale break into it and start to ruin its Classical-Northernness, he unmakes it again in scenes of apocalyptic, sunset grandeur. Casting God into a story in the form of a lion is bold and unique; the *Pilgrim's Progress* does not do as much. Aslan is an heraldic lion, bright, fearsome and wonderful, but his lion nature is appearance only – he never kills or eats. His mane is a 'tossing sea of gold'. His best appearances concern themselves only with beauty and joy. He comes frequently into the early books like an Old Testament Jehovah and less in the later ones. The most memorable occasions are those of the two girls' ride on his back in *The Lion, the Witch and the Wardrobe* and at the end of 'Prince Caspian' where he joins Bacchus, the Maenads, animals and trees in a glorious game that overcomes everything – even old age, tyranny and death. 'And so at last, with leaping and dancing and singing with music and laughter and roaring and barking and neighing, they all came to the place where Miraz's army stood flinging down their swords and holding up their hands.' When the Talking Beasts meet him they greet him as the King of the Beasts, and not with words. He seems to speak to their innocent goodness. 'They surged round the Lion with purrs and grunts and squeaks and whinneys of delight, fawning on him with their tails, rubbing against him, touching him reverently with their noses.'

It is the schoolmasterly, godlike Aslan which adults often dislike. C. S. Lewis tells in an essay (not the short piece 'It All Began with a Picture' which appeared in the *Radio Times* and was peppered with capital Hs for the personal pronoun, but 'Sometimes Fairy Tales may say best what's to be said') how he hoped to 'steal past those watchful dragons', i.e. the Sunday School inhibitions which many children may feel when thinking of religion. It is possible that children do not feel such inhibitions at all, but with many adults the watchful dragons are still there, very much awake.

At best, Aslan is the King of Beasts in an animal land where humans are put very much in their place. 'This elegant little biped' runs the giant's cookery book 'has long been valued as a delicacy. It forms a traditional part of the Autumn Feast and is served between the fish and the joint.' Humans are, therefore, just another kind of Talking Beast, with a mandate to rule under Aslan. And the only secret of happiness lies in the lumbering phrase Peaceful Co-existence, with the giants paying tribute, the Calormenes confined to Calormen keeping their nasty god Tash to themselves, and none of the Narnians eating each other (eating dumb beasts is permitted).

But the presence of Aslan does give the *Narnia* books another dimension – not of magic, but of miracle. As legends concern the presence of Gods in human affairs, and the Old Testament the dealings of one God with one race, so C. S. Lewis has written of a world where God constantly takes a hand in person. It makes for strange retributions and rewards, miraculous happenings, healing and punishment, prophecies and destinies that do not occur in *The Lord of the Rings* – the only other comparable work, where God is never present and never even mentioned. It can even lead to pantomime situations such as that of the boastful horse whose audience would have shouted 'Look behind you' had they not been rooted to the spot in awe.

The real test is that, in spite of a few awkward particles, the mixture works. The *Narnia* stories have magical invention, great beauty,

enormous and compelling epic drama. Together they form a unique
literary classic that will surely remain, like the Lord Octesian's
ring, hanging 'as long as that world lasted', on an odd, unreachable
pinnacle.

16 Animals are Equal: a bear in a London family

'*Where on earth have you been?*' *cried Mrs Bird.* '*We've been looking everywhere for you.*'

'*Are you all right?*' *asked Mrs Brown anxiously.* '*You don't look very well.*'

'*Oh, I'm all right, thank you, Mrs Brown,*' *said Paddington vaguely as he recovered himself.* '*And I haven't been on earth – at least, I have, but I didn't think I had and it cost me two shillings.*'

'Trouble in the Bargain Basement,' Paddington At Large,
Michael Bond

Paddington is a bear who has joined the human race without the transition really showing, the greatest achievement of an animal character since Brer Rabbit. He inhabits a totally realistic human world while retaining some trace elements of animal nature – the amount that he has forfeited is the price of integration. On the whole, Paddington must be considered to have made a very good bargain. What are bears like, after all? Brer B'ar was not a pleasant character and his end was unfortunate, and sticky. Fictional bears are, if treated with any realism, equivocal. The attractive, furry, plump, cuddly and rounded exterior hides a nature that can be mean, dangerous and unpredictable. Their gait is often described as shambling, or awkward, or rolling; they are unintelligent, yet wily. They can be comic, yet dangerous creatures who bully and crush, yet are sometimes cowardly, like the bear in *White Fang*, met on a narrow ledge, who retreats out of trouble; as cubs they can be enchanting, when old, curmudgeons, as are the more senior bears in the pit at Berne. Mary Plain managed a happy life by using talent and charm and never growing up, existing in perpetual cubhood and dependence on her keeper, the Owl Man. Winnie the Pooh and Albert managed it by adopting the disguise of Teddy, or toy, and living in a land that never was, which is not joining the human race at all, only giving an indirect contribution to its mythology. Paddington takes the bold step of combining the roles of mascot or toy, with pet, and youngest son and has a privileged and independent life; but he needs the family before he can achieve reality. Baby and pet are positions that are similar. They fulfil the need for someone or something demanding protection and care so that the rest of the group can feel grown up, or clever, or motherly: someone that can either be a butt or a joker, sometimes both; someone who is often able to take on some task which the others are too intelligent or adult or dignified to fulfil. This character – always a successful one – is a persistent reminder of the fictional power of the family group and is a psychological necessity for its completeness, from *The Three Bears* to the trio on *The Coral Island*, from *The Wind in the Willows* to *Dick Barton, Special Agent*.

Paddington at first has all the appeal of a toy, pet, or cub. He is young (he has to be), he has something of the charm of the Teddy from which he was created. The invention and popularisation of the Teddy has altered every child's attitude towards the species.

Whether prompted by Theodore Roosevelt or Edward VII, Teddies have re-created imaginary bears and have changed themselves since the original ones broke all records at the Leipzig Fair in 1903, steadily becoming more furry and rounded, with shorter limbs. Besides this history behind him Paddington is the answer to every child's wish that his pet could talk or his toy could walk and become, in a human capacity, a licensed small boy or younger brother; but Mr Bond's real master stroke is to give Paddington, right from the start, some of the behaviour and reactions of an adult foreigner. In the nine books that appeared at the rate of almost one a year since 1958, Paddington's adventures continue on one level of slapstick farce and on another of a more subtle kind of social comedy in which the laugh is not on the bear at all. He acts with a strange logic of his own so that his success in the various situations in the stories is of quite an adult kind: he outshines the humans and shows up their weak spots, often making them – though in a good-humoured way – look mean, or crooked, or slow.

Right from his first appearance, Paddington is as different as possible from Winnie the Pooh. His foreignness, which gives him from the beginning a well travelled near-sophistication, may be, like many masterstrokes, a combination of accident and design. Did the original model for Paddington – a stuffed Teddy, not a bear from the Zoo – have honey-coloured fur and black ears and the rather eager, almost slim appearance which Peggy Fortnum gives him in her drawings? Paddington is discovered on the platform of the station that gives him his name, sitting on a suitcase. '(Mrs Brown) peered at it more closely. It seemed a very unusual kind of bear. It was brown in colour, a rather dirty brown' (a bath soon changes this) 'and it was wearing a most odd looking hat with a wide brim. Seeing that something was expected of it, the bear stood up and politely raised its hat, revealing two black ears. "Good afternoon," it said in a small, clear voice. "Er, good afternoon," replied Mr Brown doubtfully. There was a moment of silence. The bear looked at them enquiringly, "Can I help you?" '

This character, established in this paragraph, is maintained and enlarged in this and subsequent books until the hat, the suitcase and the small clear voice become Paddington's nature and his psyche and establish his conservatism (he will not part with old clothes) his hoarding instinct (he uses the suitcase both for food

and for the past, for he keeps his memoirs in it) and the rather bale-
fully obstinate self-assertion by which he manages to get his own
way and deflate the pompous and bossy characters who are the only
villains that Mr Bond writes about. A few paragraphs later it is
established that he has stowed away on a boat from Peru, living
on marmalade, which again becomes a staple ingredient of Paddington's life.

From these firm beginnings, Paddington grows. It is obvious
from the start that the bear will have adventures of the homely
slapstick, rather than the exciting, kind. This is implicit in the
situation. The bear is unusual, so his surroundings by contrast must
be as ordinary as possible. Rupert, though a bear, is shown to be
normal, the child of the bear family in an animal village. His adventures can be totally unusual and fantastic if necessary, as the space-
man hero of cosmic strangeness has to be an ordinary chap. If he
has deviant views or appearance, he is there to observe or upset
some stable order and give point or excitement to social or moral
comment. Paddington is cast in the role of the observant stranger
or foreigner which he fulfils at the same time as being a live object,
the lost or strayed pet that has to be adopted and cared for.

From the first, the Browns are not stunned into silence by hearing
a bear speak – this is one of the conventions of the genre – but they
show mild surprise; throughout the *Paddington* books this is the
standard attitude towards the bear. No one is amazed that he speaks
English, answers the telephone, helps with the shopping, goes to
restaurants and tries to mow the lawn. No one exclaims over him as
if he were a delightful cuddly pet (if they did, Paddington's hard
stare would freeze them stiff).

The joke carried throughout the series is that he is a bear trying
to be, and succeeding in being, a person, with the inevitable farcical
mistakes. Not only is human life foreign to him, but English human
life as well, as he comes from Peru. He is both a child trying to
grow up and a character from Mars observing the contemporary
scene. The combination of the two types of humour is a comic
success which has made Paddington genuinely and unforcedly
funny, and also endearing in the way that Charles Pooter is endearing, because one laughs at what he is, what he is trying to be, and
at the social surroundings that have shaped both him and his
aspirations.

The first few *Paddington* stories establish the nature of the comedy. The bear is adopted by the Brown family, and there follow some of the topics, or institutions with which he becomes involved such as the theatre, the seaside and the London Underground. The emphasis at first is on messy custard pie adventures with sticky buns, bath water and shaving cream, but there are some subtleties; when introduced to a room of his own, Paddington identifies the bed, but not the rest of the furniture, which he sees as a series of boxes. When told they are cupboards or drawers to put things in, he admits rather touchingly to no possessions at all other than a scrapbook, a picture of his Aunt Lucy from Lima, and some centavos. The Browns are doubtful about the legality of keeping him – not because the RSPCA would be interested, but because he might be arrested as a stowaway.

'I'm not sure how much pocket money to give a bear,' said Mr Brown.
'He can have one and sixpence a week, the same as the other children,' replied Mrs Brown.

It is as if Paddington is another child, with fur instead of clothes. But he is quick to learn and very logical, never behaving in a way in which a child would behave, but in the manner of an adult who is learning about civilised life because he has been brought up on a desert island. When shown a bath, he jumps in as one might into a lake, or the sea; there follows the great mistake that most children make once, overfilling the bath by displacement so that the water is above the taps and they cannot be seen to be on or off. Paddington does not merely yell for help; he bales the water out on to the floor which is the obvious thing to do if you are used to boats rather than baths. Later, in *Paddington goes to Town* he has taught himself about baths and reached the stage at which he takes one voluntarily in order to be smart for the Prices' wedding. He is seen using a sponge in quite an adult manner, with no mess at all – but the joke in this story is *weddings* and not baths, and Paddington has lived through seven volumes and can make telephone calls and summon the fire brigade to get himself out of trouble.

Paddington's painful adventures on the Underground and in a department store start the series of common enough experiences with which he comes into contact and views in a totally new light, making the reader see them with comic objectiveness. Paddington is often disconcerted – as a man from Mars might be – by an escalator, a lift, a shop-window display. He takes a theatrical performance literally, not merely booing the villain, but going round to his dressing-room to reprimand him. He paints an abstract picture which wins a prize when it is shown at an exhibition – the wrong way up.

Gradually introduced are the characters who act as foils and props for his adventures. The Brown family are too ordinary to be true – Mr Brown, 'a big jolly man with a moustache', Mrs Brown (very like him), the two children, Jonathan and Judy, as alike as twins except that Jonathan prefixes most remarks with 'Crikey'. They represent the LCMs of English family life as it might be, as many hope it always is and will be. Mr Bond wisely ensures that the two children go to boarding schools so that the bear is not tied to children's adventures but can mix with adults, as he eventually does, as an equal. The solidity of the Brown family ensures that whatever goes wrong, whatever scrapes Paddington gets into, he is in the privileged position of a child with adult protection. He has all the advantages. He does not have to go to school, does not have to work – apart from the odd jobs he does to help Mrs Brown and her rather ambiguous housekeeper, Mrs Bird.

Mrs Bird's character is an extended mother figure with considerably more personality than Mrs Brown. She is not a Daily, nor a cook, nor a nanny, but a combination of all three, with an old-fashioned proprietary air towards the family. Her nanny qualities ensure that Paddington is treated as a child – censured, but indulged. Out of all the people he meets she alone sometimes has the upper hand, sees through him, suspects him, is frequently justified, and of course, loves him enough to forgive. Her rather too often reiterated 'h'm', reflects Paddington's hard stare. They are almost equally matched, but Paddington has the advantage of being small, and animal and forgivable. Mrs Bird's position in the Brown household is rather odd by contemporary standards, but then so is Paddington's; they understand each other very well. They have an equal appreciation of food and a careful estimation of what it costs – he quickly wins her approval by striking hard bargains in the Portobello Road, where he meets his great friend, Mr Gruber.

Mr Gruber, the antique dealer, is a quiet, shy man, almost a recluse. He appears to have no family and to be touched and gratified when invited out. His shop has everything and spills out on to the pavement. He was in South America as a boy, and discusses it with Paddington. In their friendship they are both two old men and two children together, but Paddington's status in Mr Gruber's world is that of adult and equal. To Mr Gruber, Paddington is 'Mr Brown'. They chat over their cocoa and buns at the back of the shop; Peggy Fortnum's drawings show the bald, rather ascetic-looking man in spectacles, the old-fashioned coke stove and vast overstuffed sofa on which the pair sit, both similarly hunched over their mugs. Both are occasionally scolded for getting into trouble by the more responsible adults, but each is an adult to the other and they enjoy the same things except that one is teaching and the other learning. Mr Gruber introduces Paddington to several new scenes, especially in the later books where the merely family happenings are reinforced by others taken from a wider area. Paddington goes with Mr Gruber to a band concert, an antique auction, Madame Tussaud's and the Stock Exchange, helps him to drive a vintage car in a carnival parade, and learns a good deal about the Trade, for which Paddington seems a natural recruit. One young bear, with a knowledge of antiques and an eye for a bargain is worth his weight in gold. 'Mr Gruber disappeared into his shop for a moment and when he returned he was carrying an old vase. "What would you say this is, Mr Brown?" he asked casually, holding it up to the light. Paddington looked most surprised at such a simple question. "That's an early Spode, Mr Gruber," he replied promptly'.

The third main character to appear is the next-door neighbour, Mr Curry, who is Paddington in reverse – mean and inquisitive without Paddington's adult-child charm. Mr Curry is not an evil character, but a comically bad one: always trying to get more than his money's worth, always finding fault, ending by being disconcerted, losing face and property at the same time. He arrives at Paddington's parties uninvited because there is a free tea, and stays to criticise; he is a Mr Padge without Mr Padge's immobility and monosyllabic speech. He is, in opposition to Paddington, an adult behaving like a child. Naturally it is *his* watch that is smashed in Paddington's conjuring trick, and his suit that gets put on the Guy by mistake at the bonfire party, his wall that gets knocked down, his plumbing ruined, his table sawn in half. Of course, it is his own fault for trying to get something for nothing. He returns for punishment in every new book, the lesson unlearned.

Other characters make only brief appearances, apart from the grocery assistants Harold Price and Deidre Flint who belong to the Amateur Dramatic Society and afterwards have a smart wedding with Paddington as usher. Walk-on characters and officials usually start by finding Paddington exasperating, end by loving him. There are a few useful Indian Uncles about, benefactors who turn out to be the head of the firm, bank manager, restaurateur, or marmalade king who ends by inviting Paddington to visit his factory in return for having been amused.

This is an English, middle-class world, very cosy, where nothing really unexpected can ever happen; as in farce, the banana skins never produce broken bones and a small boy adult foreigner never comes to harm but always succeeds unexpectedly and is always approved and loved. The only situation that turns in the least serious is where Paddington is ill – this strikes almost a false note. When the Browns are ill themselves in *Paddington Helps Out*, it is a mere two days in bed so that Paddington can show what he can do in the house by himself. His own illness is a more serious affair brought on by the effects of snowballing on a bear used to a hot climate. Mrs Bird sits up with him all night, shaking her head, unable to speak, and even Mr Curry calls at the house with calves' foot jelly. It is the only emotional scene that happens in any of the stories. It occurs in the second book and is never repeated, though it appeared at one time that Paddington was returning to Peru to visit his Aunt Lucy – perhaps Mr Bond was tired of him – at the end of *Paddington Marches On*; but back he came with a few shipboard adventures to add variety to his London ones.

From the bear's point of view such institutions as theatre, cinema, cricket match, gymkhana, carol singing, golf tournament, barber's shop and restaurant are at first odd and incomprehensible, to be judged and assessed by his previous experience. Later they present problems which are always, in some manner, surmounted and added to his total of successes. He hardly ever retires beaten, but usually pulls success out of disaster by presence of mind, by the goodwill of the bystanders and the logical if rather peculiar thinking of the stranger who is not conditioned by having been always in a place where money comes out of banks, washing out of the launderette and pictures out of television.

Paddington's adventures with the more static and solid aspects of

English life mark his maturity and are among the most amusing of his escapades because the humour is more logical, the absurdities less obvious. The most usual plot device concerns his accidental involvement with the institution or occasion by being frequently, and interestingly, mistaken for someone else – usually (such is the force of the bear's personality) an official. Thus, his participation is taken for granted and he carries off his new identity with growing confidence. By the end of the episode he cannot put a paw wrong. Mistaken identity is hardly a stock situation in animal fiction, but here it is a measure of Paddington's almost, yet never quite complete, human *persona*. The longer he lives with the Browns, the more complete this becomes. In *A Bear Called Paddington* a crowd collects outside the window of a department store, amazed and amused to see a bear piling up goods in comic window dressing; they think it is some kind of advertising stunt. Nine books later, in *Paddington Takes the Air*, he has a different attitude to shop windows. He has read a few detective stories and his mental processes are more like those of a rather old-fashioned small boy such as Richmal Crompton's William. When he sees a bearded man removing a model from a window, he does not think it theft, nor normal, but attempted kidnapping. He reasons that the models *may* be hypnotised victims, and the only way to solve the problem is to take a job in the shop. He gets one as a sandwich-board carrier, without the lady at the appointments desk giving way to much surprise other than saying that she could not put him behind a counter as he might have trouble seeing over the top. The storeman takes him on, gloomily, with the words: 'I suppose they 'as to take what they can get these days: but I shouldn't go joining no pension scheme if I was you.' The adventure ends in hilarious disarray in the staff canteen, with coffee cups and a cash register. Mistaken identity stories give Paddington the part of a comic outsider, a new hand at the marmalade factory, rather than a bear: he is genuinely taken for a human rather than accepted as a talking pet in a new role (the more usual convention of this kind of story). The linked stories 'A Visit to the Hospital' (to see Mr Curry, naturally) and 'Paddington finds a Cure' (*Paddington goes to Town*) find Paddington dressed as a doctor in operating gown and mask, not only mistaken for a real one, but for 'one of those gentlemen from overseas'. This kind of situation ridicules the institution rather than the bear, whose success hints that animals are better, funnier, more clever – naïve than humans, and deserve to succeed while humans look silly thus; having hired a dress suit from Heather and Sons for a party ('the young – er – gentleman's legs are a bit – ahem – and we may have to do some rather drastic alterations') Paddington goes into a restaurant by himself and is mistaken for the author of a Good Food Guide. He is offered, by the delighted manager, pot-fresh lobster, Dover-fresh sole, farm-fresh escallop of veal or oven-fresh steak and kidney pudding. Paddington decides to try them all, adding that he would like some tin-fresh cocoa. He is seated in the window which slowly becomes black with faces (who seem to be watching the gargantuan meal rather than the bear in the top hat) and all goes well until the bill. 'A *cover* charge?' he exclaims hotly. '*Seventeen shillings* for a bombe surprise?' Paddington's meanness over money is only equalled by Mr Curry's. The story ends in triumph with the invasion of the restaurant by crowds of interested patrons; no one can be angry.

Paddington's childlike literalness, money mindedness, capacity for argument and ability to fall on his feet, have much in common with William Brown. It seems no accident that the two share a surname; Paddington only lacks William's imaginative flights (unusual now in a boy of his age). They share a touching faith in instruction books and never lose hope in their accuracy and the success they are bound to have. William is addicted to *One Hundred and One Things a Boy can Do*, while Paddington takes to plumbing, cookery, making toffee, operating a sewing machine and various aspects – more suitable for the sixties – of Do-It-Yourself. He is sure that he has only to master a few simple skills – until the emergency comes which the book never caters for. Emergencies happen as regularly as sunrise and sunset and can usually be resolved by a marmalade sandwich from suitcase or hat, but greed is less of a staple than it is in Winnie the Pooh. Paddington's money anxieties keep him firmly in this world, with none of Pooh's poetry or Rupert's morbid enchantments; his human nature is reinforced. Taking pound notes to the bank in his suitcase, he is waylaid by a confidence man and persuaded to part with it for a bogus oil share. 'Pardon me, bear,' says the con man, disguised as a city gent; the 'excuse me, sir' of Paddington's world into which he now fits quite naturally. The man hoodwinks him by suggesting that the bank is not a safe place for money, using one of the two arguments likely to influence his victim most. 'You look like a bear of the world,' he says, reducing the price of the share to the amount in the suitcase, enticing him with promises of interest (the other argument), a system which by this time – the seventh book – Paddington understands quite well.

Paddington's horror when he finds he has been duped, puts him off his food – but he does not tell Father and Mother. He goes to the Stock Exchange on his own, on the Underground, to try to sell his share to someone else. He is seen by the police, who arrest him. 'Clever disguise,' they say. 'I always pictured Jim the Dandy as being much taller, somehow.' He escapes and hides (as a child might) in the hall cupboard. But the police trace the criminal through Paddington's having carefully written down the numbers of the notes in the suitcase – a typical perspicuity.

Paddington's exploits in cricket and golf – both of which games he joins by mistake – result in his usual triumph. Paddington, 'not even an old bear, let alone an Old Boy', helps his side to win by a series of mischances that are not in the rule book, and at the golf tournament wins a prize by sending the ball into the cab of a train. In one of the funniest stories of *Paddington Abroad* he wins a prize in the Tour de France by joining in a section of the race downhill on a brakeless tricycle. His money sense often leads him to buy antiques that turn out to be valuable. He obtains these, for pocket money, usually sixpence, because they are objects which ought to and obviously will not work; an old camera, a sewing machine, an antique marmalade jar. None of Mr Bond's other animals – Parsley and Dill, Olga, Thursday the mouse – have quite the personality or popularity of Paddington, with fan clubs and sales all over the world. He is believable, natural, attractive without being sentimental, and his celebrated hard stare and ruthless logic regularly floors such characters as bankers, policemen, doctors, dentists and once, memorably, a psychiatrist – figures whose authority one enjoys seeing deflated.

Of course, if Paddington were a hairy dwarf no one would laugh at all, and if he were a child he might be unlikely and annoying. But he relies, in the end, on being a bear, and so everyone is kind. The luckless Mr Curry is the only person who ever gets really angry with him, and that is almost in the family. Nothing is ever very

serious – Paddington reacts to mainly middle-class life of the sixties
and bounces back, his character strengthening and growing from
book to book. Mr Bond has only to think of the situations. Paddington will act and react. He is as dependable and as completely dead
pan as a first-class comedian, reliably making one laugh whatever
his material – and while some of Mr Bond's early material was
rather predictable, it is mostly very good indeed and time has improved it. Paddington never smiles – animals do not – and Peggy
Fortnum makes him animal enough to look serious, satisfied, woe-
begone, blissful, anxious, hopeful, inquisitive and replete: to have,
indeed, the full range that animal expressions can have. Paddington
never laughs. Peggy Fortnum makes it quite clear that he is no
Teddy. He has the endearing appearance of a bear-cub with dark
ears, a sharp snout, and the dishevelled shagginess of an untidy
child with the slight rotundity of a more middle-aged character
with a liking for honey, sugar and marmalade, and a few suggestions of the hard stare which reduces superior or pompous opponents to half their size. He has the minimum of clothing. The battered hat from which he will never be parted assumes larger and
more grotesque shapes as stories and illustrations continue, but he
is not averse to hats of other kinds and is equally at home in topper,
cloth cap, sun hat, woolly cap and French beret. His suitcase goes
with him, as does his duffle coat. The variety of expression and atti-

tude in Peggy Fortnum's drawings, which show Paddington with impressionistic vigour but merely suggest the characters and surroundings that make his background, is considerable. The explosive accidents and sticky mischances which happen in his early adventures are indicated with a confident economy that supplements the text. E. H. Shepard succeeded in the same way with Winnie the Pooh. While Paddington is shown in Churchillian pose with a cigar (*Paddington At Large*), practising his French with shrugging gestures (*Paddington Abroad*), hopefully reading one of his instruction books (*Paddington Marches On*), or riding his brakeless tricycle in hunched-up terror in the Tour de France, he is never stylised, never the same, always himself. The human life and character in everything he does make other fictional bears seem cardboard by comparison.

Human reactions are often predictable. Paddington's are no more so than those of his elders and betters. Scrooge and Marley might have lived in such an atmosphere of mutual mistrust as Paddington and Mr Curry – each trying to score off the other with Mr Curry as aggressor, getting Paddington to mow his lawn, mend his pipes, carry his golf clubs, fetch his laundry, all for a ridiculously small amount, and Paddington determined not to be taken advantage of. Mr Curry's furious roar of 'Bear!' when he sees the damage Paddington has probably done is matched by the scorn that Paddington can put into the word 'Sixpence!' when he thinks that he has been underpaid or overcharged. When Paddington discovers that he has tipped a liftman two shillings by mistake he goes rigid in a kind of catalepsy. ' "Thank you very much . . . very kind of you it was," said the liftman. "And now if you'll excuse me I've another load to take up." With that he clanged the doors shut leaving Paddington fixed to the spot as if he had been turned into a pillar of stone. He was still rooted to the spot several minutes later when Mrs Brown and Mrs Bird came hurrying up.' (*Paddington At Large*) On the other hand, when Paddington accidentally joins a line of buskers and happens to be holding his hat out at the time he almost becomes, like Bottom, translated. ' "Is anything the matter, dear?" asked Mrs Brown, catching sight of the expression on his face. "You look quite . . ." '

Unlike Pooh, who is always emphasising his lack of brain, Paddington is really rather conceited. He is proud of being a foreigner, proud of not being human, keeps adding to his numerous scrapbooks and his diary. We are never allowed to see it, apart from glimpses of a few oddly spelled lists. His authority-deflating personality (though he knows very well the exact moment to retreat, disappear, or hide in the hall cupboard) is achieved by logic as hard as his legendary stare:

'Watch the birdie' said the photographer. Paddington, (who could not see it,) went round behind the man and tapped him. The photographer, who appeared to be looking for something, jumped and then emerged from under his cloth. 'How do you expect me to take your picture if you don't stand in front?' he asked in an aggrieved voice. 'Now I've wasted a plate, and' – he looked shiftily at Paddington – 'that will cost you a shilling!'

Paddington gave him a hard stare. 'You said there was a bird,' he said. 'And there wasn't.'

'I expect it flew away when it saw your face,' said the man nastily. 'Now, where's my shilling?'

Paddington looked at him even harder for a moment. 'Perhaps the bird took it when it flew away,' he said.

He floors Mr Heinz the psychiatrist with word reactions that have almost the speed of light, and has cast-iron arguments with which he can defeat policemen, workmen, store managers, dentists and taxi drivers. Perhaps his greatest triumph is his appearance on television where he defeats an unpleasantly jokey quizmaster. Quelling the latter's puns with his usual hard stare he answers questions on mathematics with characteristic sharp literalness and insistence on what Bears do being different from what People do until the quizmaster is reduced to a shuddering wreck (he should have known that this was England, in which animals always win). Paddington donates part of his prize to the home for retired bears in Lima (he is consistently loyal to his animal progenitors) and puts the rest into the bank. A bank account is something which comes to him quite naturally. Mr Toad doubtless had one, but since this Edwardian peak the only animals to deal successfully in human currency have been those educated by Dr Dolittle. Paddington progresses from his standing order for buns to having his bills paid – probably by Giro – for he is nothing if not regular and law abiding. That all is not well with his bank – Flloyds – appals him. He takes a serious view of life. At the seaside he is more likely to enter a sandcastle-building competition than to join in beach games. He prefers to sit chatting with Mr Gruber the antique dealer rather than do what a child might do – find other children and play with them.

Paddington continues to adjust to each new experience. He has achieved a delightful symbiosis and would be very stupid indeed if he became too human for his own good, or started to grow up too much. However, as animals of his sort by-pass adolescence completely and childlike middle age is the norm, this is not very likely. He is fixed in the role of a licensed jester who deflates pomposity. explores familiar situations as if for the first time so that children can both feel more worldly wise, yet still admire his capacity for dealing with the riotous results. His restrained middle-class background probably adds to the fun of his many adventures. Anyone from the year two thousand reading these books could get a general, though rather old-fashioned picture of a a certain kind of London family in the sixties. The amiable but colourless Browns go for days out in the car, have holidays abroad, do their own decorating, celebrate Christmas without religion, visit their children's schools for cricket matches or Open Days, go to the cinema and theatre, are concerned about appearances – ' "I hope you're not wearing that hat," said Mrs Brown.' They shop for clothes in the West End, go out to restaurants for family celebrations (where even Paddington may be rejected for not wearing evening dress), their pipes freeze in the winter, their garden grows prize marrows, their children go carol singing and join in gymkhanas. Paddington is an agent who upsets these occasions and turns orderly life into an accelerating series of comic accidents which Bergson explains by a row of ninepins and atomic scientists by chain reaction. Real life is speeded and arranged. Outside the visual arts (and Paddington is very visual) life seldom obliges with unrehearsed joke effects. The very boring normality of the proceedings makes Paddington's impact greater.

One begins to list the things that Paddington has *not* done, experienced, or been to – the supermarket, the parish fête, football match, Battersea funfair, multistorey car park, Post Office Tower, and to hope that a wave of bear-immigration from Peru will start, and that Paddington will be the first bear to own a credit card.

Small faults of style, cliché and repetition are lost in the pace of the narrative. It does not really matter much that people exclaim too often instead of merely saying, that Mrs Bird's favourite word is

II

'h'm' and Jonathan's 'crikey', that everyone 'hurries' here and there instead of walking. If anything, it adds to the jerky, cinematic speed. Mrs Brown has only to say 'Even Paddington can't come to much harm in half an hour' for everyone to know that the worst – and more, and better – will happen. Soon some official will be enquiring for that young bear, young gentleman, young bear gentleman, or even, crazily, of Mr Brown 'Are you that young bear's next of kin?' But one knows that in this Utopian setting no one will be too angry with that awful child (for he isn't) that dreadful animal (he isn't that either) that hairy little man; he evades all these categories. Being an animal in England he is loved almost automatically, being adult he can answer back and win arguments, and being a childish stranger he can say about almost every new situation he meets – Look, no clothes. Children accept and love him and it is only adults who, accepting and loving him and most of his kind, can say with mixed, puzzled pleasure the opposite of what the child said to the Emperor – Look, he's a bear, and no one has noticed; or, in other words – Look, he's dressed.

Postscript

We still have longings for Eden and the old days when the beasts could speak, or understand without speech, our equals and partners, our second, good selves. Contemporary taste favours truth rather than fantasy; not Mrs Blow, Clanworthy and Hopdance united by enchantment after death, but stories about real animals that the writer has known – not merely by observation, but personally as companions such as Elsa the lioness or the animals and birds in the books of writers such as Monica Edwards, Gavin Maxwell, or Derek Tangye. It does not matter where the story happens or to whom as long as *somewhere* there was – or preferably *is* – a Gull on the Roof or an Incredible Journey. We want Eden here and now, if possible.

However in fiction not only are animals equal these days but, in the present mental climate which is in its way as full of guilt and repentance as the world of Kingsley and Mrs Barbauld, they seem much better than we are: even dragons, snakes and reptiles are no longer evil. The new villains are the industrial humans who pollute and destroy, imprison and commit sins which are concrete and far reaching. One fears less about nebulous, old fashioned things like pride, envy and avarice, but more about their actual results. The new heroes in the wake of *The Animals Conference* are the innocent creatures who, no longer caricatures of men or symbols of their vices, make societies of their own in opposition to the human ones. Such are the laboratory rats in *Mrs. Frisby and the Rats of NIMH* (Robert C. O'Brien, 1971), who, having achieved and in some cases passed human intelligence, have certainly reached a higher moral plane. Compared with them, the eighteenth-century Tabby and Grimalkin are stage characters performing in lurid lighting. The rats, determined to live without stealing or scavenging, found a new Shangrilaa in a distant valley, sowing, reaping, and living in uncontaminated pastoral bliss. One feels that they will survive after the humans have died out.

Poor humans, with their weak legs, vulnerable spines, lunatic aggressions and eroding self-doubt, they seem ill equipped for this planet. Rats, or rabbits – or cats – might well do better, as is suggested by André Norton in *Breed to Come* (1973). Eden as it now appears, is for animals only; they are, some writers seem to suggest, the new humans, putting right the wrongs of the old, corrupt societies. To such a degree are the tables turned that a heroic saga of tribal conflict, full of excitement and its own mythology, turns out to have been about rabbits all the time (*Watership Down*, Richard Adams, 1972). The rabbits may be secondary human symbols but they are their own biological selves, their drama heightened with the help of human characteristics while not depending on them. Hazel and Fiver may be *like* William Golding's Ralph and Piggy from *Lord of the Flies*, Holly and Bluebell *like* Bear and the Fool, but they are serious, adult heroes in their own animal right, and we see that Brer Rabbit has survived as a rabbit myth as well as a human one.

The animals in fact and fiction will not leave us alone. Perhaps that is well, we love them, and as in all good tales, want to be loved by them, and live with them happily for ever. They teach us about themselves – and ourselves – and can give us those amusing, thoughtful, bookish holidays that are as refreshing as the physical kind. Long may they continue to do so.

Bibliography

CARRINGTON, CHARLES, *Rudyard Kipling, his Life and Work*, Macmillan, 1955.

CHITTY, SUSAN, *The Woman who wrote Black Beauty*, Hodder and Stoughton, 1971.

CROUCH, MARCUS, *Treasure Seekers and Borrowers*, The Library Association, 1962.

DARTON, F. HARVEY, *Children's Books in Britain*, Cambridge University Press, revised edition, 1958.

DE LA MARE, WALTER, *Animal Stories* (introduction on Beast Fable), 1939.

FIELD, ROBERT D., *The Art of Walt Disney*, 1942

FISHER, MARGERY, *Intent upon Reading*, Brockhampton, 1961.

GREEN, PETER, *Kenneth Grahame*, Murray, 1959.

GREEN, ROGER LANCELYN, *Tellers of Tales*, revised edition, Edmund Ward, 1965.

JAMES, PHILIP, *English Book Illustration 1800-1900*, King Penguin, 1947.

JANSSON, TOVE, *A Sculptor's Daughter*, Ernest Benn, 1969.

KIPLING, RUDYARD, *Something of Myself*, centenary edition, Macmillan, 1965.

LANE, MARGARET, *The Tale of Beatrix Potter*, Warne, 1946.

LEWIS, C. S., *Of Other Worlds* (preface by Walter Hooper on 'Animal-Land'),

MEIGS, CORNELIA, AND OTHERS, *A Critical History of Children's Literature*, Macmillan, New York, 1953.

MUIR, PERCY H., *Children's Books of Yesterday* (a catalogue compiled for an exhibition held at the National Book League), Cambridge University Press, 1946.

—*English Children's Books 1600-1900*, Batsford, 1954.

QUAYLE, ERIC, *The Collector's Book of Children's Books*, Studio Vista, 1971.

STREATFEILD, NOEL, *Magic and the Magician* (on E. Nesbit), Ernest Benn, 1958.

TOLKIEN, J. R. R., *On Fairy-Stories, Tree and Leaf*, Allen and Unwin, 1964.

TOWNSEND, JOHN ROWE, *Written for Children*, J. Garnet Miller, 1965.

TURNER, E. S., *Boys will be Boys*, Michael Joseph, 1.48.

WHITE, T. H., *The Book of Beasts* (a bestiary translated and edited), Jonathan Cape, 1954.

I would like to thank Nigel Temple for letting me see and take examples from his superb collection of early children's books; and for his kindness in lending illustrations for *Animal Land*.

Margaret Blount

Index

Index compiled by Gordon Robinson.
NOTE: *Bracketed names are authors*

Munro, H. H., 119, 123, 193, 194, 239
My Friend Mr Leakey, 124

Napoleon the cat, 146
Napoleon the pig, 66, 67
Narnia books (C. S. Lewis), 107, 126,
 209, 228, 229, 236, 237, 284, 285,
 286, 287, 288, 291–305
Nesbit, E., 18, 48, 96, 99, 100–2, 104,
 119–20, 121, 124, 171, 275, 291, 301
Newberry, John, 43
Nibbins the cat, 191–2, 193
Nichols, Beverley, 17, 58
Nimble the mouse, 48, 245
Noah, 283
Norton, André, 324
Norton, Mary, 142, 160
Null-P, 84
'Nun's Priests' Tale', 23, 33–4
'Nurse and the Wolf, The', 38

O'Brien, Robert C., 323
Odyssey, The, 275
O'Farrell, Mary, 175
Oh For a Mouseless House, 154
Old Brown (Potter), 137
Old Lady in Babar books, 274, 275
'Old Lion, The', 276–7
Old Man who said Hugh, 79
Old Man in a Marsh, 79
Old Man with the Owl, 79
Old Man in the Tree, 79
'Old Man of the Sea, The', 213–14,
 215–16
'Old Mother Hubbard', 71, 71–2, 73
Old Possum's Book of Practical Cats, 195
Old Woman and her Little Red Hen,
 140
Once and Future King, The, 65, 262
One Hundred and One Dalmatians, 271–2
Only Toys, 171
Orlando the cat, 271, 272–4
Orwell, George, 17, 26, 58, 65, 237
Out of the Silent Planet, 63–4, 284,
 285–7, 296
Owl (Milne), 178, 180
Owl Man (Rae), 203, 204, 307
Owl and Pussy Cat, 79
Owl Service, The, 112
'Oxen, The', 265

Packet family (Baker), 142
Paddington books, 161, 241, 275, 310,
 311
Paddington Brown, 18, 24, 178, 197,
 201, 202, 203, 204, 270, 274, 275,
 307–22
'Paddock and the Mous, The', 40
Parables from Nature, 44, 53–4, 55
Peacock at Home, The, 132
Peake, Mervyn, 190
Peep behind the Scenes, A, 188
Penelope the spider, 260
Peregrine Pickle, 206
Perelandra, 121, 285, 286, 288–9, 290–1
Perrault, Charles, 25, 95, 213
Peter (C. S. Lewis), 293, 294, 297
Peter Pan, 18, 229
Peter Rabbit, 19, 30, 48, 135, 136
Phoenix (Nesbit), 99, 100, 101–2, 103,
 104, 121
Phoenix and the Carpet, The, 100, 101–2
'Pie and the Patty Pan, The', 137, 217
Piglet, 178, 180
Pigling Bland (Potter), 70
Pilgrim's Progress, The, 57, 275, 304
Pilgrim's Regress, The, 286
Pilkington, Mrs, 49–50, 75
Pinocchio, 56–7, 91, 173, 185, 209
Pip, Squeak and Wilfred, 208, 209
Pitchford, Denys Watkins, 16, 146
Plane Crazy, 91
Pluto the pup, 90, 91
Podgy Pig, 220–1
Poe, Edgar Allan, 97, 99
Poll Parrot Picture Book, 72, 274
Polynesia the parrot, 51, 199, 204
Pompey the dragon, 124
Pompey the Little, 50, 206–7, 245, 261
Pong Ping the Peke, 221
Pongo the Dalmatian, 272, 273
Poo Poo and the Dragons, 121
Postgate, Oliver, 281
Potter, Beatrix, 16, 28, 30, 70–1, 135,
 136, 138, 139, 140, 153, 154, 156,
 157, 163, 218, 260, 274
Precocious Piggy, 70–1, 72
Priestley, J. B., 175
Prince Caspian, 293, 304
'Prince Humpty Dumpty', 214
Princess and Curdie, The, 104–7
Princess and the Goblin, The, 104